Boston College

Glimpses of the Past

Over the mantle of the fireplace in the British Catholic Authors Room of Burns Library is a stone carving that represents Boston College's history. A tree symbolizes the University's life. At its roots stand the original College building in the South End and the Church of the Immaculate Conception, which was built beside it. Above is the full tree, with Gasson Hall seemingly growing out of it. Devlin Hall and Bapst Library flank Gasson, resting on shields that reflect the evolution of the College seal.

Boston College

Glimpses of the Past

Charles F. Donovan, S.J.
UNIVERSITY HISTORIAN

The University Press of Boston College
Chestnut Hill, Massachusetts

This book and its cover were designed by Janis Owens of Duxbury, Massachusetts.

The text typeface is Sabon, with Garamond used for special matter. Coghill Composition Company of Richmond, Virginia, was the typesetter. The printer and binder was Hamilton Printing Company of Rensselaer, New York.

Front cover: two of the four bells in Gasson Hall tower, each inscribed with a Latin dedication to a Jesuit saint. The largest, weighing half a ton, is named St. Ignatius. A fifteen-pound hammer strikes it for the quarter hour chimes, while a twenty-five-pound hammer helps it proclaim the hours of the day. *Back cover:* the garden enclosure behind St. Mary's Hall. At the far end of the building, protruding from the Jesuits' residence, is the exterior of the sanctuary of St. Mary's chapel. Our Lady's statue graces the center of the garden.

Cover photographs by Lee Pellegrini.

Library of Congress Catalog Card No. 94-60470

ISBN 0-9625934-1-9

PRINTED IN THE UNITED STATES OF AMERICA

To Rev. J. Donald Monan, S.J.,
twenty-fourth president of Boston College

"My feet you made swift as the deer's,
You have made me stand firm on the heights."

Psalm 18, v. 34

Preface

THE CHAPTERS of this book appeared originally as a series of pamphlets, *Occasional Papers on the History of Boston College,* which were shared with the faculty and staff of the University over a period of a dozen years. They explore facets of Boston College history that seemed too detailed for inclusion in the formal history of the University that appeared several years ago: *History of Boston College: From the Beginnings to 1990*. In book form, the present studies offer those interested in the development of the University interesting glimpses of its evolution.

The author is deeply indebted to his editor, Eugene Bailey, both for encouragement of the project and for impeccable editorial oversight. The university historian's secretary, Rose DeMaio, has been an invaluable assistant in research, in the production of the original papers, and their preparation for publication as a book. Thanks go also to two recent graduate assistants, Sister Nancy Surma, O.F.M., and Kelli Armstrong Griffin, for superb research assistance.

The Occasional Paper on Boston College's Boston priests (Chapter 15) was dedicated, appropriately, to His Eminence Bernard Cardinal Law, as the shepherd of Boston's priests as well as an honorary alumnus (S.T.D., 1984). Chapter 9, on the rotunda of Gasson Hall, was dedicated in original form to the man who suggested the topic, Professor Heinz Bluhm of the Germanic Studies Department. His death in November 1993 deprived the University of an outstanding scholar beloved by the community. Thanks are repeated to former university librarian, Thomas

O'Connell, for his suggesting the theme of Chapter 15: Boston College's priests of the Boston archdiocese.

The author acknowledges with gratitude the generous cooperation of university photographers Gary Gilbert and Geoffrey Why. Gilbert provided the photographs for Chapters 9 and 14. Thanks are due the archives of the Boston archdiocese for permission to copy seven of the photos in the last chapter. Finally, the efficient help of university archivist Ronald Patkus and his assistant, Dennis Scott, are gratefully acknowledged.

Feast of St. Ignatius
July 31, 1994

Charles F. Donovan, S.J.
UNIVERSITY HISTORIAN

Contents

PART ONE

The Early Days

PART TWO

A New Beginning

PART THREE
Vignettes of College Life

PART FOUR
A Tradition of Service

About the Author

Charles F. Donovan, S.J. (Boston College Class of 1933), was founding dean of the School of Education. From 1961 to 1968 he served as academic vice president, then became senior vice president and dean of faculties. Since 1979 he has been university historian. In addition to this book, he was co-author of the *History of Boston College: From the Beginnings to 1990*.

PART ONE

The Early Days

I

The College's First Boston Brahmin Friends

WHEN THE FOUNDER of Boston College, John McElroy, left Ireland for America in 1803 at the age of 21, he came not to Boston but to Baltimore. Forty-four years later, in 1847, fate and the bidding of his Jesuit superior brought the seasoned Jesuit priest to Boston just at the time wave after wave of McElroy's countrymen were arriving in the city in flight from the Irish famine. McElroy was a realistic observer of the immigration phenomenon. Writing to Father General Jan Roothaan in 1848, he estimated the Catholic population of Boston as 30,000.[1] Only six years later, in a letter to Roothaan's successor, Father General Pieter Beckx, he put the Catholic population of Boston at 70,000.[2]

The authority on Boston's nineteenth century immigrants, Oscar Handlin, gives somewhat more modest figures: 35,000 Irish in 1850 and 50,000 in 1855.[3] McElroy was reporting the total Catholic population, whereas Handlin focussed specifically on the newly arrived Irish. In any case, both McElroy and Handlin point to a near doubling, in a very brief period, of the population they were counting. Commenting on Handlin's figure of 50,000 Irish in 1855, the historian of Boston's topography, Walter Muir Whitehill, observed that 50,000 was more than double the entire population of Boston in 1800[4] and was better than a third of the city's population at mid-century. Not just the size of the population growth through immigration but its suddenness had what Whitehill calls a "devastating" impact on once sedate residential areas of the city such as the North End and Fort Hill.

Understandably some of the established residents of Boston resented the problems attendant upon the unanticipated explosion of a foreign population. The fact that the newcomers were "Papists" was a further irritant to the Protestant majority, and there were occasional demonstrations of anti-Catholicism. One such was a petition signed by 925 Bostonians in 1853 asking the city's Committee on Public Lands to prevent Father McElroy from building a church on land he had purchased in the North End.[5] This became the famous Jail Lands controversy that dragged on for four years before McElroy finally admitted defeat, sold the Jail Lands property, and bought alternate land in the newly developed South End of Boston, where he erected the Church of the Immaculate Conception and the original collegiate building that was Boston College's home for 50 years.

McElroy was 71 when the Jail Lands struggle began, and a less intrepid spirit might have yielded to discouragement or despair. But besides his stout heart and confidence in God's grace, the venerable priest was buoyed by unexpected support from 25 of Boston's most powerful and respected Protestant citizens. The petition of these men in support of McElroy's hopes to build a church on the Jail Lands was not immediately successful, but their friendly gesture was a public expression of tolerance that even today brightens a page of Boston's history. The impact of their action can be judged by considering their standing in the Boston community. Among them was a United States senator and a former senator, a former president of Harvard and a former dean of Harvard Medical School, a noted historian, a judge, the man known as the arbiter of Boston society, as well as some of the most substantial businessmen of the period.

The article concerning the petition on behalf of Father McElroy that appeared in the *Pilot,* May 28, 1853, listed the 25 signatories in what may have been their order of signing: Rufus Choate, Abbott Lawrence, William Appleton, George Ticknor, George B. Upton, Sidney Bartlett, James Reed, Robert C. Winthrop, C. H. Warren, Thomas Hopkinson, Amos A. Lawrence, Samuel Law-

Amos A. Lawrence, a well-to-do Boston businessman, befriended Father McElroy in his legal struggle for land. A few years later he created an unexpected future tie with Boston College. In 1862 he purchased as a summer retreat the Chestnut Hill farmland that Father Thomas Gasson was to acquire in 1907 as the site of the new Boston College.

rence, Ezra Lincoln, George S. Hillard, Thomas G. Cary, J. Thomas Stevenson, N. A. Thompson, Philo S. Sheldon, William H. Prescott, Peter Harvey, J. C. Warren, Francis B. Crowninshield, C. H. Mills and Company, Edward Everett, and Thomas Wetmore. The prominence of these men is evidenced by the fact that only six of them failed to be included in either Appleton's *Cyclopedia of American Biography* (published in 1887) or in Abner Forbes' 1852 edition of *The Rich Men of Massachusetts.*[6] Both Appleton's and Forbes' works listed 13 petitioners, and 13 of the 25 signers were given space in Mary Crawford's *Famous Families of Massachusetts.*[7]

Probably the best known of the signers among Massachusetts people was Edward Everett, for he had been their governor for four years. Appointed professor of Greek at Harvard at age 21, he became editor of the *North American Review,* served 10 years in Congress, and, after being governor, served as president of Harvard from 1846 to 1849. When Daniel Webster died, Everett served briefly as Secretary of State and began service as elected U.S. senator in March 1853. He was thus a senator at the time of the Jail Lands petition.

The esteem of his fellow-citizens for Everett was expressed by Oliver Wendell Holmes, who said that Bostonians "all carry the Common in our heads as the unit of space, the State House as the standard of architecture, and measure off men in Edward Everetts as with a yardstick."[8]

As one reviews the lives of public men of the nineteenth century, one is struck at the significance of oratory in their careers. In this apparently random group of 25 people, at least four were noted for their eloquence, and their oratorical style has been described by their biographers. Everett was one of the eloquent voices of his day; he was the featured speaker at Gettysburg when Lincoln gave his memorable address. Another was Rufus Choate, whom his biographer in Appleton's *Cyclopedia* likened to Lord Erskine in this regard. A lawyer by profession, Choate served in Congress, and when Daniel Webster became Secretary of State in 1841, Choate was elected senator.

A different career path was followed by George Ticknor. Though he studied law after graduating from Dartmouth, he felt a calling to literary scholarship and studied for four years in Germany. He was one of the first to bring German university influence to American higher education, accepting appointment at Harvard in 1819 to a chair of Modern Languages and Literature. He retired from the Harvard faculty after 15 years and held court at his home at Nine Park Street, where he served as the cultural and social arbiter of the city. In *George Ticknor and the Boston Brahmins,* his biographer, David Tyack, portrays him as the Brahmin prototype. Such was Ticknor's social position in Boston that friends suggested the city should be renamed Ticknorville.[9] Ticknor was one of the founders of the Boston Public Library, and at the time of the Jail Lands controversy, both he and Everett were trustees of the new library. In 1849 Ticknor produced his scholarly opus, *The History of Spanish Literature,* in three volumes. Somewhat later he published a two-volume biography of another petitioner for Father McElroy, William Hickling Prescott.

Nearly blinded from a college prank while a student at Harvard, William Prescott devoted his life to the study (with the help of readers) and writing of history and became one of America's great nineteenth century literary historians. His major works were *Ferdinand and Isabella, The Conquest of Mexico, The Conquest of Peru,* and *Philip II of Spain.* It is interesting to note the interrelationships between signers of the Jail Lands petition. As Ticknor became Prescott's biographer, Prescott wrote the memoirs of Abbott Lawrence, uncle of Amos A. Lawrence, former owner of much of the present Boston College campus. Incidentally, Prescott is included in a six-panel window in Bapst Library representing American historians. The window is in the Hon. Thomas P. O'Neill room on the second floor.

Another profession was represented by John Collins Warren, a physician. He was a dominant figure in Boston medicine in the nineteenth century. As dean of Harvard Medical School, he moved the school from Cambridge to Boston in 1820 and became a co-founder of the Massachusetts General Hospital. He was also one of the moving forces in starting the *New England Journal of Medicine.* A prominent public figure in Boston, he served as president of the Society of Natural History and founded the Thursday Evening Club. Amos A. Lawrence recorded in his diary that when his father died on January 1, 1853, "Dr. Warren and my brother William were called."[10] William Lawrence was himself a physician. It is significant that at the critical moment, the great John Collins Warren was summoned—another connection among Father McElroy's supporters.

George Stillman Hillard graduated from Harvard in 1828, became a lawyer, served as a state senator, as City Solicitor of Boston, and later as United States District Attorney. These occupations did not keep him from literary interests. Besides publishing tracts on such diverse topics as *The Dangers and Duties of the Mercantile Profession* and *The Relation of the Poet to His Age,* he brought out a five-volume edition of *The Poetical Works of Edmund Spenser.* Again we see the closeness of these men: After the death of George Ticknor, Hillard joined Ticknor's wife in writing his biography.

Robert C. Winthrop anticipated Boston College's Congressman Thomas P. O'Neill by better than a hundred years in having the distinction of serving both as speaker of the Massachusetts House of Representatives and speaker of the United States House. Winthrop graduated from Harvard in 1828 and studied law under Daniel Webster. After his career in elective politics, he was named U.S. senator to fill out the term of Daniel Webster when the latter was named Secretary of State in 1850. In *Romantic Days in Old Boston,* Mary Crawford credits Robert Winthrop, whom she calls "long one of the first citizens of Boston," with bringing the brilliant Episcopal churchman and preacher, Phillips Brooks, from Philadelphia to Trinity Church.[11]

The judiciary was represented among Father McElroy's supporters in the person of Thomas Hopkinson, who presided over the Court of Common Pleas. Hopkinson was president of the Boston and Worcester Railroad. His daughter Grace, some time after her father's death, became the wife of Charles W. Eliot when he was president of Harvard.

George Upton's career reads like a Hollywood script about a nineteenth century New England merchant. After studying at Harvard he settled in Nantucket, where he engaged in whaling, ship-building, and manufacturing, while also serving the district both as representative and senator. In 1846, he moved to Boston and became an importer, a builder of clipper ships, and treasurer of the Michigan Central Railroad. In the year of the Jail Lands petition he was serving as a member of the Executive Council of the state.

Ezra Lincoln was a civil engineer and surveyor. The files of the Massachusetts Historical Society show that he drew up plans for the Public Garden, as well as a plan for the streets of Boston. In 1849, when there was a movement for filling in and developing Back Bay, Lincoln was one of three commissioners appointed by the legislature to study and recommend settlement of the claims of business interests and of the people of Roxbury and Boston in that area.[12]

Thomas Wetmore was president of the Cochituate Water Board, which in the preceding decade had built the aquaduct from Natick to Boston.

The other 15 signers of the Jail Lands petition were businessmen.

The largest number were in the import business, called "commission merchants" at the time. In this category were Philo Sheldon, Charles H. Mills, Peter Harvey, James Reed, Thomas Cary, and Thomas Stevenson, as well as William Appleton and the three Lawrences. Harvey, considered the closest friend of Daniel Webster, served in both branches of the state legislature and was president of the Kilby Bank.

Newell Thompson is listed in the contemporary *Boston Directory* as an auctioneer and notary public. In manufacturing were C. H. Warren, Thomas Cary, and Francis Crowninshield. The latter served in the state legislature and was speaker of the House of Representatives.

A number of these men were officers of railroad companies. Besides those already mentioned, there was C. H. Warren, president of the Boston and Providence Railroad; Thomas Stevenson, treasurer of the Lowell Railroad; and Francis Crowninshield, president of the Old Colony Railroad.

William Appleton and the Lawrences were, of course, pioneers in American manufacturing. Appleton was the father-in-law of Amos A. Lawrence. He was president of the Massachusetts General Hospital and served in Congress from 1851 to 1855. In fact, he was representing Suffolk County in Congress when he signed the petition in Father McElroy's favor.

The 13 signatories listed in Forbes' *The Rich Men of Massachusetts* were Appleton, Bartlett, Cary, Crowninshield, Abbott Lawrence, Amos A. Lawrence, Samuel Lawrence, Mills, Prescott, Stevenson, Ticknor, J. C. Warren, and Winthrop.

Another measure of financial substance and reputation in nineteenth century Boston was association with the Provident Institution for Savings.[13] The leading moneyed men of the city were proud to have started in 1816, with no personal gain, a savings bank for people of modest income, and election to serve the Provident, either as trustee or officer, was a significant mark of recognition.

Five of the pro-McElroy signers were associated with the Provident Institution for Savings: Crowninshield as a trustee for 17 years and a member of the Board of Investment for 15; Amos A. Lawrence as a trustee for 6 years and his uncle, Samuel Lawrence, as a trustee for 3; and Robert Winthrop as a trustee for 8 years.

The longest and most impressive service was given by Amos A. Lawrence's father-in-law, William Appleton, who was a trustee of the Provident for 21 years and president from 1848 to 1861.

Only by a liberal extension can this distinguished assemblage of Bostonians be called early friends of Boston College. Throughout the Jail Lands controversy the focus was on a church, without mention of a college. Maybe Father McElroy felt or was advised that this approach would have special public appeal. The eloquent plea presented on Father McElroy's behalf before the Joint Committee on Public Lands, on April 18, 1853, by Nathaniel Bowditch, conveyancer, was entitled, "An Argument for a Catholic Church on the Jail-Lands."[14] But there is no doubt what was in McElroy's mind. As soon as he gave up on the Jail Lands and obtained the Harrison Avenue property, he began simultaneous construction of a church and a college: It was considered one project. Only one cornerstone, that of the church, was laid.[15]

In befriending Father McElroy regarding a church in the Jail Lands, the petitioners thus were implicitly—though unconsciously—furthering his dream of establishing a college. Certainly, by supporting the aging Jesuit, they countered discouragement and confirmed his determination. Their generous act of fairness and tolerance was a significant prelude to the fulfilment of McElroy's mission. Men and women of Boston College, beneficiaries of the labors, trials, and eventual triumph of Father John McElroy, have reason to be grateful to the generous Bostonians who supported his cause.

ENDNOTES

1. Cited in Gilbert J. Garraghan, "Origins of Boston College, 1842–1869," *Thought*, 17 (March 1942), p. 637.
2. *Ibid.*, p. 641.
3. Oscar Handlin, *Boston's Immigrants* (New York: Atheneum, 1976), p. 52.
4. Walter Muir Whitehill, *Boston: A Topographical History* (Cambridge, Mass.: The Belknap Press, 1963), p. 112.
5. Garraghan, *Origins of Boston College,* p. 639.
6. Abner Forbes, *The Rich Men of Massachusetts,* second edition (Boston: Redding and Co., 1852).
7. Mary Caroline Crawford, *Famous Families of Massachusetts* (Boston: Little, Brown, and Co., 1930).

8. Cited in David B. Tyack, *George Ticknor and the Boston Brahmins* (Cambridge, Mass.: Harvard University Press, 1967), p. 158.
9. Tyack, *George Ticknor,* p. 183.
10. William Lawrence, *Life of Amos A. Lawrence* (Boston: Houghton, Mifflin and Co., 1888), p. 68.
11. Mary Caroline Crawford, *Romantic Days in Old Boston* (Boston: Little Brown, and Co., 1910), p. 359.
12. Justin Winsor, ed., *The Memorial History of Boston* (Boston: Ticknor and Son, 1881), vol. IV, p. 35.
13. Walter Muir Whitehill, *The Provident Institution for Savings in the Town of Boston, 1816–1966* (Boston, 1966).
14. Nathaniel I. Bowditch, *An Argument for a Catholic Church on the Jail Lands* (Boston: John Wilson and Son, 1853).
15. Charles F. Donovan, S. J., David R. Dunigan, S. J., and Paul A. FitzGerald, S. J., *History of Boston College: From the Beginnings to 1990* (Chestnut Hill, Mass.: University Press of Boston College, 1990), p. 21.

2

Joseph Coolidge Shaw:

First Patron of the College

THE FIRST GIFT to Boston College—a gift of money and of books—was made in the will of a dying priest in the year 1851, thirteen years before the College accepted its first students. The donor was Father Joseph Coolidge Shaw, S. J. The relevant part of the will, which he dictated to a Jesuit friend, was as follows:[1]

> The deed of four thousand dollars in the Massachusetts Life Insurance (now in Father Rector's possession) I give to Father Provincial to be used with any interest that has accrued on it in establishing a school or college of the Society in Boston. . . .
>
> My library at home (consisting of about 1200 volumes on theological and spiritual subjects and 5 or 600 more on lighter topics) I intended for such college or colleges and Seminary of the Society as should be established in Boston. . . .

The great founder of Boston College, Father John McElroy, S. J., had come to Boston in 1847 to preside over Saint Mary's parish in the North End and to collect funds for the eventual establishment of a Jesuit college in the city. In 1851, when Father Shaw's will was dictated, Father McElroy was scouring Boston for a suitable location for a large church and for college buildings. Father Shaw knew Father McElroy. Indeed, immediately after his ordination in 1847, Father Shaw filled in for Father McElroy at St. Mary's parish, while McElroy gave a retreat to the other priests of the diocese.[2] Shaw mentions Father McElroy explicitly in his will, leaving to him certain relics and reliquaries, some church linens and rosaries for use at St. Mary's Church.

Shaw undoubtedly knew of Father McElroy's hopes and plans for a college in Boston. But, after all, there already was a Jesuit college 45 miles west of Boston—Holy Cross. When he dictated his will, Shaw was in the Jesuit novitiate at Frederick, Maryland, not far from the first American Jesuit college, Georgetown. And just before entering the Society of Jesus in 1850, the young priest had completed his theological studies at St. Joseph Seminary, conducted by the Jesuit fathers at Fordham, New York. So why was not one of these established Jesuit institutions the recipient of Father Shaw's money and library? The reason seems to be that Joseph Coolidge Shaw was a committed and proud Bostonian.

In her *Famous Families of Massachusetts,* Mary Caroline Crawford wrote that Father Shaw belonged to "one of the most remarkable families in the history of Massachusetts, a family which for two hundred years has played important parts in Boston's military, civic, and social life."[3] His mother was a Parkman, aunt of the historian Francis Parkman, who is represented on a stained glass window in the O'Neill office in Bapst Library. His nephew, Robert Gould Shaw, died leading a black regiment in the Civil War battle for Fort Wagner, South Carolina, and is memorialized by the Augustine St. Gaudens sculpture on Boston Common across from the State House. The Shaws were related to such famous Boston families as Agassiz, Sears, Lyman, Lowell, Sturgis, Eliot, and Higginson. So it is understandable, perhaps somewhat provincial, but certainly touching that young Father Shaw, educated theologically in Rome, familiar with cardinals and popes, and now for a few brief months an apprentice in a religious organization with worldwide apostolates, should on his death bed direct his modest patrimony and his library to his native city and to the Jesuit college that was to be established there.

Joseph Coolidge Shaw was born into a Unitarian home in Boston on January 22, 1821. After attending several schools and academies, he entered Harvard College in 1836. At Harvard he became proficient in French, Italian, and German, as well as in the traditional classics. This is significant because the study of contemporary languages in American colleges was only gaining a foothold in Shaw's time, and his later travel and study in Europe and his purchase of books in several European languages no doubt are related to his early mastery of languages other than English, Latin, and Greek. Shaw was a member of the Hasty Pudding Club at Harvard, and before his graduation in 1840 he was elected to Phi Beta Kappa.[4] After graduation, Shaw spent three years in Europe, studying German philosophy and literature in Berlin and Heidelberg and visiting the principal cities of Europe as well as the French Provinces in Africa.[5] Since Shaw was an avid book buyer, his travels can be partially mapped by the inscriptions he frequently wrote in the books he purchased, noting the city and date of purchase. We can follow his path by noting book entries such as these: Munich, September 1841; Heidelberg, 1841; Berlin, January, 1842; Vienna, September, 1842; Frankfort, November, 1843; Paris, November, 1843.[6]

According to Father Meagher's brief biography of Shaw as a preface to the Shaw diary, the young Harvard graduate's Unitarian faith was shaken by his contact with German rationalists. On a boat trip to Rome, however, he chanced to meet the future Catholic priest, Frederick William Faber, a leading member of the Oxford Movement, who was still an Anglican clergyman at the time. Faber introduced Shaw to a Jesuit, Father Thomas Glover, in Rome, and very abruptly, one month later, Joseph Shaw was baptized and confirmed by Charles Cardinal Acton in Rome.[7]

Shaw returned to Boston in 1843 and attended Harvard Law School for a year. A fellow student at the Law School was his friend and classmate from undergraduate years, Edward Holker Welch. The lives of the two men were intertwined. Like Shaw, Welch had become a Catholic while traveling in Europe in 1841. He followed Shaw into the priesthood and into the Society of Jesus. After studying theology in Paris, Welch was ordained in Rome in 1850 and was then admitted to the Society of Jesus. He was sent to the Jesuit novitiate in Frederick, Maryland, where Joseph Coolidge Shaw was also a novice, and when Shaw was deathly ill, it was Welch who wrote down the contents of his will.[8] Twelve years after Shaw's death, when the dream of a Jesuit

Rev. Joseph Coolidge Shaw in the garb of a priest of the Boston archdiocese, for which he was ordained in September 1847. Three years later, with the blessing of Boston's Bishop John Fitzpatrick, he entered the Society of Jesus as a novice. He died five months later, after willing his library to the future Jesuit college in Boston.

college in Boston approached realization with the granting of a charter by the Commonwealth of Massachusetts, Shaw's friend Edward Welch was one of the incorporators whose signature is on the Boston College charter, and he became one of the first trustees of the University.

After one year at law school, Joseph Shaw felt called to the priesthood. In 1844 he was accepted as a student at the Roman College. At his father's request and with the approval of Father Glover, his confessor and advisor, he returned to Boston in the summer of 1847. In September Bishop John Fitzpatrick ordained him in the old cathedral of the Holy Cross on Franklin Street.[9] Ordination to the subdiaconate and diaconate and then to the priesthood took place in a span of four days in September. Father Shaw had a sense of the importance of his family in Massachusetts, for he wrote in his diary three years later:[10]

> The ordination was a species of triumph for the Church in Boston, not of course as regards me personally, but from the circumstances of my family, etc. My Father and Mother who were present themselves at the three ordinations invited a great many of their friends, & especially at the last ordination the church was full of Protestants, & the papers talked a good deal of the matter.

Since he had not completed his theological studies in Rome, young Father Shaw, after some pastoral experience in the New England area, went to St. Joseph Seminary with the Jesuit fathers at Fordham, where he spent 21 months in further study. By 1850 Father Shaw was convinced he should join the Society of Jesus, and after some months of appropriate consultation he entered the novitiate at Frederick, Maryland, on September 7, 1850.

Shaw's diary shows a preoccupation with his books. He never comments on his various acquisitions, but every time he moved there was special reference to his books. For example, when he was leaving Rome to return to Boston for ordination, he noted: ". . . packed up about half of the 900 or 1000 books I had collected, and sent them by Plowden and Cholmeley, leaving the rest under the charge of Wm. Clifford. . . ."[11] Clifford was a fellow-seminarian who later became a bishop in England.

When he was about to leave St. Joseph Seminary for a final trip with his family before entering the novitiate, Shaw noted in his diary: "On Monday, Aug. 2nd (having packed up all my books & other things during the two preceding days), I took leave of Fordham with much gratitude to the Fathers . . ."[12] When he paid his last visit to the family home in Boston, where the bulk of his books had been left during his stay at Fordham and were to be left when he entered the Society of Jesus, he noted: "I remained in Boston till the 17th, packing my books, open not nailed however, & to remain in the house."[13] Since he was talking about 1700 or more volumes, one can picture them lined up neatly in wooden boxes, but with the covers not nailed for shipment.

Shaw's life in the Society of Jesus was to be a sadly short

one—six months and two days. In the fall of 1850 his diary recorded cheerfully the simple routine of novitiate life—prayer, spiritual conferences, waiting at table, washing dishes, gathering evergreens for liturgical festivals. The last entry was made on January 21, 1851: "I read in the Refectory all last week, which was pretty fatiguing as I had a bad cold & cough & today F. Minister has regularly put me on the sick-list. . . ." His sickness was apparently tuberculosis, and he spent his remaining weeks in bed. In February he decided to make a will, and on two days, the 16th and the 18th, dictated it to his priest-friend, and fellow novice, Father Edward Welch.

The will begins: "As God may very probably withdraw me from this life shortly I wish to make a disposition of my few effects as appears best for His service." The will consists largely of intimate small gifts to members of his family. The more businesslike part of the will and the only bequests of substance have to do with the money and books for Boston College. The family part of the will was dictated on February 16:[14]

> . . . To my brother Frank I give the Arab coat, cap etc. now in his possession. To Sarah Russel the gold pen & pencil case (which is here) and the purse with gold rings which she gave me. To my Bro. Parkman I give my gold shirt buttons. To Robert the scimitar now in his possession. To Mary R. the silver paper cutter she gave me (that is in my trunk I believe upstairs). To my sister Anna, the silver napkin ring given me by her and Lizzie. To Howland the silver shaving brush he gave me. To Quincy my oriental pipes, gun sword, pistols, etc. To Marian my painted German pipe (as an ornament) with the Arab purses and other little articles in mother's possession. To Frank's little Effie the prettiest little coral & silver rosary that can be found in my collection, with my blessing. Finally to my Father & Mother I leave the bronze crucifix on the table in my room with the tenderest love and respect and gratitude for their unwearied kindness and liberality, my sorrow for everything by which I have offended them and my prayers for their welfare & happiness and that they and my brothers and sisters may be brought to the bosom of the Catholic Church before God calls them to follow me.
>
> N. B. The articles above mentioned are mostly in my wardrobe at home.

This is the part of the will dictated on February 16, 1851. It illustrates Shaw's meticulous attention to detail and his delicate thoughtfulness toward each member of his family, so clearly expressed just three weeks before his death. Shaw's was a large family. Besides his five brothers and three sisters mentioned in the will, a brother William had died in infancy and a younger sister Elizabeth had died in 1850.

When Shaw continued dictating two days later he turned his attention to other than family matters—mostly to the as yet nonexistent Jesuit college in Boston. He began:[15]

> Whatever money, books or other effects of mine may be in this house [the novitiate] at the time of my death or may by chance be sent here for me after it, I give to F. Rector for the use of the Novitiate or Tertianship. Except the gold pen and pencil case and the silver paper cutter above mentioned and except any *odd* volumes of books, which should be sent to Boston that the set may not be broken.

Every bibliophile and librarian reading this will applaud the dying Shaw's concern that no set of books be broken. Implicitly he was concerned for the integrity of the Boston College library collection. But they will applaud even more warmly a parenthesis Shaw inserted later in the will: "(A list of the greater part of my theological and spiritual books will be found in a little green account book which is either here or in my bookcase at home.)"[16] How he loved his collection and how proudly he recorded it—a thousand entries in his own hand. But, alas, the little green book has disappeared. Perhaps, when after Shaw's death the cases of books presumably were shipped to the Jesuit Provincial's office in Maryland, it was thought that with the books in hand, Shaw's listing of them was unimportant. What a treasure that little green book could be as part of our collection in Burns Library!

We now turn to the final section of the Shaw will that concerns his books. Immediately after the paragraphs quoted at the beginning of this chapter, concerning the $4,000 for a school or college of the Society in Boston and his library of 1200 volumes on theological and spiritual subjects and 500 or 600 more on lighter topics intended for a college to be established in Boston, Father

Shaw added, ". . . but as there is no immediate prospect of such being established I give them to Father Provincial either to be left in Boston or to be brought here for the use of the Tertianship or in fine to make such distribution of them as he judges best."[17] This is a critically important condition to which we will return. At the end of the will was the name "J. C. Shaw" and beneath it in parentheses, "per E. J. Welch."[18]

Father Walter Meagher writes of Father Shaw:[19]

> Six days before his death he received the last Sacraments of the Church, and then, according to the custom of the Society, he was allowed to make his vows. Notwithstanding his great weakness, he read them so as to be heard all over the room. He then gave his blessing to the novices and scholastics of the community, wishing them all the grace and perserverance in their holy vocation.

Joseph Coolidge Shaw died on March 10, 1851, at the age of thirty.

Of the 1700 books collected and treasured by Father Shaw, 350 are in the Burns Library. Obviously Father Ignatius Brocard, the Provincial in Maryland, acted upon the clause at the end of Father Shaw's will that said ". . . in fine to make such distribution of them [the books] as he [Provincial] judges best." Indeed, in 1851 there was no immediate prospect of a college opening in Boston. Not only was Father McElroy to run into political opposition, but a catastrophic Civil War was to intervene before McElroy's and Shaw's hopes were to be realized. The Shaw family may well have been anxious to have son Joseph's precious boxes removed from their home. Georgetown was the prominent Jesuit college at the time, and plans were afoot to establish a seminary in the Province. Actually Woodstock College, the Jesuit seminary, opened in 1869, five years after Boston College accepted its first students. It is known that some Shaw books are in the Georgetown library. As noted elsewhere in this volume, the man who wrote Shaw's will for him, Father Edward Holker Welch, signed the charter of Boston College and was a member of the first board of trustees in 1863. Had he felt that Shaw's will regarding the disposition of the books had been violated, he presumably would have made representation on his friend's behalf. Fifty-seven years after Father

Shaw's death Father Welch wrote a memorial of him in the Jesuit journal, *Woodstock Letters*. He recalled the deathbed dictation of the will:[20]

> his father at the time of his ordination had given him the sum of $3000. This with the interest which had accrued he now left to the college of the Society that was to be built in his native town, and which is known as Boston College. To the same institution he left his valuable library collected partly in Germany, but principally in Rome. He is thus the earliest benefactor of that now flourishing Institution.

Father Welch notes and applauds the intention of the dying Father Shaw to benefit Boston College. That circumstances intervened to keep Shaw's hopes from being fully realized, Welch did not think worth mentioning. Obviously he was satisfied with the division that had been made of the Shaw library and felt that Boston College was the principal recipient of the young Boston priest's benefaction.

Those who are downcast at the realization that only 350 of Father Shaw's 1700 volumes eventually came to Boston College may be reminded of the most famous gift of books to a college in American history—John Harvard's donation of his library to the infant institution in Cambridge in 1638. His library consisted of 320 books.[21] There are startling similarities between Joseph Coolidge Shaw and John Harvard. Both were clergymen. Both died very young, apparently of tuberculosis, Shaw at 30 and Harvard at 32. Both made wills on their deathbed. Both are best remembered for their benefactions of money and books, one to a nascent, the other to a pre-nascent institution of higher learning in the Greater Boston area. Shaw left $4000 for Boston College. John Harvard's bequest was £779, but Harvard historian Samuel Eliot Morison says that only £375 was received by the College.[22]

The Shaw books in Burns Library are an impressive collection, especially as the work of a sole collector who apparently used no agent. The collection is overwhelmingly theological. The largest item, though not necessarily the most valuable, is Gian Domenici Mansi's monumental series of tomes on the Councils of the Church, *Sacrorum Conciliorum nova et amplissima collectio* in 31

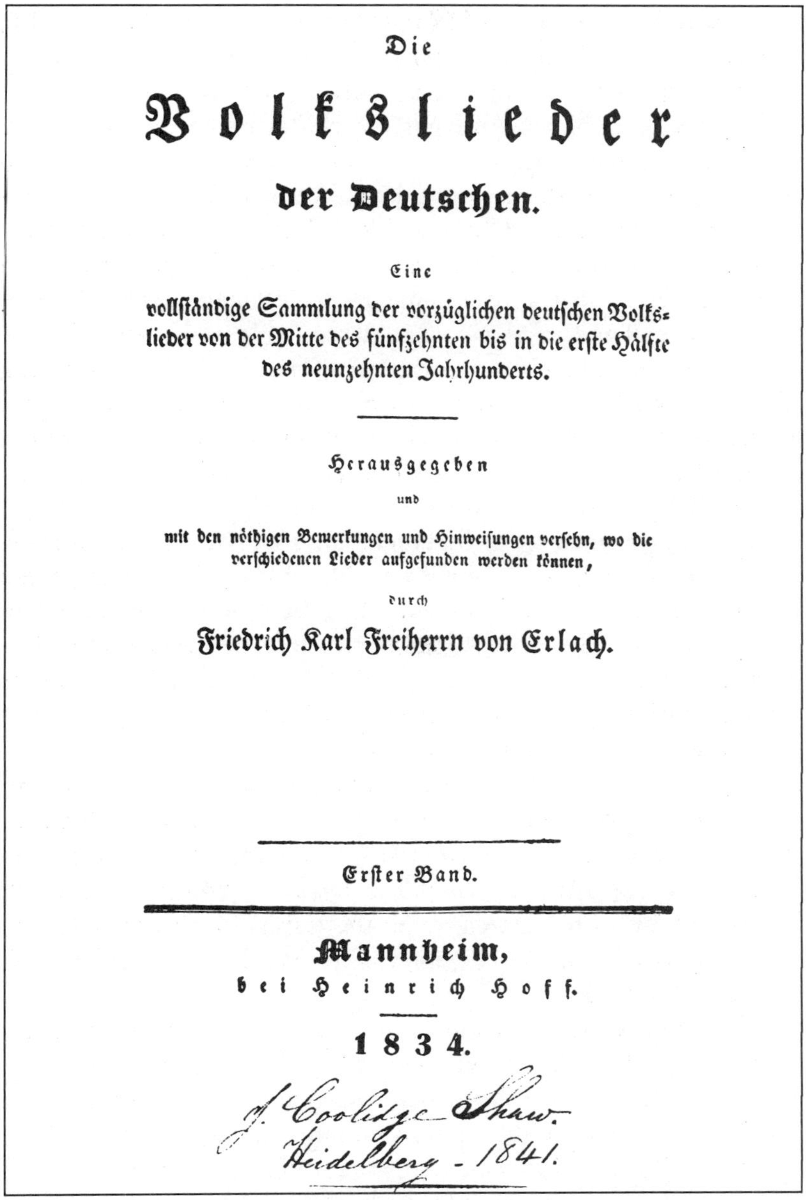

Die

Volkslieder

der Deutschen.

Eine

vollständige Sammlung der vorzüglichen deutschen Volkslieder von der Mitte des fünfzehnten bis in die erste Hälfte des neunzehnten Jahrhunderts.

Herausgegeben

und

mit den nöthigen Bemerkungen und Hinweisungen versehn, wo die verschiedenen Lieder aufgefunden werden können,

durch

Friedrich Karl Freiherrn von Erlach.

Erster Band.

Mannheim,

bei Heinrich Hoff.

1834.

J. Coolidge Shaw.

Heidelberg - 1841.

After graduating from Harvard in 1841, Joseph Coolidge Shaw spent three years in Europe, studying languages, attending lectures, and buying books. One of his early purchases was a book of German folk songs which, appropriately, he purchased in Heidelberg, as can be seen from his inscription.

folio volumes covering the councils from the early church to the Council of Florence in 1438. The volumes were published in Latin, with some Greek, from 1758 to 1798. Despite Father Shaw's warning against splitting a set, Boston College does not have volumes 29, 30, or 31. An equally ambitious piece of scholarship is the 26-volume work of Henri Francois Vence in French, called *Sainte Bible de Vence,* giving the Latin text with French translation of every book of the Old and New Testaments plus elaborate commentaries. Shaw's edition, the fifth, was published in Paris in 1827. There is also a 10-volume *Histoire Generale de L'Eglise,* published in Paris in 1841. That date, incidentally, was the first year of young Shaw's European trip, and it reveals something about Shaw as a collector. It is surprising how many of the books in the collection, even works written centuries earlier, bear a recent publication date—e.g., 1830 to 1845. A good example is St. Robert Bellarmine's *De Controversiis,* published in Rome in 1836. There is however, a set of St. Augustine's works in nine volumes, published in 1768. And there is one extraordinarily well preserved volume of commentaries on St. Thomas Aquinas, published in Venice in 1559. But one gathers from surveying the entire collection that Shaw, in the various cities of his travels, did not shop as an antiquarian but visited bookstores where most volumes would bear recent dates of publication.

Shaw's purchases showed his growing interest in the Society of Jesus. In January 1847 in Rome he purchased a life of St. Ignatius by a Fr. Muriani, *Vita del Patri S. Ignazio,* that was published in Venice in 1845. And on May 13, 1848, he bought an English translation of a French treatise on the Jesuits by Father DeRavignan, *On the Life and Institute of the Jesuits,* that was published in Philadelphia in 1845.

His secular volumes include a number of books in German and French on philosophy as well as large volumes of Tasso and Dante, Gibbon's *Decline and Fall of the Roman Empire, The Poetical Works of Thomas Gray,* a four-volume edition of Shelley, the poetry of William Cowper, and an edition of Thomas Carlyle's *The French Revolution,* published in Boston in 1839, with an inscription on the flyleaf, "Joseph Coolidge Shaw from his Friend and classmate Moses William Weld. August 26, 1840." That was the summer after their graduation from Harvard and may have

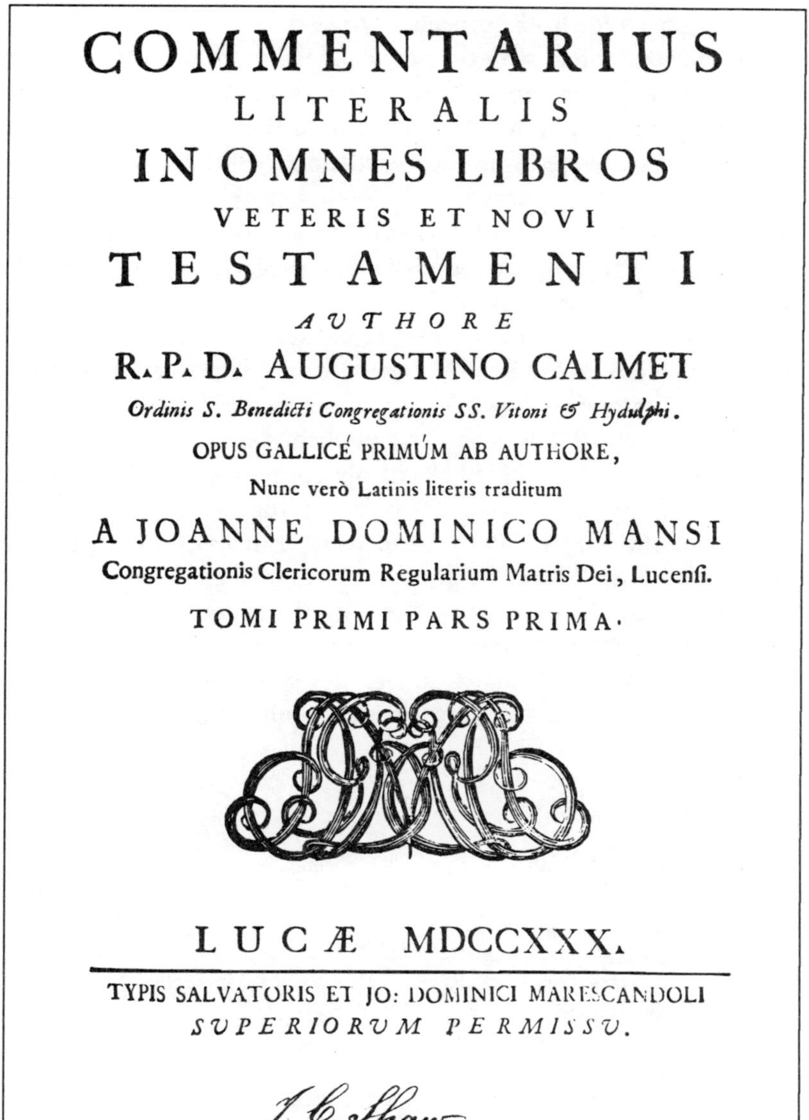

COMMENTARIUS
LITERALIS
IN OMNES LIBROS
VETERIS ET NOVI
TESTAMENTI
AUTHORE
R. P. D. AUGUSTINO CALMET
Ordinis S. Benedicti Congregationis SS. Vitoni & Hydulphi.
OPUS GALLICÉ PRIMÚM AB AUTHORE,
Nunc verò Latinis literis traditum
A JOANNE DOMINICO MANSI
Congregationis Clericorum Regularium Matris Dei, Lucensi.
TOMI PRIMI PARS PRIMA.

LUCÆ MDCCXXX.

TYPIS SALVATORIS ET JO: DOMINICI MARESCANDOLI
SUPERIORUM PERMISSU.

J. C. Shaw
Rome, Mar. 1845.

In 1845 Shaw purchased a multi-volume set of over-sized Latin commentaries on the Bible, published in 1730. The set is part of the Shaw collection in Burns Library.

been a graduation present or perhaps a going-away present as Shaw prepared for his European adventure.

To come in contact with the Shaw collection, to feel the bindings and smell the pages and note his elegant signature or initials with date and place of purchase in so many of them and to remember that all of them were carefully recorded in the little green book by the purchaser is to marvel that, even before its existence, the Boston College library had a patron as assiduous and discriminating in book collecting as Joseph Coolidge Shaw. He is, indeed, a patron saint for Burns Library.

The first formal account of the Boston College library was written by Father Edward I. Devitt, a gifted president, for the 1893–94 catalogue. The collection had now been in existence for thirty years, and this was the first published acknowledgement of various special gifts. Father Devitt appropriately gave first notice to Father Shaw. He wrote: "The stately tomes, which form the nucleus of the Theological alcove, were contributed by the Rev. Joseph Coolidge Shaw, S. J. who, after his conversion to the Catholic Church, went abroad and with the cheques of a generous father bought many volumes in Paris and Rome." To that generous father, Robert Gould Shaw, and to the generous-spirited, book-loving son, Boston College is forever, happily, indebted.

ENDNOTES

1. Rev. Walter J. Meagher, S. J., ed., "*A Proper Bostonian, Priest, Jesuit.*": *Diary of Fr. Joseph Coolidge Shaw, S. J.* (1821–1851), privately printed, pp. 77–8.
2. Meagher, *A Proper Bostonian,* p. 11.
3. Mary Caroline Crawford, *Famous Families of Massachusetts* (Boston: Little, Brown, and Co., 1930), vol. I, p. 233.
4. Meagher, *A Proper Bostonian,* p. ix.
5. *Ibid.*
6. It is worth noting that a well-known precedent for Shaw's academic "grand tour" in Europe with book buying as a prime byproduct was set by Harvard professor George Ticknor, who, incidentally, was the person responsible for gaining respectability at Harvard for the teaching of modern languages. In his *Three Centuries of Harvard,* Samuel Eliot Morison records (p. 266) that in 1815 Harvard sent two promising faculty members in their early twenties to the University of Göttingen for two years—George Ticknor and Edward Everett. Morison says that both

men made purchases in Europe on behalf of the Harvard library, and he cites at length a letter Ticknor wrote from Göttingen in 1816 stressing the great catch-up problem facing American college libraries. It is quoted here because of its relevance to Shaw's assiduous collecting for Boston College.

> . . . One very important and principal cause of the difference between our University [Harvard] and the one here is the different value we affix to a good library, and the different ideas we have of what a good library is . . . We found new professorships and build new colleges in abundance, but we buy no books; and yet it is to me the most obvious thing in the world that it would promote the cause of learning and the reception of the University ten times more to give six thousand dollars a year to the Library than to found three professorships. . . . I cannot better explain the difference between our University in Cambridge and the one here than by telling you that here I hardly say too much when I say it *consists* in the Library, and that in Cambridge the Library is one of the last things thought and talked about,—that here they have forty professors and more than two hundred thousand volumes to instruct them, and in Cambridge twenty professors and less than twenty thousand volumes. . . .

We note with satisfaction that, nearly four decades after their European sojourn, both Ticknor and Edward Everett befriended Father John McElroy in his struggle, against Protestant opposition, to acquire land in Boston for the Jesuit college he wished to found.

7. Meagher, *A Proper Bostonian,* pp. ix, x.
8. *Ibid.,* p. x, p. 84.
9. *Ibid.,* p. x.
10. *Op. cit.,* p. 10.
11. *Op. cit.,* p. 5.
12. *Op. cit.,* p. 47.
13. *Ibid.*
14. *Op. cit.,* p. 77
15. *Ibid.*
16. *Ibid.,* p. 78.
17. *Ibid.*
18. *Ibid.*
19. *Op. cit.,* p. xi.
20. *Woodstock Letters,* 26 (1897), pp. 446–450.
21. Justin Winsor, "Libraries in Boston," in *The Memorial History of Boston*

(Boston: Ticknor and Co., 1881), vol. IV, p. 279. Winsor was librarian of Harvard University.

22. Samuel Eliot Morison, *Three Centuries of Harvard* (Cambridge, Mass.: Harvard University Press, 1936), p. 9.

3

Nineteenth Century Boston College:

Irish or American?

IN HIS GENERALLY IMPRESSIVE HISTORY of the American collegiate curriculum from Colonial times to the present, Williams College historian Frederick Rudolph remarked of nineteenth century Catholic colleges, "Their [Catholics'] colleges were mostly Irish colleges, along with some German colleges, before they were American colleges."[1] To be sure, there were Catholic colleges whose students were almost all of Irish or German extraction, and to that extent the institutions might be called Irish or German. But when they are called Irish or German before American, what does that imply? That such colleges were more Irish or German than American? Or that they were somehow Irish for a while and later American? It is not clear, but Rudolph's statement led to the examination of one college in a city with a large Irish population, Boston College, to explore its "Irishness" in the last century.

Scholars of nineteenth century Irish-Catholic history point to the Irish Catholic newspaper as the standard and vehicle of Irish spirit. It therefore might be reasonable in assessing the Irish tone or style of a college to compare its student paper—in this case, the Boston College *Stylus*—with the local Catholic paper, the Boston

Pilot. In his 1960 volume, *To the Golden Door: The Story of the Irish in Ireland and America,* George Potter observes:[2]

> Next to the Church as a cultural influence was the Catholic Irish newspaper. The newspaper stood to the Catholic Irishman as school and college in one, his library, guide and companion. The impress of the Catholic Irish weekly upon the emigrants cannot be overemphasized . . . . Critics have dwelt upon the untoward influences of the Catholic Irish press; that it kept alive Irish sentiments, that it agitated Irish passions, that it flattered the Irishman instead of telling him the truth, that its results were divisive and exclusivist inside the American community . . . . Of the numerous Catholic Irish journals in the United States, many of which had only a brief and fitful life, the best and most important was the Boston *Pilot* . . . . The highest tribute to the value of the *Pilot* is to say that no history of the Catholic Irish in the United States can be written without it. Its pages were in the marrow of the Catholic Irish.

Already more than a half century old when *The Stylus* began publishing in 1883, the *Pilot* had served the immigrant Irish during the painful years at and after mid-century, when they thronged to Boston's shores. Boston's Irish may have needed the *Pilot* more in 1850 than three decades later. By the 1880s the Irish were on their feet. They had an imposing new cathedral. They had their college. They had a seeming galaxy of new churches, not only in Boston, but in the growing suburbs. And one of their own was Boston's mayor. One might expect their weekly newspaper to become more local or national, less Irish, in emphasis. But the *Pilot* of the 1880s and 1890s lived up to Potter's judgment: It left the impression that the United States was a suburb of Ireland rather than a different country.[3]

Front page articles dealt mostly with Ireland and Irish news or problems. A regular feature on page 3 was "Latest Irish News," giving rather gossipy items from or about each county of Ireland. A popular department right through the nineteenth century was "Information Wanted—Missing Friends," in which Irish all around the United States and Canada advertised for relatives or friends whom they wanted to contact.

The flavor and emphasis of the *Pilot* can be gleaned by examining the contents of the first page of several issues. In the year of the birth of *The Stylus,* the November 17, 1883 *Pilot* carried the following headlines on its first page: "An American View of Ireland," "How English Papers Concoct Irish-American News," "James Stephens' Reminiscences in Dublin's Freeman's Journal," "Failure of St. Alban's (Vt.) Trust Co.," "Gov. Butler on His Defeat," "Michael Davitt's Address in England," "A sensible Reform in Time-Keeping," and "Ancient Irish Art." Five of the eight articles were about Ireland.

In 1890 the May 17 issue of the *Pilot* gave first page prominence to the following articles: "American Prelate at our Italian Pilgrimage," "The Tramp of an Army—Laborers of the World on the Move," "The Tories in Danger" (containing a prediction that the British government would have to sacrifice part of their Irish Land Purchase Bill), "Democrats Control R.I." (explaining that as soon as a constitutional provision limiting the vote to people owning real estate worth $134 was repealed, the Republicans of Rhode Island were defeated), "Immigrant Girls—Cardinal Gibbons speaks for them in N.Y." (the cardinal left no doubt about the immigrants he extolled, praising "the Irish maiden"), "The Celt in London—Irish Writers Ought to Take Irish Subjects," and "The Mouth of the Columbia—Rich Irishmen Married to Indian Women."

When the first issue of *The Stylus* appeared, Boston College lads, whose families read on the front page of the *Pilot* that week articles about nine Irish-American judges, Mr. Parnell's great speech in Cork, and Michael Davitt's trip to England to speak on behalf of the Irish poor, presented their readers a poem of welcome to *The Stylus* by "the priest-poet of the South," Father Abram Ryan, an exposition of the need for a college paper, an essay on the importance of scientific study in a technological age, an invitation to alumni to subscribe to *The Stylus,* an account of the decorations and activities for Christmas at "the Immaculate" (the College church), an essay on a two-day summer visit to Salt Lake City in which the Mormons were described as "a sullen, cross, dissatisfied and unhappy set," news and odd items about college and class activities, several poems, an essay on reason, and a piece of fiction. Not a word about Ireland or the Irish, although that first *Stylus* carried on a back page an advertisement for the *Republic,* a newspaper proclaiming itself to be the leading Irish-

American journal of the east. To support that contention the ad gave testimonials from other papers, such as, "Takes an aggressive stand on Irish affairs"—*Boston Transcript*; "May it live to see Ireland a Republic"—*Boston Commercial Bulletin*; and "A vigorous and efficient advocate of Ireland's rights"—*Hartford Catholic*. The *Pilot* and the *Republic* were avowedly, aggressively Irish. No trace of their spirit or mission is found in the first issue or, as will be seen, in most later issues of *The Stylus*.

To give one more comparison, in the first year of the new century, the front page of the November 10 *Pilot* had stories with these headlines: "Three Yankees in Ireland," "British Atrocities in the Orange Free State," and "Anglo-Saxonism and Catholic Progress." A non-Irish item was headed "Cardinal Gibbons on the National Election," with the reassuring subheadline, "The Republic is Safe Whoever Wins." In the same month *The Stylus* offered its readers six poems on subjects such as autumn and evening and essays on the Jew of Malta, Macbeth, youthful types in Homer and Shakespeare, and universal peace. There were the usual domestic tidbits about college societies, alumni, class activities, and exchanges. Again the contrast is complete: the *Pilot* preoccupied with Ireland and things Irish, *The Stylus* with no reference to Ireland or Irish themes.

In all the issues of *The Stylus* between 1883 and 1900 there were only three articles on Irish topics. In the March 1899 *Stylus* there appeared an essay on the Irish poet Lionel Johnson under the title, "An Irish Lyrist." Considering the many articles on British, French, American, and classical authors carried by *The Stylus* during those years, the single article on Johnson shows no absorption with Irish literature. The April 1900 *Stylus* reprinted an article from the *Messenger of the Sacred Heart,* "A Catholic University for Ireland," which called for a government-funded Catholic university similar to the British-supported Presbyterian universities of Scotland.

The most "Irish" of the three essays, and the one most like those in the *Pilot*, appeared in February 1888, under the unpretentious title, "A Word." It is a reply to an article that had appeared in the *Boston Beacon,* which described itself as a weekly magazine of social progress and was part of Boston's journalistic scene from 1876 to 1904. The *Beacon* article opposed home rule for Ireland because, it stated, "We believe Home Rule in this connection would mean Rome rule." To this the *Stylus* writer riposted: "How smoothly flows the rhythm here! Home and Rome. But methinks 'tis the voice of a bigot, the phantasma of whose life is the mythical Rome that has passed back into the misty, legendary realms whence it was first conjured up by some *imaginative* Puritanic enemy of Rome." The *Stylus* article continued in the same vein, reacting to the *Beacon's* mention of "the unlovely characteristics" of the Irish race and its statement that "the two greatest sources of trouble are the ignorance and thriftlessness of the majority of the people."

The *Stylus* author ended with an apology for having dwelt so long on the *Beacon's* anti-Irish article, and his excuse is significant: "Our indignation at what we have no hesitation in styling its *un-Americanism* has perhaps led us beyond the limits of the reader's patient indulgence." The italics were the author's. True, he had accused the *Beacon* writer of religious and ethnic bigotry; but his final salvo was that the adversary was un-American. That charge of un-American reveals a ready faith in the fairness of American principles and laws, an ease and pride in being American. The young author of "A Word" was irate at slurs on the Irish, but he sounds as if he would have been equally indignant at an intimation that he was Irish before American.

Still, the contrast between the Irish emphasis of the *Pilot* and the near absence of Irish topics in *The Stylus* is striking. What accounted for that difference? It could be that the very dominance of the *Pilot* in the Boston and American Catholic scenes and the national standing of its eloquent editor, John Boyle O'Reilly, made the college students realize that an attempt to duplicate or compete with the *Pilot* in style or emphasis would be vain, and it seems likely that they would have been so advised by their Jesuit mentors. There may also, however, have been some reluctance on the part of the youthful editors to concentrate on issues that preoccupied their elders.

Before considering *The Stylus* from another viewpoint, in the context of American collegiate journalism, it is pertinent to examine a second institution that preserved Irish spirit, the Irish militia company. The first in Boston was the Montgomery Guards, founded in 1837, a decade before the explosion of Irish immigration. Of the Montgomery Guards, George Potter wrote:[4]

> The company had been formed for the praiseworthy purpose of military service and association with the life of the city and state; it was an affirmative expression of a will by the Irish to be Americans. Pride of race and sentimental attachments to the motherland prompted a distinctively green uniform, on their caps the emblem of the eagle bearing a harp symbolic of amalgamation, their motto: "Fostered under thy wing, we will die in thy defence." Each member wore a piece of lace in the form of a shamrock sprig. A deep psychological necessity urged the Catholic Irish to express membership in the American community in terms of their racial identity—a pattern consistent with emigrant peoples; but the means of fulfilment through this symbolism struck highly nationlistic America as unpatriotic and unsatisfactory hyphenation.

Militia companies in towns and on campuses were part of the American scene throughout the nineteenth century. The Irish seized upon this American institution and made it their own. In *Boston's Immigrants* Oscar Handlin wrote:[5]

> Militia companies were friendly social organizations, less attractive for their martial exploits than for the small bounty, the opportunity to parade in uniform, and the dinner and speeches that followed target practice and parade. Though others [it is clear from a footnote that Handlin means other immigrant groups] joined American companies, the Irish formed their own. Their earliest, the Montgomery Guards, had disbanded in 1839 after a dispute, but the Columbian Artillery, the Bay State Artillery, and the Sarsfield Guards took its place by 1852. Dissolved by the governor in 1853 as a result of Know-Nothing agitation, they continued their activities in new skins. The Columbian Artillery became the Columbian Literary Association, while the Sarsfield Guards became the Sarsfield Union Association, and their balls, picnics, and lectures suffered no loss in popularity.

With the outbreak of the Civil War, the Columbian Artillery was re-established, and Irish units were recruited around the country. A number of them bore distinctively Irish names. There were Montgomery Guards from Cincinnati and Detroit, Emmet Guards from Albany, the Jasper Greens of Savannah, and the Hibernia Greens of Pittsburgh.[6] Sarsfield and Emmet, of course, were Irish military heroes, Patrick Sarsfield being the seventeenth century defender of Limerick and Robert Emmet the late eighteenth century romantic rebel. General Richard Montgomery was a Dubliner, a career officer in the British army, who became a naturalized American and led American troops during the Revolutionary War in the capture of Montreal, only to be slain in the assault on Quebec.

In contrast to the social Irish military units and the volunteer Irish brigades with Hibernian names and emblems in the Civil War was Boston College's cadet company. It started during the presidency of Father Fulton and flourished in the years 1870 to 1884. It was called the Foster Cadets, not after an Irish hero but after a New Hampshire Yankee, John Gray Foster,[7] a West Point graduate who served with distinction in the Civil War and was converted to Catholicism during the North Carolina expedition of 1861. One of the early cadet officers, who wrote his reminiscences for *The Stylus* twenty-five years later, described the cadet uniforms as Civil War style, dark blue in color, with large brass buttons stamped with the College monogram down the front, and white duck gaiters over blue trousers. The officers wore crimson sashes under their sword belts.[8] No green, no shamrocks, no harps.

But when we look not at Irish militia brigades but at cadet organizations on Catholic college campuses during the nineteenth century, we get a different perspective.[9] None of the other Catholic colleges, many of which had largely Irish student bodies, had any Irish touch in their titles or uniforms. In fact, most of the cadet units took the name of the college. Here are a few, with the date of the formation of the cadet organization: Georgetown College Military Cadets, 1836 (they were brightened by a red braid and a red sash); Spring Hill Lancers of Spring Hill College, 1843; the Mountain Cadets of Mount St. Mary's College, Emmitsburg, Md., 1836; St. Louis Cadets of St. Louis College, 1851; Santa Clara Cadets of Santa Clara College, 1856; Continental Cadets (seniors) and Washington Cadets (juniors) of Notre Dame, 1859; St. Xavier Cadets of Xavier University, Cincinnati, 1875; and St. John's Cadets of Fordham (with scarlet uniform), 1891.

Harvard anticipated Notre Dame by having a military corps

The Foster Cadets uniform was a single-breasted dark blue sack-coat and trousers of the same material and color, with white duck gaiters. "No green, no shamrocks, no harps."

named after Washington as early as 1812. Later in the century, at the time Boston College's Foster Cadets flourished, an organization called the Harvard Rifles was formed in 1875. A random selection of other non-Catholic colleges reveals that Allegheny, Baylor, Brown, Cornell (Iowa), and Dartmouth Colleges had cadet groups carrying the college name. So Boston College seems to have done the unusual in naming its cadet corps after a person, and the fact that the College honored John Gray Foster, a Civil War veteran and a Catholic, reflects both patriotism and Catholic pride.

To return for a moment to the *Pilot*, George Potter commented:[10]

> A reading of the *Pilot* in the pre-Civil War years underlines the wide gulf between cultured Boston and the Irish community. The Golden Age of New England letters coincided with the years of greatest Irish emigration. Nothing in the *Pilot* indicated that the great literary figures of the time exercised the slightest influence on the Boston Irish.

Of course, Potter was speaking of the literary era that Van Wyck Brooks called the "flowering" of New England, whereas Boston College in the last decades of the century was in the season that Brooks termed New England's "Indian summer." Longfellow, one of the luminaries of New England's literary circle, died in 1882. Three years later the Class of Poetry at Boston College held a commemoration in Longfellow's honor. It was a formal symposium with an artistically printed program. The exercises consisted of essays and poems about the author and readings from his work. This rather touching tribute to Longfellow—Yankee, Brahmin, Harvard professor—of course manifested a familiarity with the poet and his fame, but it also proved the absence of any parochial Irish or Catholic bias against him. The event might be seen simply as a small but significant example of acculturation and of pride in regional lights of whatever ethnic background. But perhaps there was more to it than that. In his book, *The New England College in the Age of the University,* George Peterson noted that the graduating class at Williams College during the 1880s, as one item in a general poll of class opinions, regularly named Longfellow as the world's greatest poet.[11] (One year Tennyson was ranked second and Shakespeare fourth.) There is no record that the Boston College students' admiration for Longfellow went to such lengths, but it is perhaps more than coincidence that students at an "Irish" college and a Yankee college shared similar enthusiasms at roughly the same time. One can speculate that for the Boston College students, the primary reference group was not the local Irish community but the general collegiate population.

Lending some credence to such a hypothesis is the fact that, from its inception, a regular feature of *The Stylus* was "Exchanges," which acknowledged and commented on student papers received from other colleges. Not surprisingly, journals from Catholic colleges were listed: Georgetown, Holy Cross, Fordham,

Notre Dame, Villanova, and Niagara. But there was also a good representation from private and public non-Catholic colleges: Dartmouth, Brown, Amherst, Wesleyan, Tufts, Northwestern, Minnesota, Illinois, and Virginia. Clearly the editors and readers of *The Stylus* did not have their intellectual horizons limited either to Suffolk County or to the Boston *Pilot*.

This speculation to the effect that their status as collegians caused Boston College students to be more like than unlike their peers elsewhere led to a comparison of the entire contents of *The Stylus* in the last two decades of the nineteenth century with the contents of student papers at Brown and Williams during the same period. The similarities of focus, concern, subject matter, and style are strong. The students at all three colleges showed a partiality for the essay in the style of Lamb, as seen from these titles: from Brown's *Brunonian,* "A Day Off," "Withered Leaves," "The Art of Conversation," "Dreams;" from *The Williams Literary Monthly,* "Jogging through Some Old Ruts," "Duck Shooting," "The Poplars in the Berkshires," "That Dress Suit;" and from *The Stylus*, "Day Dreaming," "A Lamp Post's Soliloquy," "Cycling under Difficulties," and "An Evening Stroll."

The longer and more serious articles in all three journals tended to be scholastic and philosophical rather than political or social. This is seen in such titles from *The Brunonian* as "Pedagogy in Our Colleges," "Religious Tolerance in College," "Civilization and Selfishness," "The Bible in the College Curriculum," "An Evil of the Elective System;" from *The Williams Literary Monthly,* "The Christian Element in Plato," "Doubt and Belief," "The Psychology of Belief," "College Journalism;" from *The Stylus* "The Need of Religious Education," "The Moral Value of Education," "Catholicism and Science," "The Literary Study of the Bible," "Dr. McCosh on Electivism."

While *The Brunonian* carried almost no articles with strictly literary themes, the Boston College and Williams College papers featured pieces about major and some minor British and American authors and their works. The Boston College students showed two of their distinctive loyalties by articles about Catholic writers such as Cardinal Newman and New England Catholic poets and by dozens of articles on classical themes and authors.

The Brunonian, The Stylus, and a second Williams College

paper, *The Williams Weekly,* carried many domestic features having to do with college activities, athletics, and life. All exhibited a certain moralism in editorial comments, as witness such headings as "Cramming for Exams," "Cribbing," "Student Decorum," and "Decline of College Spirit" in *The Brunonian*; "Chapel Etiquette" and "Ungentlemanly Acts on Campus" in *The Williams Weekly*; and "College Spirit," "Evils of Smoking," and "Copying Themes" in *The Stylus*. Baseball was the central athletic interest for the papers of all three colleges in the 1880s, while in all three football gained equal space and concern in the 1890s. *The Brunonian* carried such articles as "Nuisance at Ball Games," "Base-running," "The Double Umpire System," and "The Importance of Interest in Football." *The Williams Weekly* felt called upon to rebut the charge of giving too much space to baseball and had articles on the need for financial contributions from the students for both football and baseball. *The Stylus* called for a college song and a new cheer to help the athletic teams, and at different times it both urged support for the football team and decried the baseball team's poor performance.

In keeping with the starting-point of this chapter, mention may be made of an article in *The Brunonian* of 1896 by one Thomas Hamilton Murray entitled, "The Irish Chapter in the History of Brown University" and of an 1890 report in *The Williams Weekly* of a debate between two Williams literary societies on the question, "Resolved that the British Government should grant Home Rule to Ireland," in which the affirmative side was declared the winner.

The nineteenth century was an era of oratory. Public occasions called for a profusion of speakers. Commencement was the college's oratorical showcase, often featuring a Latin oration and, besides the salutatory and valedictory, a philosophical oration, a classical oration, and six or seven other orations. Commencement programs of Brown and Williams show that in the late nineteenth century there were at least 10 senior orators at Brown and as many as 14 at Williams. Boston College was more restrained, or more humane, since it usually had four and never more that five student addresses.

Commencement in the nineteenth century, as it had been since Colonial times, was a public exhibition, a display of student talent and college accomplishment. Hence, the topics of commencement orations offer significant insight into the values and concerns of both the colleges and their graduates. Once again, by this norm the Boston College seniors were more like than unlike their Brown and Williams counterparts. The following commencement themes are representative. From Brown, "Belief and Character," "Science and Philosophy," "The Growth and Influence of Physical Science," "Law and Liberty," "A National University"; from Williams, "The Influence of Intellect on Character," "Science and Revelation," "Law, the Interpreter of Truth," "Christianity and Scientific Progress," "Moderation," "Social Inertia"; and from Boston College, "The Existence of God and the Belief of Nations," "Anarchy and the Synthetic Philosophy," "Shall the United States Found a National University?" "The Rights of Inferior Nations," "The Ethics of Competition," "The Church and Education."

The topics tended to be abstract and were frequently philosophical or religious. If a random selection were made of thirty commencement topics from each college without identifying the campus where the orations were delivered, one would be hard put to identify one list as Boston College's rather than Brown's or Williams'. What might complicate such a challenge is that in 1884 a Williams commencement topic was "Justice for Ireland"; in 1886 and 1887 Brown audiences heard orations on "Ireland for the Irish" and "The Moderation of Daniel O'Connell"; and in 1895 a Williams senior spoke on "The Irishman and His Case," while the following year a Brown orator expounded on "The Patriotism of the Irish-American." During that period no Boston College senior spoke on an Irish theme.

So, while we started out prepared to explain and perhaps defend an Irish emphasis at Boston College, we end up wondering why, in an actively Irish community, Boston College was not more Irish. We have to ask whether there was, on the part of the College authorities or of the students, an attempt to tone down and mute Irish sentiments, interests, and themes. Had the Jesuits subscribed to Orestes Brownson's outrageous mid-century suggestion that the Irish cease being Irish as soon as possible and assimilate themselves to the Anglo-Americans? In the best—or worst—tradition of nativism, Yankee Brownson, a convert to Catholicism, wrote in *Brownson's Quarterly Review:*[12]

> The American nationality will never be Irish, German, French, Spanish, or Chinese; it is and will be a peculiar modification of the Anglo-Saxon, or, if you prefer, Anglo-Norman, maintaining its own essential character, however enriched by contributions from other sources. This is to be considered as settled and assured as their starting point by all immigrants from foreign countries. They should understand at the outset, if they would avoid unpleasant collision, that they must ultimately lose their own nationality and become assimilated in general character to the Anglo-American race.

Brownson had more particular advice for the Irish:[13]

> What the Irish should aim at is not to excite pity for the misfortunes of their country, or tears for the wrongs they have for so many ages endured. The restoration of a nation is hopeless when it can only boast a greatness that has passed away, or chant, though never so sweet and musical, a wail of sorrow.

The Anglo-American sage further admonished the Irish:[14]

> They must study to avoid, as far as possible, wounding the national sensibility, or adopting modes of action or expression likely to offend it. Let them not make their new home an arena for fighting the battles of the country they have left; let them organize no military companies composed exclusively of foreign-born citizens; let them publish no journals, and organize no associations for political purposes to be effected in foreign countries. These things give offence, and not unreasonably, to the national feeling.

However naïve Brownson was in thinking his condescending advice would be welcomed by the Irish, his sentiments undoubtedly expressed the thought of the dominant Protestant population of the Boston area. Could it be that Boston College was seeking to "avoid unpleasant collision" and was fostering assimilation with the native majority? The answer appears to be no. There are too many contrary indications to justify the assumption of a set policy at Boston College of disowning or deliberately downplaying the Irish heritage. For example, from the earliest days, St. Patrick's Day was a college holiday. Again, an account of a lecture at Boston College by an English Jesuit that appeared in *The Stylus* in 1883 expresses sympathies Brownson would not have approved. The lecturer was Father Richard Clarke, S. J., late Fellow of Oxford. His address took place in the College Hall, though the article did not specify whether he spoke to a student or to a more general audience. His subject was, "My Visit to Ireland," and *The Stylus* editor commented:[15]

> The vivid and sympathetic story which he tells, under this caption, in a recent number of the "Month," is simply a record of actual facts and impressions gathered during a brief visit to the country. The harrowing details are much more moving than pen or tongue can describe. Yet, when such strong confirmation of the sad recital comes from an English witness of so high a character, there is hope for a larger acceptance of the facts in the case, and readier sympathies with them.

Several humorous anecdotes in *The Stylus* reveal that the students were quite comfortable with their Irish identity. One, tongue in cheek, expostulated against the painting of a wooden building in the college yard a color that the writer perceived as British red. Another poked fun at a group of upperclassmen who were so enchanted by the Irish airs played by an Italian street musician on the eve of St. Patrick's feast that they forgot to offer the usual appreciative donation.

Rather than postulate a policy or tradition of muting Irish emphasis at Boston College in its early decades, the following factors seem sufficient to account for the kind of low-keyed "Irishness" we have noted. The students were surrounded at home and in their neighborhoods by successful organizations and agencies such as Irish Clubs, the *Pilot*, and the rest of the Irish press, all of which vigorously and effectively promoted Irish causes, news, and themes. There was no need, nor little point, in college students duplicating the work of such organizations. It is also clear from the evidence that the Boston College students were quite conscious and proud of their Americanism, which would naturally lead to emphasis on topics of local and national interest. Finally, the students of Boston's Jesuit college are revealed as preoccupied with their life as college students, absorbed in their classical literary, philosophical and religious studies, and sharing the interests and preferences of their contemporaries at non-Catholic colleges.

It would, of course, be disingenuous to attribute student attitudes and interests in nineteenth century Boston College solely to a self-generated student culture. The Jesuits were close to students both in class (the typical teacher had the same students in three or four subjects for as many as 15 hours a week) and in out-of-class activities. Whereas in the twentieth century the Jesuit assigned to supervise a debating or dramatic society was termed a "moderator," which implied occasional tempering of student exuberance, in the nineteenth century the Jesuit assigned to guide the student editors of *The Stylus* was called the "director," a word that suggests an active role in the setting of publication policy and tone.

Considering the relatively non-Irish tone of the early *Stylus*, one might wonder whether the Jesuit directors may have been of non-Irish backgrounds and, hence, not particularly sympathetic to Irish emphasis. Between 1883 and 1900 *The Stylus'* Jesuit directors were: Michael Byrnes, Martin Hollahan, Willian Stanton, Patrick Mulry, Thomas Gasson, Patrick Cormican, and Edward O'Hara. Father Gasson was born in England. All the others were of Irish extraction. One must conclude that the predominantly Irish faculty approved or abetted the low key approach to Irish themes and emphasis manifested by the nineteenth century Boston College students.

Although the evidence permits a variety of interpretations, one thing is clear: Nineteenth century Boston College was not Irish before it was American.

ENDNOTES

1. Frederick Rudolph, *Curriculum: A History of The American Undergraduate Course of Study Since 1636* (San Francisco: Jossey-Bass Publishers, 1977), p. 170.
2. George Potter, *To the Golden Door: The Story of the Irish in Ireland and America* (Boston: Little, Brown and Company, 1960), pp. 598, 599, 603.
3. Potter, *To the Golden Door,* p. 601.
4. Potter, *To the Golden Door,* p. 312.
5. Oscar Handlin, *Boston's Immigrants, 1790–1880* (New York: Atheneum, 1976), p. 157.
6. Potter, *To the Golden Door,* p. 475.

7. Foster, prominent enough to find a place in both the *Dictionary of American Biography* and the first *Catholic Encyclopedia,* served with the Army Corps of Engineers after the war and conducted extensive survey and construction operations along the New England coast. He published a well known treatise, "Submarine Blasting in Boston Harbor," and was in the Boston area when the College's student battalion was formed.
8. Rev. Patrick H. Callanan, "Reminiscences," *The Stylus*, XI (November 1897) pp. 454–55.
9. Information concerning cadet activity at the colleges mentioned was obtained by correspondence with the institutions and, in a few cases, from institutional histories.
10. Potter, *To the Golden Door,* p. 607.
11. George E. Peterson, *The New England College in the Age of the University* (Amherst, Mass: Amherst College Press, 1964), p. 78.
12. Orestes Brownson, "A Few Words on Native Americanism," *Brownson's Quarterly Review,* II (July 1854), pp. 336–37.
13. Brownson, *Native Americanism,* pp. 341–2.
14. Brownson, *Native Americanism,* p. 352.
15. *The Stylus,* II (December 1883), p. 13.

4

Student Enrollment in the Nineteenth Century

UPON CONSULTING the Boston College catalogues of the nineteenth century, one finds that the enrollment in 1870 was 128, that it topped 200 (202) in 1877, went over 300 (334) in 1890, and was 472 in 1898. But those overall figures take on a different meaning when it is recalled that, during this period, the curriculum at Boston College was a seven-year program that embraced a preparatory as well as a collegiate division, with the majority of students in the lower division. Thus, if we look only at the upper three classes, we see that in the year the College awarded its first A.B. degrees, 1877, there were 36 collegiate students. The collegiate enrollment reached 91 in 1880, 101 in 1885, and 186 in 1898.

It was not at all unusual in the nineteenth century for colleges to have preparatory departments. Private academies were limited in number and location, high schools were in an incipient stage, and colleges found that they had to provide transitional preparation for grade school graduates to bring them up to college entrance level. One historian of higher education, Frederick Rudolph, says that in 1870 only 26 colleges in the country were not operating preparatory departments.[1] So there was nothing "unAmerican" about running a preparatory department, except

Rev. Jeremiah O'Connor, fourth president of Boston College, 1880–1884.

that Boston College was not doing it as a stopgap to meet a temporary educational problem in the United States but in conformity with a centuries-old Jesuit educational tradition.

The famous European Jesuit colleges of the seventeenth and eighteenth centuries, following the code for liberal education established by the Society of Jesus for all its colleges in the *Ratio Studiorum,* took students through a graded classical education, starting with rudiments of Latin and Greek and culminating six, seven, or eight years later with the course in philosophy that finally led to the bachelor's degree. The same pattern had been followed at Georgetown, Fordham, St. Louis, Santa Clara, and other Jesuit colleges founded in America before Boston College. All had a seven-year program (later eight years) that embraced preparatory and college years in a continuum, with all the students sharing the same campus and buildings and (as at Boston College until 1899, when for the first time separate catalogues were published for the two divisions) a common catalogue that listed students alphabetically, with their class or grade after their name. Thus, a 14-year-old C. Murphy in lowest rudiments came before a 21-year-old D.

Murphy who had attained the eminence of the class of philosophy. That the older or collegiate students did not dissociate themselves from the younger is attested by an item in *The Stylus* in 1888 that reported on enrollments in the 26 Jesuit colleges in America in the academic year 1886–87, noting that the average enrollment was 231 and rather proudly stating that Boston College exceeded the average by more than 40. Since there were only 96 students in the upper three classes in 1886–87, it is clear that the editors were reporting and accepting as applicable the total enrollments of Jesuit institutions with preparatory and collegiate divisions combined.[2]

Compared with today's huge college enrollments and Boston College's current annual freshman class of over 2000, the number of students in the College prior to 1900 seems tiny. But these numbers must be seen in the light of circumstances at the time. In 1870 only 1.7 percent of young people between the ages of 18 and 21 were attending college, and the number had gone up only to 3 percent by 1900.[3] Another way of judging size of collegiate enrollment in the nineteenth century is to look at the number of students being prepared for college. Boston school records show that in 1864, the year Boston College opened, the venerable Boston Latin School graduated only 11 young men. Ten years later the number of graduates was 31, and in 1898 Latin School graduated 49.[4] Thus, even the city's principal supplier of candidates for entrance to college did not produce large numbers.

Colleges with enrollments under a hundred were commonplace in the nineteenth century. Frederick Rudolph notes that in the middle of the century the two colleges then existing in New York City, with its half million population, had a combined enrollment of only 247. At about the same time, the board of trustees of Lafayette College was larger than the student body, and just before the Civil War there were 22 colleges in Ohio with an average enrollment of 85.[5]

At the end of the century the small-enrollment college remained the mode in American higher education. In 1898 the Secretary of War published a report concerning 101 institutions with federally supported military cadet programs.[6] Only five of the colleges had enrollments over 1000 (three of them being Harvard, Yale, and

MIT), while eight had enrollments between 500 and 1000. That year, which was the first year the college division extended to four years, the Boston College enrollment was 186. Compare that with the enrollments of selected colleges listed in the report of the Secretary of War (see table below).

College	Number of Students
Massachusetts Agricultural College	75
University of New Hampshire	75
University of Rhode Island	67
Rutgers	162
Fordham	140
Michigan State	190
Purdue	60
Maryland	109
Seton Hall	72
Alabama	120
Louisiana State	185
Tennessee	179
Washington	117

On the Secretary's representative list of American colleges were many with enrollments larger than Boston College's in 1898, but the number of institutions with comparable or smaller enrollments shows that, even with fewer than 200 college students, Boston College was by no means on that account a feeble or unusually small college at the time.

Boston College's first graduating class of 12 young men in 1877 seems small, especially since the college had been in existence for 12 years before the first great prefect of studies (as the dean was then called), Father Robert Fulton, would permit the class of philosophy to be added, completing the curriculum leading to the bachelor's degree. But, again, that figure of 12 graduates takes on a different significance when it is compared with the number graduating the same year from the older Jesuit colleges. The catalogues of the several Jesuit Colleges for the year 1876–77 show the numbers of students awarded the bachelor's degree at commencement in June (see the table on the next page).

Boston College in the nineteenth century. The photo was probably taken from the roof of the old Homeopathic Hospital, site of the present Boston University hospital. In the left foreground is the Jesuit residence fronting (extreme left) on Harrison Avenue. Beyond the residence, still on the left, is the roof of the grand church of the Jesuits, the Church of the Immaculate Conception. The College building, looking here like a wing of the Jesuit residence, extended along James Street (parallel to Harrison Avenue) and went as far beyond the residence toward the church as it extends beyond the residence in this photo.

College	Year Founded	Number Graduating
Georgetown	1789	7
St. Louis	1818	3
Spring Hill	1830	3
Xavier (in Cincinnati)	1831	7
Fordham	1841	5
Holy Cross	1843	13
Santa Clara	1851	11
Loyola (in Baltimore)	1852	0
College of St. Ignatius*	1855	1

*Now the University of San Francisco

In light of those numbers, Boston College's first graduating class must have seemed almost robust.

By June 1900, after its twenty-fourth commencement, Boston College had granted the bachelor's degree to 423 men, a small band, to be sure, but how relative size is. It was representatives of that small band that Father Thomas Gasson stirred a few years later when he told the alumni in May 1907 that he needed the sum of $10 million to move the College from the South End to a more expansive setting, to add to the faculty distinguished lay professors, and to strengthen the physical sciences.[7] A heady challenge for an institution with fewer than 500 alumni. Those may have been small-number days, but they were not days of small dreams or hearts. The challenge—not the precise financial challenge, but the challenge to plan and act boldly—was met, and we marvel today at the scale and quality of the achievement.

ENDNOTES

1. Frederick Rudolph, *Curriculum: A History of the American Undergraduate Course of Study since 1636* (San Francisco: Jossey-Bass Publishers, 1977), p. 160.
2. *The Stylus,* VI (October 1883), p. 45.
3. Rudolph, *Curriculum,* p. 152.
4. *Annual Report of the School Committee of the City of Boston,* 1864, 1874, 1898.
5. Frederick Rudolph, *The American College and University: A History* (New York: Alfred A. Knopf, 1962), p. 219.
6. U.S. Serial Set 3630, 55th Congress, 2nd Session, Dec. 6, 1897–July 8, 1898, pp. 226–233.
7. The *Pilot*, June 1, 1907.

5

The Foster Cadets

WHEN THE THIRD PRESIDENT of Boston College, Father Robert Fulton, established military drill for all students in 1870, he was following a tradition popular in nineteenth century America in both civic and collegiate circles. One chronicler of Post-Revolutionary Boston recalled eight militia companies—the Winslow Blues, the Boston Light Infantry, the Independent Fusileers, the Washington Light Infantry, the New England Guards, the Rifle Rangers, the Cadets, and the Ancient and Honorables—who stored their arms in the upper floor of Faneuil Hall.[1]

Military units served social as well as patriotic ends and were often formed along ethnic or political lines. It is interesting that the historian of the city of Newton included in a chapter on "Culture and Recreation" an account of the organization of the Claflin Guards in 1870, the same year Boston College's cadet brigade began.[2] In his book, *Enter the Irish-American,* Edward Wakin tells how immigrants, imitating the native tradition, started their own militia companies as sources of social activity and expressions of ethnic pride. He writes:[3]

> The Irish organized militia companies, a practice common among immigrant groups but pronounced among the Irish. These military

> units were mainly social and a great excuse for parties, dinners, and rhetoric-drenched speeches. They were also highly visible since the units loved to parade whenever they had a chance. New York had the Emmett Guards, the Irish-American Guard and the Mitchel Light-Guard; Brooklyn boasted the Shields Guard. Compared with German companies, which totaled 1700 in 1853, the Irish had 2600 militiamen. Philadelphia had Hibernia Guards . . . Boston the Montgomery Guards, the Columbian Artillery, the Bay State Artillery, and the Sarsfield Guards . . . . Such units were formed even in smaller towns, evoking considerable newspaper comment about their penchant for parading.

Collegiate military groups were as colorful in uniform and quick to parade as were their non-collegiate counterparts. Except in times of national emergency, however, their purpose seems to have been physical exercise and recreation. Many nineteenth century colleges, like early Boston College, had few facilities for recreational exercise, and cadet drill provided an inexpensive form of exercise that the whole student body could engage in, whether in a small hall or yard or on neighboring streets.

The Baylor University catalogue for 1888–89 explained the presence of military drill this way:[4]

> A healthy, sound body is next in importance to a cultivated head and a pure heart. To promote health and physical development, we have organized a fine military company—the Baylor cadets—for our young men . . . . The students are thoroughly drilled, as a means of health and graceful movement, and become greatly interested in drill and calisthenics, but never lose sight of their studies.

The University historian of Baker University in Kansas wrote: "It seems that the decision for the introduction of such [military] training came about concurrently with the abandonment of intercollegiate football as a sport too dangerous to life or limb, in 1894. The University had only very limited facilities for physical education . . . ."[5]

The president of Georgetown College (Kentucky) cited from the official college history the reasons for military drill: "The college administration suggested that drill was needed to encourage grace of carriage and inculcate habits of promptness, regularity, and order."[6]

The historian of Oklahoma State University indicates that that institution borrowed the rationalization of the Kansas Agricultural College in inaugurating military drill:[7]

> First, military science was throught to have merit as a means by which to impart manliness, alertness, respect for authority and consideration for others. Second, the faculty, in a day when the harmful effects of German academic practices were being widely publicized, believed time devoted to physical culture would promote health, bodybuilding, and correction of unnatural posture. To these two concepts the Oklahoma A and M College added one more. It thought that military instruction and drill could be used to combat the indolence and indispositions always found to exist in a warm climate.

Military drill was regarded by some colleges as a means of fostering discipline[8] and was also considered by some to have moral and even religious value, though no such justification is found in any Boston College documents of the time. Father Fulton evidently felt no compulsion to put a religious or moral blessing on battalion drill as did the University of Tennessee (Nashville), which proclaimed that military discipline is invaluable as a means of moral training, teaching two great moral principles, subordination and method; or as Amherst did in declaring that the military spirit, when worthy of the name, is the true Christian spirit.[9]

The collegiate military tradition long antedated Boston College's Foster Cadets. Harvard had military companies during the Colonial period, and at the time of the War of 1812 it formed the Washington Corps.[10] Dartmouth had five military groups at various times starting in 1832: the Dartmouth Phalanx, the Dartmouth Greys, the Dartmouth Zouaves, the Dartmouth Cavalry, and the Dartmouth Cadets.[11] St. John's College, Annapolis, introduced compulsory military drill in 1826.[12] Five Jesuit colleges, Georgetown, Spring Hill, Holy Cross, St. Louis, and Santa Clara, had pre-Civil War cadet companies. Seven Jesuit colleges joined Boston College in establishing military brigades after the Civil War: Xavier, Fordham, Canisius, St. Peter's, Creighton, Gonzaga, and Loyola in New Orleans.

Collegiate military activity was given impetus by the Morrill Act, passed during the Civil War, which established land grant colleges in the several states and mandated the availability of military training in them. During the next ten years, government-supported military departments were also introduced in private colleges.[13] Boston College did not apply for such a relationship with the War Department. The only Jesuit colleges to apply for and receive such federal aid were Fordham, St. Louis, and Gonzaga. In his history of the American college curriculum, Frederick Rudolph states, "Military training in the colleges, land grant or otherwise, has been generally a postwar phenomenon, a passing enthusiasm"[14] While there is undoubtedly some truth in his statement, it is belied as a generalization by the number of colleges (some named above) that had military training in periods of national peace. Rudolph's statement implies a patriotic or martial motivation in having cadet activities in colleges. Particularly in the private colleges such as Boston College, non-martial motives such as morale, wholesome physical exercise, discipline, and public relations seem to have been dominant. A contemporary scholar, Christa Ressmeyer Klein, writing of New York City's Jesuit colleges of the nineteenth century—namely, Fordham and Xavier (now defunct)—said both colleges introduced military drill as a method of updating the discipline and the public images of the colleges.[15] A similar interpretation is given by the historian of Gonzaga University, who noted that the Jesuit fathers did not take military training as a serious commitment (though it was government-subsidized at Gonzaga). They appeared to regard it "as a kind of disciplinary program for gentlemen-boys. It was so nice to have them in uniforms, marching around on formal occasions. It gave the school status."[16]

A corroboration of the nonmartial inspiration of many collegiate cadet groups is the fact that a few colleges had ladies' battalions, among them Kansas State,[17] Cornell College[18] in Iowa, Oklahoma State University,[19] and DePauw.[20] At DePauw the coed company was said to afford "the ladies of the University an easy, healthy and interesting mode of exercise, and gives them for a time, at least, a style of dress conforming to the much-abused rules of hygiene."[21] The women's drill was identical to the men's except that they carried wooden guns.

It is worth noting that the Harvard Rifle Corps of 1875 to 1878 flourished during the period when Boston College's cadet corps existed. A Harvard historian wrote of the Rifle Corps that it was "apparently the only instance where the undergraduates drilled spontaneously, uninfluenced by public opinion or public emergency."[22] A current member of the staff of the Harvard University archives speculates that the formation of the Rifle Corps may have been inspired by the anticipated centennial celebration of Bunker Hill.[23] There is no suggestion in any Harvard source that the existence of the Rifle Corps was connected with any postwar sentiments.

The motivation of Father Fulton in starting military drill in 1870 and the eager response of the student to the new activity is probably well summed up by one of the first cadets, writing his reminiscences 20 years later: "We had no gymnasium, no playground, no foot-ball team, no opportunity, in fact, for anything in the line of athletics except an occasional base-ball game."[24] Military drill promised regular exercise, camaraderie, and an instrument for building school pride and spirit.

The introduction of military drill at Boston College came suddenly and simply, announced by a brief paragraph appended to general information in the college catalogue for the year 1869–70:[25]

> The State authorities having granted a supply of arms, a drill-master will be appointed, and due notice will be given as to the style of the uniform, and the time by which it must be procured.

In 1869–70 Father Robert Brady was president. He served as Boston College's second president just that one year and then was called to be pastor of St. Mary's parish in the North End, with responsibility for building a new church there. He was succeeded as president by Father Fulton. But Father Fulton had been prefect of studies (dean) since the opening of the college in 1864, and under the first two presidents all academic decisions were his. So apart from the fact that the cadet corps became a reality in Father Fulton's first year in office, even the preliminary planning for the new program was Father Fulton's, as a contemporary witness testified.[26]

In October 1870 the student body, which at that time included both preparatory school and college divisions, was called together

Rev. Robert J. Fulton, first dean of Boston College, 1864–1870, and twice president, 1870–1880 and 1888–1891. He launched and staunchly supported the Foster Cadets during his first presidency.

in the College Hall where Father Fulton introduced to them their military instructor, Sergeant Louis E. Duval, a regular in the United States Army, then in charge of the troops at Fort Warren in Boston Harbor.[27] Though rifles were eventually supplied by the state and though a regular Army man was instructor, this arrangement did not involve a contractual relationship with the War Department. The instructor had other full-time duties; indeed he devoted only two hours a week to the College drill, for which he was paid five dollars an hour.[28]

From the first, the Boston College cadets carried the name of the Foster Cadets in honor of a distinguished Army man, General John Gray Foster, a recent convert to Catholicism and a friend of Father Fulton's, who is said to have been instrumental in persuading Father Fulton to establish military drill.[29] General Foster was a significant enough figure to have found his way into the *Dictionary of American Biography, The Twentieth Century Biographical Dictionary of Notable Americans,* and *The Catholic Encyclopedia,* as well as a 1907 volume entitled, *Distinguished Converts to Rome in America.*[30] Foster was a graduate of West Point, served under General Winfield Scott in the capture of Mexico City, was chief engineer in the construction of Forts Sumter and Moultrie, and was commandant of the Departments of the Ohio, of the South, and of Florida during the Civil War. After the war he was superintending engineer of river and harbor improvements at Boston and Portsmouth. In 1869 he published a volume that became a classic in its field, *Notes on Submarine Blasting in Boston Harbor.* He died in 1874 at the age of 51.

Accounts of military battalions of the nineteenth century abound in detailed and colorful descriptions of the uniforms. So much attention was given to the style and dash of the uniform that one might conclude that a certain amount of male preening was a factor in the popularity of cadet activity. Fordham mourned the passing of the spiked helmets and scarlet uniforms of its nineteenth century cadets.[31] The Georgetown University Military Cadets were described as "resplendent" and "brilliantly uniformed."[32] An account of military traditions at Notre Dame gives this description of the uniform of the Continental Cadets, founded in 1859:[33]

> The uniform of the cadets was copied from the Buff and Blue of the old Continental Line; a blue coat with buff facing, braid and brass buttons, the vest was buff colored and a white tie was worn. The breeches were blue, knee length with brass buttons at the knee, white, knee length stockings were worn. The boots were black with a buff colored strip at the top. The hats were blue, tricornered, with buff colored braid and a red and white cockade. From all reports, the Cadets were a brave and martial sight to behold and were in great demand locally for drill performances and parades.

An earlier uniform was that of Dartmouth's Phalanx, founded in 1832. A student paper carried this description of the uniform:[34]

> Trousers—white in summer and black in autumn—strapped down (as was the fashion of the day) over boots, polished "ad unguem" (no patent leathers were then known); black dress coats, beaver hats with cockade on left of crown, white crossbar straps for cartridge box and white gloves completed the tidy outfit. The three commissioned officers were more elaborately attired in dark green close fitting coats trimmed with gold lace and epaulets, and with ostrich plumed beaver hats.

In the first year of their existence, the Foster Cadets trained without uniforms and without guns. During that year there was a lively debate concerning the style of uniform to be adopted. Some students advocated a very showy affair, while others, more practical-minded, wanted a uniform that would not be expensive, since the students were going to have to pay for them.[35] Patrick Callanan, who was a student when the Foster Cadets were inaugurated and rose in rank to become major and, indeed, drillmaster while still an undergraduate, wrote some lively reminiscences of his cadet days for *The Stylus* in 1897 and 1898. He gave this description of the cadets' uniform:[36]

> The uniforms of the Foster Cadets, though simple in make up, and inexpensive, were very neat, and the boys were very proud of them. A single-breasted sack-coat, dark blue in color, snug-fitting at the neck, with a row of large brass buttons, neatly stamped with a B.C. monogram, [perhaps, in 1871, the first use of "B.C."?] constituted the body covering. The trousers were of the same material and color, and the head-gear was a fatigue cap, with a B.C. monogram worked in silver thread, over the visor. White duck gaiters completed the outfit. When the belt and bayonet-scabbard and the great big well polished United States buckle were added to the equator of each lad, he felt still more like a soldier, but he became a positive warrior when he shouldered his big Springfield rifle.

Incidentally, Callanan attested that the rifles were the 1863 issue of muzzle-loading Springfield rifles, which were returned to Springfield when the state militia were equipped with modern breech-loaders.[37]

At Boston College, as elsewhere, the officers' uniform was especially resplendent, as attested by one who wore it:[38]

> The officers' uniforms were of the same color and material as those of the privates, but in all else they were different. The coat was double-breasted, and had a double row of extra large brass buttons, about five inches apart and running down the entire front from collar to hip. The cap was not unlike that of the privates, but was elaborately trimmed with gold braid, and instead of a silver monogram, had a gold B.C. monogram over the visor. A gold stripe ran down the trousers' legs on either side. Every officer was a

> broad, square-shouldered chap, thanks to the tailors' art, and the chest measurement was simply immense,—one-third flesh and bone and two-thirds of padding! The gilt shoulder-straps topped off the rig to perfection. But this was not all. A beautiful sash of maroon color, about three inches wide, was girded around the warriors' loins, and served as a fundamentum for the shining patent leather sword belt. The swords were the regulation army style, as used by the regular militia.

Well might ex-officer Callanan recall, "I was always proud of my uniform, and I remember time and again how I imagined myself the cynosure of all eyes, as I strutted through the streets of Boston, to and fro, on my way to the College."[39]

But in the spring of 1871, not all the students were enthusiastic about the proposed uniforms. The college classes, poetry and rhetoric, were disappointed to learn that Father Fulton felt the school was not ready to crown the college course with philosophy; hence these students had no prospect of earning their A.B. degree. (The first A.B.s were granted in 1877.) Some students began to think of transferring elsewhere, while others wondered about simply giving up college studies. At any rate, they did not want to commit themselves to procuring uniforms. But Father Fulton insisted on military drill for all not excused by a physician, and the requirement of the "College uniform" for all students remained. A number of upperclassmen did drop out of college, and so in September 1871 some of the younger students, including Patrick Callanan, were thrust into positions of leadership in the cadet corps as well as in other college activities.[40] Callanan made an interesting observation. One would have thought that in his second year as president of an infant college with a tiny enrollment (149 students in the preparatory and college divisions), Father Fulton would be shaken at the loss of some of the older boys. But Callanan commented: "The situation was such that it was practically the '*ab initio est oriendum*' for Father Fulton. I believe myself the state of affairs pleased him rather than otherwise."[41] The implication seems to be that Fulton was not one to shrink from a challenge, and he saw an opportunity to achieve higher standards and esprit. Callanan continued: "To his credit, be it said, he laid the foundations sure and solid, and from this time on the watch-

Group photo of the Foster Cadets in the 1870s.

word was onward and upward until 1877 saw the first graduating class."[42] Incidentally in 1876–77 the combined enrollment was 238.

The brouhaha over uniforms at Boston College in 1870–71 anticipated a more serious problem referred to as the "Drill Rebellion" at Bowdoin College in 1873 to 1875. Bowdoin instituted a military department in 1872, under War Department auspices, with participation obligatory for all students. There was some objection, again by upperclassmen, but, as at Boston College, it was the announcement of the required uniform that sparked open rebellion. The students appealed to the trustees but were adjudged out of order for not addressing the administration and faculty first. Those who absented themselves from drill were threatened with expulsion, whereupon all members of the sophomore, junior, and senior classes pledged to share in the punishment of the rebels. The uprising received wide publicity, with Boston and New York papers castigating the students for insubordination. There were rumors that Dartmouth was prepared to receive students expelled from Bowdoin. A Visiting Committee was appointed, and eventually the students were victorious in that military drill was made optional and the War Department affiliation transferred from Bowdoin to the Agricultural College at Orono.[43] This episode of Bowdoin's drill rebellion is cited as evidence that, in most aspects of college life, the Boston College experience was not unique.

Despite the loss of senior cadets, the 1871–72 year was one of enthusiasm and excitement for the Boston College cadet corps. The new uniforms were worn proudly. Guns, belts, knapsacks, and bayonet scabbards came from Springfield. Father Fulton donated a dozen drums, a drum major was appointed, and a fife and drum corps established. But the greatest stir was caused by the College's persuading Captain George Mullins, a commander of the Montgomery Light Guard, to take over as drillmaster, a post he was to hold for four years. Mullins had gained national attention in the spring of 1871 by issuing a challenge to any military company in the United States to meet his Montgomery Guard in competitive drill. The challenge was taken up by a Roxbury company of volunteer militia and a contest was held on Boston Common. Captain Mullins' men won as they had won similar contests in several parts of the country. So the students were proud to have as military instructor one of the premier drillmasters in the army.[44]

The high point in the history of the Foster Cadets was the St. Patrick's Day parade in 1875.[45] The success and public acclaim of Boston College's military corps led to the formation of parish or regional cadet companies among the Catholic youth of Boston. South Boston had the Johnson Cadets, Charlestown the Supple Cadets, and East Boston the Noddle Island Cadets, and they were followed by groups representing a number of parishes. By 1875 there were over a thousand well-drilled young men in various organized companies. Seeking to capitalize on and coordinate this fine resource, the great John Boyle O'Reilly, poet and editor of the Boston *Pilot*, suggested in an editorial that the Catholic cadet companies should show the world what they could do by way of a military display on St. Patrick's Day. O'Reilly visited Father Fulton and recieved his pledge of the participation and support of the Foster Cadets. O'Reilly sent a circular to all pastors whose parishes had cadet companies, and he himself presided over the initial planning meeting in the basement of St. Francis de Sales Church in Charlestown, which was attended by a hundred delegates. It was decided to form a brigade. Precedence was given to the College cadets and a Boston College representative, none other than Patrick Callanan, was chosen as brigadier general. As befitted his office, the brigadier general was to head the parade on horseback, accompanied by eight mounted aides. Father Fulton agreed to underwrite the expenses of providing horses and trappings for the College men who formed the General's staff. Fifteen or twenty organizations, averaging fifty members, made up the parade. Here is how Father Callanan recollected it:[46]

> Those who took part in the parade will never forget it. Snow began falling on the previous evening and the streets were in a horrible condition on the morning of the 17th of March. Snow and rain and sleet and slush, however, did not frighten the boys; for on to the rendezvous came the gallant young lads, and when the procession started every company and every lad was in line. The fellows on foot envied us on horseback, I am sure; but I now confess that I would be willing to walk from 9 A.M. till 4 P.M. rather than be obliged to sit on a saddle for the same length of time, especially on a horse that was prancing with fright from morning till night at the sound of the martial music. Think of it! a wild horse with his nose just over a brassband, and a man on his back who was not accustomed to the business, and from 9 A.M. till 5 P.M.! The fellows who walked did not come to college the next day, but I did not get to school again for a week!

Out of deference to Father Fulton and Boston College, the parade passed the College along Harrison Avenue. The cadets gave the College a salute, while all the Fathers, lay professors, and Jesuit scholastics stood on the front porch and steps and gave the Boston College contingent a great cheer. Bishop Williams reviewed the parade from an upper window of his residence on the corner of Union Park and Washington Street. The mayor and the board of aldermen reviewed the parade on School Street in front of City Hall.[47]

A contemporary of Father Callanan's, Father Myles McLoughlin, S. J., of the class of '78, published some recollections of old Boston College in the 1930 edition of the Boston College High yearbook, *The Botolphian*. Part of Father McLoughlin's five-page article touched on the Foster Cadets and the famous St. Patrick's Day parade of 1875. Here is what Father McLoughlin wrote some fifty-five years after the events:[48]

> Military drill was part of the college activites in the "seventies." The various evolutions were performed in the college yard, and later on, when some proficiency was attained the hour for drill was finished by a parade through the adjoining streets greeted with the attention of the neighborhood, always—like people elsewhere—alive to the appeal of the marching line, the bugle note and the roll of the drum. In the meantime, far removed from glory in the college yard, "the awkward squad" paced to and fro under summary command and harsh discipline until they would deserve a place in the regular ranks. One of the patient trainers of the squad was Jeremiah Millerick of the Senior Class, afterwards a devoted priest of this diocese. On St. Patrick's Day the entire military arm of the college was mobilized and on the line of march scaled the ascent of Beacon Hill, and passed the State House one hundred percent Irish and Catholic, saluting the Governor and his Staff. In those days it was also true that "every little added to the little that we had made a little bit more." In other words, those who are wise know that our progress in earlier days was often over disputed ground. Everybody on the other side seemed to be from Missouri—and they were shown!

Father McLoughlin introduces a Catholic versus Yankee note that is absent in Callanan, whose account was only two decades from the events he recalled. McLoughlin can be forgiven for one lapse of memory, the presence of the governor. Callanan dwells upon the governor's absence as a sore point in that St. Patrick's Day parade of 1875, an absence that was noteworthy enough to have been commented on in the *Boston Herald*.[49] Of course, it enhanced Fr. McLoughlin's sense of Irish triumphalism to have the parade observed by a Yankee governor, but his memory apparently played a trick on him. Indeed, the bland account by Father Callanan matches the generally non-combative, non-muscle-flexing style that Boston College students displayed in the early decades of their college paper, *The Stylus*.[50]

Another great event for the Foster Cadets in 1875 was participation in a ceremony honoring the elevation of Bishop John Williams to the post of first archbishop of Boston. The solemn installation took place in the cathedral on May 2 with Cardinal McCloskey, archbishop of New York, presiding, and the following day the Catholic Union of Boston sponsored a distinguished public reception for the new archbishop and the ecclesiastical dignitaries who had gathered for the occasion. The reception was held in Boston College hall, and Father Fulton was asked to have the College military battalion give the visitors a military welcome and reception upon their entrance into the college building. It was agreed, and for some days in advance Captain Mullins put the cadets through a number of rehearsals for the special event. Let a participant in those rehearsals give an account of them:

> Perhaps the most excruciatingly funny incident of my college career was the part good old Father Fulton ["good old Father Fulton" was 49 years old in 1875] played in these very military rehearsals. The major of the battalion was to stand at the Harrison-avenue entrance of the college, and upon the arrival of the dignitaries, after giving the military salute, was to take the Cardinal's arm and proceed with stately and military step through a continuous file of the young soldier collegians from the entrance up to the reserved seats in the college hall. Captain Mullins, at these rehearsals, took the part of the major, and good Father Fulton assumed the role of the Cardinal. Starting at the college entrance, Mullins would give Father Fulton the military salute, and then, sheathing the sword and boldly taking Pere Fulton's arm, both would start off together on their march to the hall. "Step, step, step, Father," Mullins would mutter to Father Fulton; but ye shades of the martial dead! ye living friends of the good and great Father Fulton! ye can see and feel the absurdity and ludicrousness of such an appeal to Father Fulton. Father Fulton keep step! keep step with anybody! keep step in military-time! No, no, that was beneath the good man, and such shuffling and bobbing up and down and such jostling as Mullins and Father Fulton treated us to would make the dead rise up and laugh. Bear in mind, too, that this march of theirs was made in view of the whole battalion drawn up in two single files facing each other and stretching out from the Harrison-avenue entrance to the college stage.

We are assured that despite the levity of the rehearsals, the ceremony on the day of the reception was carried out with impressive precision.[51]

In the years 1875–76 and 1876–77 Patrick Callanan was the drillmaster, pleased that Father Fulton paid him the same fee for his service that had been given to Captain Mullins. Callanan recalled that, preoccupied with preparation for the first graduation in June 1877, Father Fulton allowed interest in the drill to diminish.[52] Callanan left Boston College with the first graduating class, and the college catalogue made no mention of military drill until 1880; thereafter it included the reference through 1884. In September of the latter year the young drillmaster, Captain Matthew Callahan, died suddenly, an event that undoubtedly contributed to the decision early in the year to put military drill on an optional basis. There was a sharp drop in attendance, and the activity was not continued the following year.

Father Edward Devitt, who served as president of Boston College from 1891 to 1894, wrote about the Foster Cadets in a manuscript history of the Maryland Province: "This organization [the Foster Cadets] was quite popular for a time—but it was dissolved as the advantages of the military training were found an inadequate compensation for the time and labor expended."[53]

It would have been difficult to sustain enthusiasm such as that of young men like Patrick Callanan who were both innovators and leaders in cadet drill. The experience of flagging interest in cadet activity was common. The examples of Dartmouth and Wooster were typical. The Dartmouth Cadets were formed in 1874 and had only a two-year life. The drill instructor commented that by the second spring, "the boys did not take the trouble to attend the drills and the company died a natural death, easily and quietly.[54] Military instruction lasted six years at Wooster. A historian of the college commented: "The training . . . was of a high order, both from the point of view of physical discipline and from that of actual instruction in military science. After the novelty wore off, the boys themselves grew tired of this constant drilling . . . . When the department was withdrawn, most of the students sighed with relief."[55]

Frederick Rudolph was cited above as saying that military drill was a "passing fancy." He added: "For various reasons and at various times and places, military training was taken seriously . . . but the characteristic experience for this detour from collegiate purpose [Father Callanan and Father Fulton would undoubtedly give Rudolph an argument here] was that at Indiana, where compulsory drill was adopted in 1868 and discontinued in 1874."[56]

One conclusion of this account of military drill at Boston College in the nineteenth century is that both in the apparently isolated decision to establish a cadet corps in 1870 and in the decision to discontinue it 14 years later, Boston College was very much in the mainstream of the American collegiate experience.

ENDNOTES

1. John McHale, *Old Boston Town* (New York: George Nesbit Co., 1880), p. 13.
2. Henry K. Rowe, *Tercentenary History of Newton* (Newton: City of Newton, 1930), pp. 231–232.
3. Edward Wakin, *Enter the Irish-American* (New York: Thomas Crowell Co., 1976), p. 82.
4. Catalogue of the Officers and Students of Baylor University at Waco, Texas, 1888–89, p. 67.
5. Letter to the author from Harold Kolling, University Historian, Baker University, April 1, 1980. Boston College Archives.
6. Letter to the author from Ben M. Elrod, president, Georgetown College, February 6, 1980. Boston College Archives.
7. Philip R. Rulon, *Oklahoma State University* (Stillwater, Oklahoma: State University Press, 1975), p. 39.
8. Letter to the author from the president's office, St. John's College, Annapolis, Maryland. Boston College Archives.
9. *Report on National Military Education* (Washington, D.C.: War Department, 1867), p. 32
10. Samuel F. Bachelder, *Bits of Harvard History* (Cambridge, Mass.: Harvard University Press, 1924), Chapter II, " 'The Student in Arms' Old Style." Bachelder relates (p. 72) the interesting anecdote that the day after the burning of the Ursuline Convent in Charlestown, August 11, 1834, a rumor reached Cambridge that the local Catholics intended to retaliate by burning Harvard College. A mixed crowd of students and alumni armed themselves with muskets of the Washington Corps and spent the night waiting for the attack that never came.
11. *The Dartmouth*, XVII (May 8, 1896), 28, p. 437. Also letter to the author from Kenneth C. Cramer, archivist of Dartmouth College, March 3, 1980. Boston College Archives.
12. Letter from St. John's College.
13. Ernest A. Smith, *Allegheny: A Century of Education* (Meadville, Pa.: Tribune Publishing Co., 1916), p. 205.
14. Frederick Rudolph, *Curriculum: A History of the American Undergradu-*

ate Course of Study Since 1636 (San Francisco: Jossey-Bass, 1977), p. 122.

15. Christa R. Klein, "New York City's Jesuit Colleges, 1846–1912." Address to the American Catholic Historical Society, March 27, 1976. Boston College Archives.
16. Wilfred P. Schoenberg, S. J., *Gonzaga University* (Spokane: Lawton Printing Co., 1963), p. 162.
17. James C. Carey, *Kansas State University* (Lawrence: The Regents Press of Kansas, 1977), p. 111.
18. Letter from Charles J. Milhauser, registrar, Cornell College to the author, February 1, 1980. Boston College Archives.
19. Rulon, *Oklahoma State University,* p. 40.
20. George B. Manhart, *DePauw Through the Years* (Greencastle, Ind.: DePauw University, 1962), vol. I, p. 98.
21. Ibid.
22. Bachelder, *Harvard History,* p. 76.
23. Letter to the author from Jennifer Zukowski, Curatorial Associate, Harvard University Archives, February 26, 1980. Boston College Archives.
24. Patrick H. Callanan, "Reminiscences," *The Stylus*, 11 (October 1897), p. 387. Patrick Callanan was one of the first graduates in June 1877. He entered St. Joseph's seminary in Troy, N.Y., and was ordained a priest in 1880. He served in the Boston Archdiocese as curate at Sacred Heart in East Cambridge and St. Bernard in West Newton, and as pastor of St. Mary, Foxborough, St. John, Wellesley, and St. Peter, Cambridge. While still active in the last post, he died in 1933.
25. Boston College Catalogue, 1869–70, p. 11
26. Callanan, "Reminiscences," *The Stylus*, 11 (October 1897), p. 387.
27. *Ibid.*
28. Callanan, "Reminiscences," *The Stylus*, 12 (May 1898), p. 279.
29. Callanan, "Reminiscences," *The Stylus*, 11 (October 1897), p. 387.
30. D. J. Scannell, *Distinguished Converts to Rome in America* (St. Louis: B. Herder, 1907).
31. Robert I. Gannon, S. J., *Up to the Present* (New York: Doubleday and Company, 1967), p. 179.
32. Joseph T. Durkin, S. J., *Georgetown University: The Middle Years* (Washington, D. C.: Georgetown University Press, 1963), pp. 14, 15.
33. "Military Traditions at the University of Notre Dame." University of Notre Dame Archives.
34. *The Dartmouth,* 17 (May 8, 1896), 440.
35. Callanan, "Reminiscences," *The Stylus*, 11 (December 1897), p. 513.
36. Callanan, "Reminiscences," *The Stylus*, 11 (November 1897), pp. 453–455.
37. *Ibid.*, p. 455.
38. *Ibid.*, pp. 456–459.
39. Callanan, "Reminiscences," *The Stylus*, 11 (December 1897), p. 456.

40. *Ibid.*, pp. 513–522.
41. *Ibid.*, p. 522.
42. *Ibid.*, pp. 522–523.
43. Louis C. Hatch, *The History of Bowdoin College,* (Portland, Me.: Loring, Short, and Harmon, 1927), pp. 133–148.
44. Callanan, "Reminiscences," *The Stylus* 11 (October, 1897), pp. 391–392.
45. Callanan, "Reminiscences," *The Stylus* 12 (May, 1898), pp. 257–266.
46. *Ibid.*, pp. 266–268.
47. *Ibid.*, pp. 269–290.
48. Myles A. McLoughlin, S. J., "Reminiscences of the Eighteen-Seventies," *The Botolphian,* 1930, pp. 50–51.
49. Callanan, "Reminiscences," *The Stylus* 12 (May, 1898), p. 269.
50. See Chapter 3. Boston College Archives.
51. Callanan, "Reminiscences," *The Stylus* 12 (April 1898), pp. 202–210.
52. Callanan, "Reminiscences," *The Stylus* 12 (May 1898), pp. 277–278.
53. Edward I. Devitt, S. J., "History of the Province of Maryland." Manuscript in the Maryland S. J. Provincial Archives, p. 17.
54. John King Lord, *A History of Dartmouth College* (Concord, N. H.: The Rumford Press, 1913), p. 392.
55. Lucy L. Notestein, *Wooster of the Middle West* (New Haven: Yale University Press, 1937), p. 141.
56. Rudolph, *Curriculum,* pp. 122, 123.

In his second term as president of Boston College, Father Fulton expanded the college building 100 feet along James Street. At this time (1889), the above seal was installed on the floor of a corridor connecting the Jesuit residence to the college building, an interesting step in the evolution of the college seal. For the first time, a shield appeared, with the three hills of Boston at the bottom and an open book (to which were added the Greek words αἰὲν ἀριστεύειν in 1914). Two of the three crowns of the city of Botolph in England were introduced, with the simple cross and IHS instead of the full seal of the Society of Jesus, which also was added in 1914 . Since Father Fulton originated the primitive shield, it is appropriate that it is now installed in Fulton Hall.

PART TWO

A New Beginning

6

The Move to Chestnut Hill

BOSTON COLLEGE'S ORIGINAL BUILDING on Harrison Avenue was completed in 1860. It received the first students in September 1864. Between that academic year and the close of the century was a span of 35 years—not a long period in the life of an institution or of a collegiate building. Yet, in 1900 the realty firm of Meredith and Grew recommended to the then president, Father W. G. Read Mullan, three parcels of land in the Brighton-Chestnut Hill area (now occupied by St. Elizabeth's Hospital and Mt. Alvernia Academy, plus the University's present central campus) as possible sites for a relocated Boston College.[1]

The archives provide no antecedents to the Meredith and Grew communication. In the absence of documents explaining the decision of Father Mullan and his advisors to explore an alternate location, we are left to speculate about the reasons. What factors in the Harrison Avenue setting made it inadequate or inappropriate for the College after only 35 years?

The most obvious possible explanation is enrollment. The preparatory school and the College were housed in the same building. Were their combined numbers outgrowing available space? This does not seem to have been the case. Up to 1900 the combined enrollment never reached 500. The year the College moved to

Rev. Thomas I. Gasson, S.J., president of Boston College, 1907–1914, who moved the College from the South End to Chestnut Hill.

Chestnut Hill (1913), more than a thousand students attended Boston College High School in the former collegiate building. So it is unlikely that a preparatory-collegiate enrollment of under 500 was overcrowding the facilities on Harrison Avenue.[2]

Even if in 1900 the Jesuit Fathers were optimistic about future growth in numbers, they would have had to have second thoughts on that score as the first decade of the new century unfolded. The preparatory division experienced a 14 percent enrollment decline between 1900 and 1904, from 277 to 238. More ominous was the dip in the college enrollment, from 206 in 1900 to 113 in 1904, a 45 percent drop. Today an enrollment loss of such proportions would be reason for drastic cutbacks or even the closing of a college. But it seemed not to have fazed Boston College's administration, for Father Gasson purchased the Chestnut Hill property in 1907.

Boston College was not unique in the temporary decline in students in the early years of the present century. A table in George Pierson's history of Yale comparing freshman enrollments at Harvard, Yale, and Princeton from 1859 to 1937 shows that Harvard and Princeton experienced a drop between 1900 and 1910, while Yale hit a plateau.[3] Samuel Eliot Morison noted this phenomenon in his history of Harvard. Writing of President Eliot's era, he commented, "Enrollment continued to swell until about 1903, when the progressive advance in numbers stopped, with the immediate result of a deficit."[4]

If a crush of students was not a reason for contemplating a new site for the college, what about the dimensions of the campus? We know that Father McElroy had tried to purchase a lot containing 115,000 square feet (an entire block) on Harrison Avenue, but an outcry about the "audacious attempt on the part of ecclesiastical authorities to acquire undue and colossal power"[5] led him to make a more modest purchase. The eventual Harrison Avenue site, for the spacious Church of the Immaculate Conception, the faculty residence, and the college building, was 65,000 square feet. The land did not have adequate recreational space, which led Father Timothy Brosnahan, president in the 1890s, to purchase a large but rough tract of land of over 400,000 square feet about a mile from the College on Massachusetts Avenue in Dorchester. The College did not have funds for any elaborate development of this property for athletic or recreational purposes. Parts of it were used as playing fields for a decade. There is no evidence that College authorities ever contemplated erecting buildings at that location, and the land was sold during the construction of Gasson Hall to help defray the building costs.

The most illuminating insight as to the attitude of some Jesuits toward the Harrison Avenue location is contained in a letter written by Father Gasson in 1928 to Father James Dolan, then president. Father Gasson was giving his recollections concerning a large bequest to the College from a member of a prominent Boston family, a convert who became a Jesuit, Father Edward Holker Welch. The gift was made during Father Brosnahan's presidency (1894–1898). In the letter Father Gasson remarked, "Father Welch was anxious for Boston College to forge ahead and to emerge from the circumscribed limits of the Harrison Avenue property."[6] Welch, a Harvard graduate, no doubt had more in mind than playing fields in considering the South End property circumscribed. Gasson's ambitious plans for the Chestnut Hill campus only a dozen years later show that people at Boston College were thinking and talking of expanded facilities and property, even though there are no records of such discussions.

Another matter that must have entered into the deliberations of the faculty and administration as the nineteenth century drew to a close was the juxtaposition of the preparatory school and the college on the same property and in the same building. The Jesuits would have been aware of an article published in 1898 in *Woodstock Letters,* a journal by, for, and about American Jesuits, that criticized the commingling of high school and college students. The Jesuit author wrote:[7]

> Some of our colleges, which twenty years ago stood the proud rivals of local colleges and universities, have lost their old prestige on account of the predominance of small boys. Larger boys have told us repeatedly that they would be only too willing to attend our classes were it not that they were ashamed to be seen in the company of so many "kids."

In 1900 the president of Georgetown urged the moving of the Jesuit Theologate from Woodstock, Maryland, a rural setting, to Georgetown, adding that should this happen, the preparatory division would be abolished. The historian of Georgetown comments on this proposal:[8]

> This was an interesting suggestion. Many had long felt the presence of the "small boys" on a campus destined for mature university students was a drag on Georgetown's progress.

A similar observation is made by the historian of a West Coast Jesuit college, Santa Clara, citing an early twentieth century document to the effect that the faculty "resented the intolerable anomaly of a University frequented by boys in Knickerbockers."[9]

It is significant that the Boston *Pilot* of September 10, 1898, in an article on developments at Boston College, reported:

> The preparatory school of the college, which from its inception enjoyed an unrestrained commingling with the collegiate department, is now confined exclusively to the southern wing of the college, and the college men are located in the northern wing.

The following year the college catalogue, which for 30 years had included the names of the teachers and students of the preparatory division along with their curricula, regulations, and prizes, limited itself to data regarding the four college classes. These steps toward the separation of the college from the preparatory division undoubtedly presaged the geographical separation that was to follow.

In 1907 Father Thomas Gasson, who had been a professor of philosophy at Boston College for the preceding 12 years, became president and at once pressed with zeal for a new site and a new vision of academic prestige for the College. The Chestnut Hill property was purchased that year. Gasson Hall was under construction from 1909 to 1913, and the College moved to its new home in September 1913.

The preparatory division and the College both seem to have prospered by the separation. The enrollment of Boston College High School, which had slipped to 238 in 1904, rose to 550 the year of the purchase of the Chestnut Hill property for the College and to double that number the year after the College moved from the South End. To be sure, high school attendance was on the rise nationally at that time, but state and city records show that between 1900 and 1914 attendance at public high schools in Massachusetts and in the City of Boston just about doubled,[10] whereas Boston College High School's 1914 student body was five and a quarter times that of 1900.

At the same time the collegiate enrollment began to swing back. By 1910 it was almost at the 200 mark it had reached in 1900. The first freshman class of over 100 entered in 1911. The year of the move to Chestnut Hill, the student body was 387; three years later it was 578; in 1919 it rose to 697; it reached 900 in 1923; and finally in 1925 it topped a thousand. The enrollment of 1925 was five and a half times larger than that of 1910.

It is ironic that when Father McElroy failed to get clearance to start the College in the North End and purchased the Harrison Avenue property, some of the Catholic clergy and laity were upset.[11] They wanted Boston College in the North End where they lived rather than in the South End, two and a quarter miles away. Yet a few decades later when the decision was made to move the College out of the City of Boston, there is no recorded murmur of protest. Undoubtedly the mid-century concentration of the Irish

The rural Chestnut Hill property, the Lawrence farm, that Father Gasson boldly purchased in the first year of his presidency, 1907, as the new location of Boston College.

population in the North End and the core city was a factor in the initial negative reaction to the South End setting, but transportation may also have been a consideration. The South End was a new development in the 1860s and transportation was just getting organized, although by the mid-1880s Dexter Smith's *Cyclopedia of Boston and Vicinity* noted after the entry on Boston College, "Take Norfolk House horse-cars."[12] It was a different story with the Chestnut Hill location. The extension of the streetcar line to Lake Street in the late nineties made the campus readily accessible to a commuting student body. One who made the daily trek from South Boston to Chestnut Hill during the College's first four years on the Heights, Father Maurice Dullea of the Boston College Jesuit Community, recalled in 1980, that for him and the other students the longer ride to Newton in comparison with what it would have been to Harrison Avenue was not seen as a burden. He said the cost was the same—a nickel—and spirits were lifted by what was at the end of the line: a rural setting, a spacious campus, and the imposing tower of Gasson looking down on the then twin reservoirs.

In the half century between 1864 and 1914, the Catholic population began moving out of the crowded inner city as transportation lines extended and new neighborhoods developed. Such movement was reflected in the Boston College student body. For instance, in 1900 17 percent of the students lived in the inner city—Boston proper, North End, West End, and South End. By 1905 this proportion dropped to 7 percent, and by 1915, when the College was in Newton, to 3 percent. In 1900 51 percent of the students came from some part of Boston, 49 percent from outside the city. By 1915 the balance was reversed, with 44 percent from Boston and 56 percent from outside. One might attribute this shift to the move of the College out of Boston, but that does not seem to have been the case, since the shift to a majority of non-Boston students took place while the College was still in the South End. In 1905, for instance, 57 percent of the students commuting to Harrison Avenue were non-Bostonians.

That the move to Chestnut Hill had very little impact on the geographical origin of Boston College students may be seen by comparing percentages of students coming from selected areas in 1900 and 1915. Percentages afford a readier comparison because actual numbers of students were rising during this period (see the table).

Percentages of Boston College Students Coming from Selected Areas in 1900 and 1915

	1900	1915
South Boston	3	4
Roxbury	9	9
Dorchester	4	11
Brighton-Allston	1	4
Cambridge	4	11
Somerville	2	4
Newton	4	4
Lawrence	3	2
Lowell	1	3

Despite the more complicated transportation from South Boston, Dorchester, Cambridge, Somerville, and Lowell to Newton as compared with the South End, the percentages of students from those districts increased. Roxbury, the immediate neighbor of the South End, sent the same proportion of students to Chestnut Hill as it had to Harrison Avenue. The increase of students from the Brighton-Allston area may have been due to the increase of population there, as in Dorchester, rather than to proximity, since the proportion of students from Newton did not rise when the College moved to Newton.

As we look back from the vantage point of nearly nine decades to Father Gasson's unhesitating decision to acquire property in Chestnut Hill and locate there an imposing college campus, we applaud his daring and imagination. It would seem that his natural clientele of the time, the Catholic families of the Greater Boston area, had the same reaction, because when the College was relocated, their sons found the way to Gasson's tower on the hill in increasing numbers.

ENDNOTES

1. Charles F. Donovan, S.J., David R. Dunigan, S.J., and Paul A. FitzGerald, S.J., *History of Boston College: From the Beginnings to 1990* (Chestnut Hill, Mass.: University Press of Boston College, 1990), p. 115.
2. Enrollment and other student data are taken from the annual Boston College catalogues. Enrollment data for Boston College High School was supplied by the administrative office of the High School.
3. George Wilson Pierson, *Yale College: An Educational History, 1871–1921* (New Haven: Yale University Press, 1952), vol. I. p. 723.
4. Samuel Eliot Morison, *Three Centuries of Harvard* (Cambridge, Mass.: Harvard University Press, 1946), p. 365.
5. Donovan, Dunigan, and FitzGerald, *History of Boston College,* p. 15.
6. Copy of Father Gasson's letter in the Boston College Archives.
7. *Woodstock Letters,* 27, no. 2 (1898), p. 183.
8. Joseph T. Durkin, S.J., *Georgetown University: The Middle Years, 1840–1900* (Washington, D.C.: Georgetown University Press, 1963), p. 187.
9. Gerald McKevitt, S.J., *The University of Santa Clara* (Stanford: Stanford University Press, 1979), p. 204.
10. Massachusetts data from *Annual Reports of the Board of Education, Public Document No. 2.* Boston data from *Documents of the School Committee of the City of Boston, Document no. 9.*
11. Donovan, Dunigan, and FitzGerald, *History of Boston College,* p. 15.
12. Dexter Smith, *Cyclopedia of Boston and Vicinity* (Boston: Cashin and Smith, 1886), p. 48.

7

Boston College's Second Spring

FATHER THOMAS GASSON'S DETERMINATION in 1907 to acquire spacious property for a new campus and to engage nationally prominent architects to plan and begin the building of a series of collegiate structures must qualify as one of the most courageous and far-seeing decisions in the history of American higher education. The student body of the College at that time consisted of 150 young men from families of modest income in Boston and the outlying towns. The enrollment that year was actually one quarter smaller than it had been in 1900. There hardly seemed an immediate need for separate buildings for a library, science classrooms and laboratories, a chapel, or a college hall. Boston College's first A.B. degrees were awarded in 1877, so no alumnus was more than 30 years out of college; and since graduating classes had averaged about 18 over the 30 years, fewer than 600 alumni could be counted on to support the gigantic fund-raising effort that Father Gasson's plans obviously entailed. The magnitude of Gasson's gamble as he assumed the presidency of the tiny college on James Street in the South End can hardly be exaggerated.

There exist some contemporary accounts of Gasson's vision as it was first made public and gradually began to move toward reality. It may be helpful to reproduce them here as a recollection of and salute to Boston College's amazing "second spring."

Father Gasson became president in January 1907. In May the alumni held a reception for him at which he gave the first inkling of the magnitude of the developments he hoped to undertake. The event received front page coverage in Boston's Catholic newspaper, the *Pilot*, and the following account appeared in the Jesuit magazine *Woodstock Letters*:[1]

> The College—The Boston College alumni association gathered last evening at the hotel Brunswick to do honor to Rev. Thomas I. Gasson, S.J., who was recently elevated to the presidency of the College.
>
> It was a notable gathering and the call of the secretary brought out men prominent in church, state and city life. Archbishop O'Connell graced the occasion with his presence, and many of the leading clergymen of the city, who were graduated from the college, took advantage of the opportunity to publicly express their appreciation of the honor bestowed upon Father Gasson.
>
> Mr. Aylward '84 acted as toastmaster, and after a few brief remarks he introduced Fr. Gasson, who was tendered an ovation. The new president feelingly expressed his gratitude for the kindness evidenced by the alumni since his elevation to the presidency, and then the hearts of his audience were gladdened when he announced that he intended to make several changes in the college to meet the growing demands of the student body.
>
> "In the first place," said Fr. Gasson, "it is my intention in the very near future to have the college and the high school separated, and the college will be moved into another building entirely apart from the preparatory school.
>
> "I intend also to make an effort to get a new location for the college, where we will not be confined to one building, but we will get a big group of buildings and grounds sufficient for the uses of a big institution of learning.
>
> "It is my desire to secure a staff of distinguished laymen to join our faculty and have charge of the several scientific and modern language studies.
>
> "I must also have an advisory board consisting of members of the alumni association, who will make it a point to keep me in touch with their ideas of progress, and by this cooperation I hope to advance the college to the highest point possible in the intellectual world.

Timothy Walsh of the firm Maginnis and Walsh, architects of the new Boston College.

"I need money to accomplish these results, and I want the alumni to raise a fund sufficient to cover the expenditure of moving, the securing of a new location and the erection of new buildings. In my plans for the future, the college will not be associated with the high school in any way, and the buildings will probably be located in different parts of the city."

Fr. Gasson, in concluding, stated that he had other plans for the future also, but could not make them public just at present.

It is significant that the *Woodstock Letters* article reports that Father Gasson asked for a "sufficient fund" for his purposes, whereas the largest-type headline on the front page of the *Pilot*[2] announced that Father Gasson set $10 million as his goal. In 1991 dollars Gasson's proposal rivaled the major fund drives undertaken in recent years by some of the largest and most influential universities in the country. Of course Boston College never came close to Gasson's financial goal during his presidency, but his fund target presented a new scale of aspiration for the Catholics of Boston that befitted the noble architectural plans that were developed shortly by Charles D. Maginnis and Timothy Walsh. The Boston College contributor to *Woodstock Letters* may have omitted the reference to $10 million because negotiation with the superiors in Rome would be required before an undertaking of such proportions could be set in motion.

Father Gasson was letting the world know that he was thinking big. He wanted a "big group of buildings" for a "big institution of learning." But he wasn't thinking only of a physical plant. It is noteworthy that he specified the need for distinguished lay professors; Jesuits would not have the numbers to staff the seat of learning he envisioned. And he saw the curriculum expanding from classical-philosophical studies to embrace more fully sciences and modern languages. Indeed Thomas I. Gasson was a man of vision.

The account of the alumni dinner mentions the presence of Archbishop William O'Connell of the class of 1881. When he heard Father Gasson's challenging dream, O'Connell was coadjutor to Archbishop Williams of Boston. Three months later Williams died and O'Connell, as the new archbishop of Boston, was in a position to abet Gasson's plans. He did so enthusiastically and encouraged Gasson as he eyed a Chestnut Hill site for a campus.[3] Before the year was out, in December 1907, the energetic new president of Boston College bought the magnificent property that is now the central campus.

The following article from *Woodstock Letters* is one of the first published descriptions of the new college site. If refers to an initial plan for seven buildings, although in reality the first architectual plans included more than seven. The article echoes Father Gasson's alumni reception emphasis on the sciences:[4]

> Boston. New College Site—The trustees of Boston College have finally brought to a successful issue a project that has for many months been under consideration.
>
> For some time past the friends of the college have urged upon the authorities in charge the necessity of expansion, and the need of separating locally the high school from the college department.
>
> This project had the hearty support of the alumni and old students of the college, and, above all, of the most reverend Archbishop, himself an alumnus, who is a recognized leader in every

movement that tends towards the advancement of Catholic higher education.

The site selected for the new college is the Hinckley estate, a large tract of land—over 30 acres in extent—situated in Newton, bordering on the Chestnut Hill reservoir. . . . The land faces directly on the boulevard on the north, adjoins the reservoir on the east, is bounded by South St. [College Road], Newton, on the west and Beacon St. on the south. Deeds conveying this tract to the trustees of Boston College will be placed on record in Cambridge today, December 12, 1907. The site is, and always will be, one of the finest in New England for academic purposes.

The surroundings are extremely artistic, for the land looks out upon the clear waters of the Reservoir lakes and the wooded slopes of the environment.

The upper part of the tract has a splendid elevation, while the land toward Beacon St. affords unrivalled facilities for a fine campus and for athletic purposes.

Upon this charming site it is hoped to erect a group of buildings which, both in design and equipment, will take a high rank among the college structures of the land.

The position and shape of the land must prove an inspiration to any architect who might wish to build a lasting monument of architectural excellence.

It has been suggested that the initial plan should contemplate a recitation building, an administration building, two science buildings with ample facilities for laboratory training, an up-to-date gymnasium, a library and a college hall.

In the new plan, provision will be made for special study in technical and scientific research, for it is well known that many of the professors are ardently devoted to scientific and technical training. The scientific department will, consequently, be a marked feature in the new development.

The present facilities for reaching this favored spot are many indeed, but in addition to those now existing others are projected which, in connection with the Riverbank subway, will bring this entire region within easy reach of the railway terminals and of the great local centers of travel.

While the scheme as outlined above will call for the outlay of a large sum of money, it is felt that the wonderful progress of the Catholic Church in New England warrants belief that these plans can be brought to a successful issue in a few years by the cooperation of those who have at heart the intellectual needs of Catholic youth.

> Already steps are on foot to secure the funds necessary for the erection of the first buildings. A number of the older alumni and former students have entered into the work with enthusiasm, and it is hoped that their efforts, together with the assistance of all who are interested in higher education, will result in an early fruition of the hope of the president of the college, Rev. Thomas I. Gasson, whose energetic work since he became the head of the institution augurs much for the success of the undertaking.
>
> The present site on Harrison ave. and James st. will be kept for the academic department [high school], after the change to the new location has been made.
>
> At a mass meeting of old students and friends of Catholic Education, held in Boston College hall, great enthusiasm was shown and $50,000 were subscribed for the building of the new college.

The first building, known originally as the Recitation Building, later as the Tower Building, and now as Gasson Hall, was under construction from 1909 to 1913. An account of the arrival of the senior class on the Chestnut Hill campus in the spring of 1913 appeared in *Woodstock Letters*. It includes the touching remarks of Father Gasson, for whom the event must have been one of great satisfaction, his dream become imposing reality. There is irony in the reporter's boast that Boston College would never spill over its original 35 acres.[5]

> Boston. The New College.—It is a cause of great joy to all interested in the development of Boston College to be able to announce that an informal opening of the new building took place on Friday, March 28th. For the present, only the Seniors will hold their classes at University Heights, but in September all the college classes will have their lectures and recitations in the new building.
>
> The exercises at the informal opening were very simple. The Senior Class met the President at the South Street [College Road] entrance. Marching up the roadway, they entered through the west porch and proceeded to the rotunda. Here they halted, and Father Rector [Father Gasson] impressively said, "Members of the Class of 1913, we now, in an *informal* manner, take possession of this noble building which has been erected for the greater glory of God, for the spread of Catholic faith, for the cultivation of true knowledge, for the development of genuine science, and for the constant study of those ideals which make for the loftiest civic

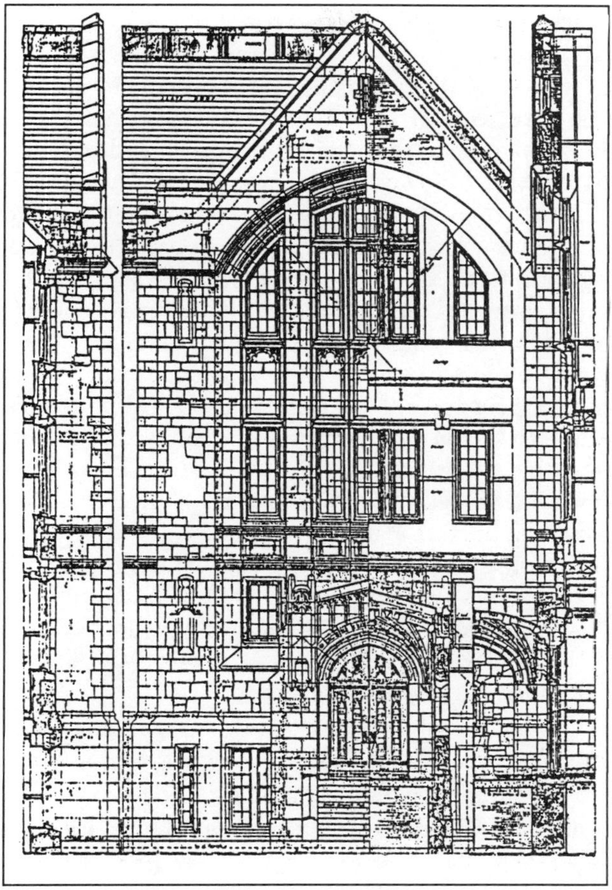

Detail of the central gable and porch on the east elevation of the Recitation Building. What architects Maginnis and Walsh planned as the main entrance to their first Chestnut Hill building now looks over the plaza that descends to O'Neill Library.

probity and for the most exalted personal integrity. May this edifice ever have upon it the special blessing of the Most High, may it ever be a source of strength to the Church and her rulers, a source of joy to the Catholics of Boston and its vicinity, a strong bulwark of strength for our Country and a stout defence for the illustrious State of which we are justly proud."

To friends of the college this event has a two-fold significance. It indicates not only that the institution is on the threshold of a new and greater era but that it has virtually completed fifty years of honorable existence.

The location of the new college is the very finest imaginable. It seems, in fact, to have been reserved for academic purposes. . . . Too many of our institutions of learning, collegiate as well as secondary, have followed the policy of purchasing land for the present rather than for the future with the result that they are to-day wondering where to turn for more room. Boston College will never find itself in that plight. It has grown rapidly in the past; it expects to grow still more rapidly in the years to come and it has governed itself accordingly.

The new building is one of the most beautiful in and around Boston and promises to be one of the show places of eastern Massachusetts. From its centre rises a majestic tower, which reaches a height of nearly two hundred feet. The structure is of the English collegiate Gothic style, and in architectural effect is very similar to the newer buildings at Princeton and the University of Chicago. It is, however, not intended that it should be left to stand alone. All arrangements and plans have been made with a group of buildings in view. Just as soon as the necessary funds are forthcoming the other structures will be erected. But the present building will ever be the dominant structure of the group.

Gasson's tower did not take long to catch the eye of the architectural community. During the first full year of occupancy of the Chestnut Hill campus, the professional journal *The American Architect* published a 16-page article on the first of Maginnis and Walsh's Boston College buildings. It gave 7 external and interior photographs and 17 floor plans, details, or elevations. The brief accompanying text is presented here in its entirety. It will be noted that the architects intended the east entrance of Gasson as the main entrance. The article indicates the varied uses the space in the new building had to be devoted to—laboratories, locker rooms, library, classrooms, and offices—because for 10 years it was to be the sole academic building on the campus. The reference to a dormitory shows that Gasson was just about a half century ahead of this time.[6]

The American Architect, Vol. CV, Wednesday, January 14, 1914, Number 1986. The Recitation Building of Boston College, Newton, Mass. Maginnis and Walsh, Architects.

The new Boston College, of which only the Recitation Building has as yet been erected, is to occupy a commanding situation on an eminence to the west of the Chestnut Hill Reservoir. The property consists of about thirty-five acres and is of varied topography. The landscape in the vicinity is in great part under the control of the Metropolitan Park Commission, so that no future development can do any prejudice to the beauty of the view. The higher ground of the site consists of an irregular plateau and here are to be situated the chief buildings of the group. The style in which the group is conceived is English Collegiate Gothic.

The axial building of the scheme is the Recitation Building, here illustrated, the tower of which is intended to dominate the group. The main entrance of this building is from the campus on the east side. This is marked by a large porch. A salient feature of the main floor is the rotunda which comes within the lines of the massive tower and rises to a point under the roof. On the northerly side of the first story corridor is the large Assembly Room, accessible from the rotunda and by the two north doors; opposite this on the south side is the Library. The rest of this floor is devoted to the Reception Parlors, rooms of the President, Vice-president, Perfect of Discipline, Registrar and teachers. The second, third and fourth stories are occupied by classrooms, lecture-halls, laboratories and rooms for the College magazine. In the basement on the North is the great locker room, sixty-eight feet long by forty-two feet wide, and on the southerly side is the large recreation room. The eastern side is occupied by the chemical and physical laboratories and their apparatus rooms; the west side by the boiler, cloak and fan rooms.

The building is constructed of rubble stone obtained from the site, the trimmings being of artificial stone. Fire-proof materials are used up to the roof of the first floor only. The building is roofed with green terra cotta tile.

On either side of the broad avenue by which the building is approached from the North and South it is proposed to locate other buildings of the group. The chapel is to be between the Library Building and Faculty Hall which are to be opposite the Biological Laboratory and Assembly Hall. The South end of the avenue is to be dominated by the Dining Hall flanked by the Gymnasium and a Dormitory House.

A generous portion of the South Campus is devoted to athletic activities of students and faculty. In the south-western corner, the foot-ball field will be the scene of physical contests as gruelling as those which Puritan forefathers may have fought in the same spot

THE AMERICAN ARCHITECT

VOL. CV, NO. 1986 JANUARY 14, 1914

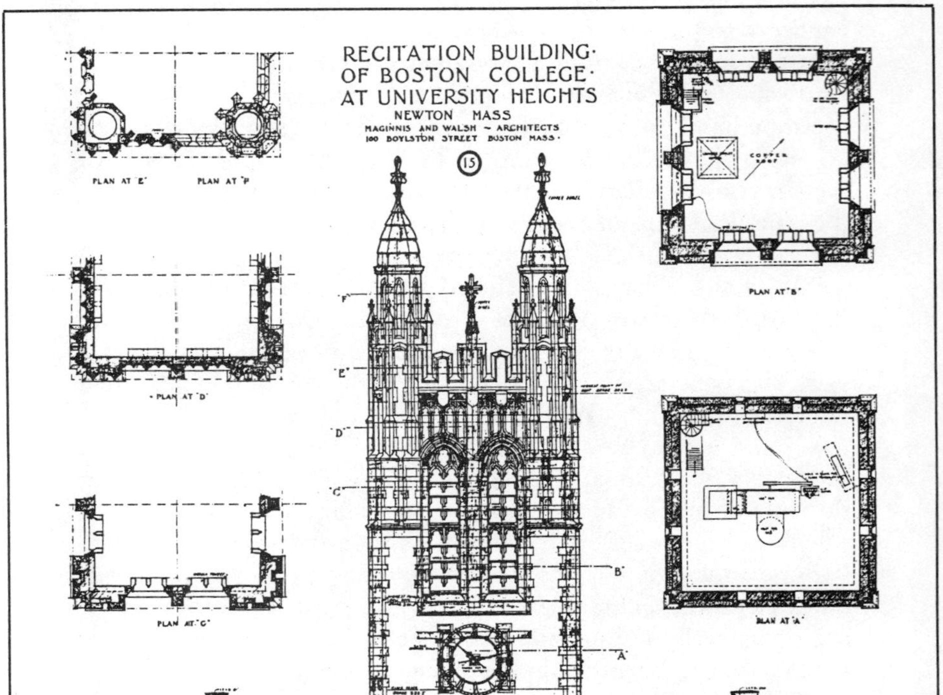

NORTH ELEVATION

RECITATION BUILDING OF BOSTON COLLEGE, NEWTON, MASS.

MESSRS. MAGINNIS AND WALSH, *ARCHITECTS*

nearly three hundred years ago. A base-ball diamond adjoins the football field, and beyond it, to the east, several tennis courts are planned.

Messrs. Maginnis and Walsh were awarded the commission for the Recitation Building—the first unit of Boston College to be erected—as the result of a competition.

The most significant professional critique of the new Boston College buildings came from the nation's leading architect in the Gothic revival, Ralph Adams Cram. Architectural historian Douglas Shand Tucci devotes a chapter to Cram entitled, "Ralph Adams Cram and Boston Gothic," in his volume, *Built in Boston*. Cram's best known local work is All Saints Church in Ashmont, although he established his national reputation with the design for the Cathedral of St. John the Divine in New York City. Thus, praise from Cram for Maginnis and Walsh's Boston College work was the highest possible accolade.

An article in *Woodstock Letters* reported the successful completion of a $2 million drive undertaken by the president of Boston College, Father William Devlin, for the erection of the science building that now bears his name. The article then quotes architect Cram's comments on Boston College's Chestnut Hill buildings:[7]

BOSTON. THE COLLEGE—
THE GREAT DRIVE FOR $2,000,000.

The splendid response given to the Boston College Fund Campaign will more than ever draw the eyes of the entire country towards this institution, which is "a monument of esthetic value" not merely to Boston, but to the entire country, while from its halls "have come forth men who are an honor to the community, an asset to good citizenship." Such is the view rightly taken by the leading Boston journals. To impress upon our readers what has really taken place in Boston, and to indicate the cultural significance of the buildings being erected there by this Catholic college, the following opening paragraphs of a descriptive article by Ralph Adams Cram deserve to be quoted entire from the Boston *Evening Transcript:*

"For some years everyone who has seen the beginnings of the new Boston College—and who has not?—has realized that something was happening here in Chestnut Hill that was immensely significant. The

> extraordinary beauty of the site and the striking qualities of the architecture make a combination that not only gives immediate satisfaction to the eye, but stimulates the imagination as to the future. Certainly, here is a scheme under way which promises to work out into one of the greatest artistic features of Massachusetts, even of the United States. Higher education demands, and has by no means received of late, the finest possible architectural embodiment, for the silent influence of good art is perhaps quite as potent along educational and cultural lines as is the scheme of studies and the discipline involved. When this higher education is knit up with religion, the demand becomes even more insistent, and when by chance this religion is the ancient Catholic Faith of the world, then indeed we have not only the greatest possible opportunity, but the most imperative demand for the best that men of today can provide.
>
> "Every architect knows, and I should say every layman as well, that in this particular case the institution itself and the architects are meeting the evident necessity in the most appreciative, intelligent and brilliant fashion. The great tower has been a landmark and a joy to the eye ever since it was erected. The faculty building began to indicate future possibilities, and now the designs that have been made by Maginnis & Walsh for the chapel, the library, the science building and the gymnasium go still further in their stimulating promise. Usually one gets in American colleges one, or perhaps two, structures conceived in the right spirit, worked out in logical style and admirable design, mixed up with heterogeneous edifices of very varied value. Occasionally, as for example at Princeton, this number is increased to a preponderant majority. Seldom, however, does the opportunity offer itself for a complete and consistent group of all the educational buildings, planned by one hand and forming a consistent whole. Boston College is one of the exceptions, and from every possible point of view the general public must look with interest on the working out of the project, at the same time giving it every possible support, financial and otherwise. There are no limits that can be set to the cultural and civilizing value of such a power as this."

Cram was praising a scheme of building as much as he was lauding the first buildings of that scheme. Regrettably, soaring costs of construction made it impossible to pursue the original grand Gothic plan, and Boston College has followed the familiar pattern of "heterogeneous edifices" of varied style. Still, the five buildings that bear the Maginnis and Walsh stamp (Gasson, Bapst, St.

Mary's, Devlin, and Lyons) form a coherent cluster that gives character and proud identity to Boston College architecturally. To these may be added Fulton Hall, the first Maginnis and Walsh building of the post-World War II era, whose recent reconstruction brought it into harmony with the original buildings.

Thanks to Father William Stinson, who was librarian from 1923 to 1933, we have some thoughts from Charles Donagh Maginnis about his work for Boston College. Bapst Library was completed in 1928. In 1933 Father Stinson wrote a lengthy and detailed article on the new library for *Woodstock Letters*. He included in it some remarks of the architect on the occasion of the library's completion.

Maginnis was an incomparable English stylist, as can be seen even in this brief piece. Had he devoted his efforts to letters instead of architecture, he could have become one of the masters of our literature. Maginnis' remarks are a fascinating disclosure of what led him to start with a tower, as well as of his sensitivity to the inspiration of the Gothic style. Here is the pertinent excerpt from Father Stinson's article:[8]

> On the occasion of the library's dedication, June 13, 1928, the architect, Dr. Charles D. Maginnis, in the quaint and pleasantly dramatic part of presenting the keys of the building to the Rector of the College, told briefly and classically how it came to pass that the buildings of the new Boston College were reared in the spirit of Gothic beauty:
>
> > "As one thinks back to its rather adventurous inception, one is gratified by the security of Father Gasson's title to the vision which first perceived such an eminence as this ground with buildings and peopled with a multitude of students. General testimony supports it, his successors unanimously proclaim it. Doubtless to him also is due the wisdom of the measure by which there was established at the very outset the large relation of building to building in completed picture, giving thereby to Boston College, in this type of organized design, priority among the Catholic institutions of America.
> >
> > "The acquisition of this superb property was surely a triumphant beginning and deserves to be a notable item of College history. The challenge to the architects which resided in its dramatic elevation, in the immensity of its vistas, in the natural and cultivated richness of its immediate frame, was clear and unmistakable. Here, in enduring

Charles D. Maginnis of the firm Maginnis and Walsh.

stone, was to be raised an adequate and convincing symbol of the genius of a unique institution of learning. The College had resolved not to build selfishly. It had preempted a vivid space in the proud suburb of a great city. It must manifest itself, therefore, in such terms of beauty as to satisfy at once the impulse of its own high self-respect and a distinct communal obligation.

"What should those terms be? For the architectural style was yet to be determined. No mathematical street leads to University Heights such as would suggest the availability of those styles of architecture which, like the Classic and the Renaissance, depend for their impressiveness on literal balance and symmetry and axial vista. One approaches on curved and oblique lines with constantly shifting perspective. Only a great tower overtopping the trees could adequately focalize the group under those circumstances. This was the first conviction which emerged from the study of the architects. With this large peg to hang the fancy on, the choice of Gothic was almost inevitable. Time only emphasizes the fortuitousness of this choice. You are familiar with the high estate of this beautiful tradition. History has no record of a system of architecture which expresses so eloquently the genius of the Christian idea. To the felicity, the poignant beauty with which it testified to its religious inspiration in the ancient days, we have still living the majestic witnesses at Amiens. Chartres, Paris, Burgos, York, Gloucester, Canterbury,—a unique literature of stone which retains a marvellous potency over the modern imagination. Now and then down the years from 1600 shifting philosophies have sought to relegate it to the sphere of archaeology, but its ingratiations seem to be imperishable. I know of nothing in the history of modern architecture, for instance, more curious than its present vitality. And I venture to say that this medieval art has never been, since 1600, so skillfully, so beautifully, so sympathetically exemplified as in this present hour in the churches, universities, and colleges of this country. Clearly the spirit of man is not to be satisfied with machinery. One is startled by the vividness of the reaction which has carried into our age in such flood this current of ancient Catholic sentiment. We see it even glorifying proud seats of learning behind whose walls is cultivated a haughty and fearful detachment from its implications.

"In the face of this development, whatever its significance, do we not perceive how becoming it is that this institution, born as it were to this great artistic heritage, should wear a Gothic countenance—a fair and proud countenance, which should grow with the years radiant and luminous as the soul behind it?"

It is fitting that we close this tribute to the spiritual and physical architects of University Heights with a quotation that includes a salute from the artist to the priest. Boston College cherishes its Gothic countenance and hopes that the soul behind it is as radiant and luminous as Charles Maginnis described it 66 years ago.

ENDNOTES

1. *Woodstock Letters,* (1907), pp. 133–134. *Woodstock Letters,* a journal published by and for American Jesuits, presented in each issue items of significance or interest about Jesuit institutions and activities.

2. The *Pilot,* June 1, 1907.

3. Robert H. Lord, John E. Sexton, and Edward T. Harrington, *History of the Archdiocese of Boston* (Boston: The Pilot Publishing Company, 1945), vol. III, p. 527.

4. *Woodstock Letters,* 37 (1908), pp. 121–124.

5. *Woodstock Letters,* 42 (1913), pp. 246–247.
6. *The American Architect,* 105 (1914), pp. 13–14.
7. *Woodstock Letters,* 50 (1921), pp. 223–224.
8. *Woodstock Letters,* 62 (1933), pp. 211–213.

8

The Spirit Maketh Alive:
A Protestant View of the Chestnut Hill Campus

GASSON HALL WAS DEDICATED in March 1913, and the senior class finished the year in the new building. The next fall, all four classes climbed the hill from Lake Street for instruction in Maginnis and Walsh's Gothic structure. Two years elapsed. The people of Newton, Brookline, and Brighton—as well as commuters along Beacon Street and Commonwealth Avenue—were getting accustomed to Boston College's tower on the skyline, when a Protestant journalist ventured onto the campus and seems to have fallen at least mildly in love with what he saw. The result of his visit was an article that appeared in the *Boston Saturday Evening Transcript*. The article reveals as much about the social milieu of Boston at the time and the relations between Protestants and Catholics or between Boston Brahmin and Irish populations as it does about Father Gasson's masterpiece.

The author expressly, if somewhat playfully, addresses himself to the Protestant community and feels obliged to introduce Boston College to them. He invites his religious confreres to "walk boldly" onto the campus, where they will be pleased to observe the "charming Irish courtesy" of the place and the "consecrated pluck" that drives it. The author's perspective on the student body and academic pursuits at Boston College were particularly refreshing. One must remember that only a half century had passed since Father John McElroy had struggled mightily against anti-Catholic prejudice just to acquire land on which to build a school. Now, here was someone in the Boston daily press saying to its Protestant readers, in effect, that these Catholics were perfectly normal people, and that they went about the education of their children in basically the same way that Protestants themselves did.

It is interesting to have this description of the campus when the Recitation Building (as Gasson Hall was originally called) was the only completed building and to recall that in 1915 the "Faculty Residence" (St. Mary's Hall) was "an affair of derricks, scaffolds, and tawny gray walls of but a quarter of their intended height." The Jesuit brother mentioned in the article who did the paintings in the rotunda, over the stage in the assembly hall, and elsewhere in Gasson Hall, was Brother Francis Schroen. As noted in Chapter 9 he did similar art work at Georgetown and Fordham and for several Jesuit churches. The author has a few reservations, hinting that the good lay brother may have had more holiness than artistic ability, and finding the tower of Gasson somewhat broad and heavy. But, on the whole, his appraisal both of the first Chestnut Hill building and of Father Gasson's plan for the development of the campus is warmly enthusiastic.

The author was Rollin Lynde Hartt, a staff columnist of the *Transcript,* and his article appeared on October 30, 1915. Were Hartt alive today he would be happy to know that his prediction of the permanent dominance of Gasson Hall has been sustained. When plans were afoot to erect the University's most massive academic structure, O'Neill Library, in the shadow of Gasson, there might have been a threat to the original building's preeminence. But sensitive planning by architects and campus advisors provided a library so positioned and shaped that it proclaims its great mission without challenging Gasson's tower as the University's signature. Following is the text of Hartt's article:

CHESTNUT HILL'S TOUCH OF OXFORD. A NEAR VIEW OF THE UNAPPRECIATED ARCHITECTURAL SPLENDORS OF BOSTON COLLEGE.

This is not written for Catholics, and they will please keep out, for we Protestants hate to be laughed at. Blandly we have gone on—fifty years, now—calling Boston College an "oh yes, one of those places where they turn out Catholic priests." Even to-day, while the institution on University Heights in Newton is inaugurating its new athletic field in a blaze of glory, you will hear passing automobilists comment, naively, "Why, it might be almost any college crowd almost anywhere! We thought students for the Catholic ministry wore cassocks." Which indicates once again that the laugh is on us.

And more properly than ever before. When Boston College hid in Harrison avenue there was some measure of excuse for the prevalent notion among Protestants. At present—well, hardly. With that lordly tower dominating the eminence above the Chestnut Hill Reservoir and visible in all its splendor for miles around, the establishment's newer conspicuousness should make the most self-satisfied ignoramus ask what, as a matter of fact, Boston College is. A Catholic divinity school? Not in the least. If you fancy there are black-robed seminarists walking meekly, two and two, beneath its Gothic vaults or kneeling in a dim chapel with candles on the altar, you will as reasonably look for that sort of thing at Amherst or Williams. Then what is Boston College? Answer: A College. Not a boy there is making himself a priest—though, out of 525 students, there are many who will study for the priesthood later on, just as at Williams and Amherst there are many who will by and by study at some Protestant divinity school.

Naturally, this revelation brings a smile when a Catholic reads it. But the facts are put strongly, in order to combat a fixed idea. Apparently, we Protestants accept the principle of a Baptist, Methodist, or Episcopal college, which turns out bachelors of arts and cannot by any means turn out bachelors of divinity, but balk at the notion of a Catholic college doing the same thing. It is high time we left off the follies. Nor is it difficult. Walk boldly in from Commonwealth Avenue, and see for yourselves, Catholics don't bite. On the contrary, they receive you with a charming Irish courtesy, sufficient reward in itself for your coming, while there are other rewards, some romantic, some aesthetic, some moral—moral, that is, in the sense that you feel a tingle of enthusiasm over the fine, manly struggle that has made the institution what it is and braves the future with a spirit of consecrated pluck very splendid to observe.

The mere walk from Commonwealth Avenue toward the magnificent Recitation Building—the one with the tower, of course, for the Faculty Residence on your left is still an affair of derricks, scaffolds, the tawny gray walls of but a quarter their intended height—has thrills you never suspected. How that majestic pile gains in beauty as you come nearer and gets its noble lines foreshortened! You might almost be strolling within the Cathedral Close at Canterbury and looking up at a wealth of Gothic loveliness and grace. To call it "one of the sights of Boston" is no extravagance. Nor do you wonder that the Catholics boast of choosing "the finest campus in America." From that undulated hillside, where twenty collegiate structures of the same tawny gray stone are to be grouped in dignified harmony when the plans are carried to completion, you look out across the twin lakes, the wooded shores, the Brookline ridges and hillocks, and, far on beyond, the dim perspective of Boston, where a faint, ghostlike campanile, the Custom House tower, seems hanging in the air.

Behind the Recitation Building, and at the foot of a steep incline, lies the newly finished athletic field, with its tracks, its "gridiron" and "diamond" and its temporary grandstand—a capital place to meet an undergraduate who will do the honors by presenting you to a Jesuit professor.

You are not surprised that Catholic youths prefer to study under such teachers as these, or that they will make daily pilgrimages from South Boston, Lowell, and even Providence for the privilege. It takes grit, though. As yet, Boston College has no dormitories, no community life for its undergraduates, and no place to lodge them anywhere near the campus. And they are not only fighting distance; a great share of them are fighting poverty. So, to a serious extent, is the institution. To be sure, the priests who serve as professors have no salaries, but fully half the students receive instruction free of charge while the regular tuition fee is only sixty dollars a year. The college is not a money-maker (what college is?) and its expenses and equipment represent continued sacrifices and struggle.

No doubt the boys who choose Boston College instead of a secular university are influenced more or less by "social suggestion." In Harrison avenue there is still an immense Catholic high school with thirteen hundred pupils. This explains the two telephone numbers opposite Boston College in the directory. The

Hartt felt that Gasson tower was a trifle too ornate and a bit too broad and heavy for the building it adorns. Had he lived with it for four years, as do undergraduates, or for decades, as do faculty members and staff, perhaps he would have modified his first judgment. (This and the following two sketches are part of a series of drawings of campus buildings by artist Jack Frost. They were published in *Crowned Hilltop,* a volume that was Cardinal Cushing's centennial gift to his alma mater. Francis Sweeney, S.J., provided text for the book.)

high school belongs to the college, and a stormy current sets from Harrison avenue to University Heights. But deterrents are nevertheless to be reckoned with. Matriculating at Boston College means giving up a lot that a boy could obtain elsewhere. There is as yet no gymnasium building. Fraternity houses are conspicuous by their absence. "College life" hardly exists. And the new "plant" is as yet without a chapel. The controlling motive, then, is apparent enough—to study in a Catholic atmosphere under Catholic professors and receive Catholic doctrine and moral instruction along with the usual courses leading to the bachelor's degree.

But while it is a severely abbreviated "plant," at this stage, few institutions have ever attempted anything more sumptuous, architecturally, than the English Gothic triumph at University Heights. Even in embryo, it is Oxford and Cambridge without their grime. One misses the grime, and yet is there not a civilized, refreshing decency in clean halls, newly chiselled groinings, and interiors whose lavishly decorated walls are still taking on the radiance of soft gold and undimmed color? Step in, and judge.

You are startled at first. So used have you become to associating dull hues with the gothic, that you forget how gorgeous were the "Dark" Ages and how daring the original color-schemes their architects supplied—precedent and to spare for what has been accomplished here. Inside the great tower and offsetting the gray of stone pillars and arches, color gleams resplendent, with lavish use of a pale, greenish gold and a rich and all but redundant profuseness in design. Gothic? In detail, perhaps not. In adherence to strictly mediaeval standards, assuredly not. You recall Viollet-le-Duc's restoration of the Sainte-Chapelle, and remind yourself that it was not in the least like this. Possibly your aesthetic traditionalism growls within you, till you wonder if the architects are not tearing their hair. Patience! The more you study those radiant decorations, the more it seems to you that they reflect the spirit of the Middle Ages.

And so they do, in a way you little dreamed. All the mural embellishments here, all those in the library, all those in the sumptuous assembly hall, and plenty more besides, are the work of a lay brother, who though not ordained, belongs to the Jesuit order and labors for the salvation of his soul and to the glory of God. Up yonder on his scaffold, you will see him, a very modern-

The rotunda of Gasson Hall is today as it was when Rollin Hartt inspected it in 1915. For a detailed treatment of the rotunda, see Chapter 9.

looking artisan in overalls—prosaic, frankly, yet with a mission like that of the Twelfth Century craftsmen, whose workmanship in stone, wood, and jeweled glass lives after them in the European cathedrals and was prompted by the same devout motive.

What matter, then, if the lay brother is in some minor respects more a saint than an artist? "The letter killeth, the spirit maketh

The sketch shows the approach to the original tower building as Hartt saw it, except that the linden trees were not at this height in 1915 and, as he said, St. Mary's Hall was only partly completed.

alive," and the spirit is perfect. There are higher harmonies than the literal ones. For that matter, sufficient harmony is already a foregone achievement in the great architectural scheme for University Heights. You begin to realize even now. If the tower that crowns the Recitation Building has appeared a trifle too ornate for the rest of the structure, the elaborate gothic traceries adorning the new Faculty Residence relieve the effect by carrying a note of lavishness over into an adjoining edifice. And if the tower has seemed rather too broad and heavy for the building it surmounts, you perceive that it is meant to dominate the entire group.

A noble group it will be, with its tawny gray halls set well apart, with lawns and open spaces between, and abundant opportunity for landscape gardening. In general, the composition is that of the new Tech or of the Harvard Medical School, only on a vaster scale and without the need of packing the separate structures close together, much less putting them under one roof. As the domed building at Tech and the colonnaded building at the Harvard Medical School are the "clous" of their group, so is the towered building at Boston College. It will remain the "clou" even when the gymnasium, the laboratories, the dormitories, and the additional recitation halls provided for are outdone in both size and splendor by the church that is to give Commonwealth avenue a "monument," as the Parisians say, and a reminder of their stately Notre Dame.

* * *

Hartt was cordial—even benign—not only to the newcomers to Chestnut Hill but also toward what we now appropriately know as Gasson Hall. His ecumenical essay is a gem of generous Protestant outreach to an ascending Catholic minority as well as a classic expression of a layman's appreciation of the wonders fashioned by Maginnis and Walsh.

To give a balancing perspective on the Protestant-Catholic gap referred to by Rollin Hartt at the beginning of his article, this author can aver that, about five years after the article appeared, he was old enough to know of the existence of the *Transcript.* From family remarks he knew it was a Yankee paper, therefore unfriendly to Catholics and therefore not allowed in the house. As he grew older the author came to think of the *Transcript* as a respected though stodgy paper that probably did not carry comics. He never saw it except on newsstands. It was still off limits because it was Yankee or Protestant. So 75 years after the engaging article on Boston College in the *Transcript,* testimony is given that the Protestant-Catholic rift Hartt regretted was a two-way rift.

Rollin Lynde Hartt's 1915 *Transcript* article is another precious bit of Boston College history rescued from quiet archives. May Hartt's kind judgment on Brother Schroen be a benediction on Boston College today: "The Spirit Maketh Alive."

* * *

There are two other recorded reactions to the new Chestnut Hill campus, written before Hartt's and by no means as sociologically significant as his. But, like Hartt's article, they are fugitive bits of the College's past that perhaps deserve a modern audience.

On January 6, 1907, Father Thomas Ignatius Gasson became the thirteenth president of Boston College. It had been agreed among the Jesuits since at least 1900 that a move out of the South End by the College was called for. Since Father Gasson's term of office was to be only six years and action was needed, he acted. Before his first year in office expired, on December 12, 1907, legal papers were passed on the Chestnut Hill property. The size and beauty of the new campus and its location in one of the most prestigious neighborhoods in Greater Boston thrilled alumni, students, and friends of Boston College. Student response was immediate.

One month after the epochal land acquisition, the January 1908 issue of *The Stylus,* the student paper, had several articles about the new property. One was an editorial by Joseph F. O'Sullivan, editor. He rightly saluted the vision and courage of those who built the South End College 50 years before. He correctly commented on the failure of the South End to blossom into an elite residential area like the Back Bay and, with classical and literary allusions, he hailed the move westward. He dared to call the new campus a fitting site for a new Parthenon. But in 1908 he could have had no idea of the architectural jewel that would rise on Chestnut Hill. O'Sullivan wrote:

> Times change and we with them, runs the old proverb. Nearly fifty years ago, the present site of Boston College was the land of promise for Catholic education. We who look at the College buildings now, and think them small for their requirements can hardly imagine how mighty a work they made for those who planned their founding. It was a heroic task. The site in those days was in the line of the city's residential growth; but after a few years the march of residences went to the Back Bay and the suburbs.
>
> Now again—as westward the course of empire has its way—the site for the new buildings is on the line of Boston's most promising growth—there above the picturesque reservoirs, between Beacon street and Commonwealth avenue. Glimpses of the Roman Campagna—as Ruskin saw it—are there, and there, too, are bits of scenery equal to portions of the far-famed Lakes of Killarney. How some old architect of Athens would have chosen the place to set

> thereon a building like the Parthenon! The Romans would have put the palaces of the Palatine upon it. We of a later age—if not as art-loving as our classic elders of Rome and Athens—will vow our devotion to our Alma Mater. Out of our purses just now there is not much to give; out of our hearts we can give priceless treasures.

The second article was longer and more intimate, since it recorded student impressions of their first visit to the future site of the College. It was written by John T. O'Hare, who on the masthead of *The Stylus* was regularly responsible for a section of the magazine called "Domi," a Latin title that means "At Home." A regular feature of the magazine from its inception in 1883, "Domi" concerned itself with items of domestic interest, including accounts of important visitors to the College, publications by teachers, and special liturgies for feast days. In it John O'Hare gave this account of a student excursion to the campus-to-be at Chestnut Hill:

> On the last day of the old year Mr. Earls, S.J., and Mr. Miley, S.J., with a party of boys from the High School, spent the entire day at the new college grounds. [The Mr. (rather than Rev.) before the names Earls and Miley indicates that these were Jesuit scholastics—that is, not yet ordained.] They prepared their mid-day meal camp fashion in the spacious, open hearths of the old homestead, and the boys passed the day playing games about the grounds and in the groves, while the big, roomy barn proved an excellent basketball court.
>
> During the day several of the college fellows appeared, and in the afternoon Captain O'Kane of this year's track team, who lives close by, brought over enough balls, bats, mitts, and gloves to equip a baseball nine and they engaged in what was probably the first, though not a formal, baseball practice on the new grounds. All were fascinated with the place and well might they be, for there is a comfortable, home-like feeling about it that makes one loath to leave. On the return home many pleasant compliments were paid Fr. Gasson on the wisdom and good sense of his selection of land for the new college.
>
> Of course this new site cannot be seen to best advantage at this bleak and desolate season of the year. To see it at its best we must wait till the coming of spring, when the grass begins to push its

green blades up through the softening earth and flower and leaf unfold in all their vernal vigor and beauty.

In expectation of all this the members of the present Senior class are planning to take possession of the new grounds for their class day exercises which shall include the planting of ivy and all the other events which are possible to graduates of an institution having extensive grounds.

Under the new order of things *The Stylus* will be very amply provided for, as it is intended that the cosy, little gate lodge of four or five rooms at the Beacon street entrance shall be given over to the future editors of our beloved college journal.

Though we of today feel somewhat envious of them, still we cordially congratulate them and pray to be admitted to the hospitality of the "sanctum" if we should call out there in future years.

The "Domi" article went on to tell of the preparations for a mass meeting sponsored by the alumni to be held on January 20 in the College Hall to inaugurate a drive for funds to pay for the new property and erect the first building. There were other references to the mass meeting in the January 1908 issue of *The Stylus,* including a speech written by a sophomore as part of a class exercise, done by all at one sitting, as a model for what a student might say on the occasion of the upcoming meeting. It is clear that the whole institution—high school, college, and faculty—were caught up in a mood of excited anticipation at the news of the purchase of the Chestnut Hill property.

Going back to the "Domi" article, this is perhaps the only firsthand description we have of the original Lawrence house and barn when acquired by Boston College. We should note the mild weather that greeted the lads on December 31, 1907, enabling them to play baseball in the afternoon. While those of us who have lived through some "winter wonderland" seasons at the Heights might take exception to the comment about "this bleak and desolate season of the year," we can certainly agree with the author's anticipation of the "vernal vigor and beauty" of spring. The students of 1908 were hardly bashful. *The Stylus* staff had already (in their own minds) preempted as their editorial offices the gate lodge that stood by the Beacon Street entrance. That lodge, later called Hancock House, has recently given way to an extension on Campion Hall. No student activity was ever located in the lodge.

Had Rollin Hartt seen a copy of the January 1908 *Stylus* he would have been confirmed in his judgment that Boston College students were just like "any college crowd almost anywhere."

9

Gasson's Rotunda:
Gallery of Art, History, and Religion

FOR A CAMPUS that has been cited as one of the most beautiful in America,[1] Boston College has little outdoor statuary. We have no signature figure in marble or bronze, like John Harvard in Harvard Yard, or Nathan Hale, Yale's Revolutionary war hero, or Archbishop John Carroll on the Georgetown campus. Our one freestanding outdoor statue is the comely figure of Our Blessed Mother on the College Road side of Bapst lawn. Early campus planners must have expected more sculpture, because Maginnis and Walsh's Bapst Library provided five exterior niches for statues, only one of which has been filled. The class of 1942 commissioned sculptor Robert Amendola of Natick to create the statue of Our Lady that stands in a niche near the entrance to Burns Library.

Perhaps the prescient second founder of the university, Father Thomas Gasson, foresaw the tardiness of his successors in adding sculpture to the site he named University Heights, because he turned the soaring rotunda of the first Chestnut Hill building into a gallery of art that includes five statues as well as four large paintings, with inspiring inscriptions over the doors and painted decorations that bring contrasting warmth and life to the rotunda's Gothic stonework.

Statue of St. Michael overcoming Satan.

The dominant feature of the rotunda is, of course, the gigantic marble group representing St. Michael triumphing over Satan, based on the New Testament Book of Revelation, 12:7. The sculpture, almost as old as Boston College, was commissioned in 1865 by a wealthy Boston merchant, Gardner Brewer, whose stately mansion stood at 29 Beacon Street. The Brewers were eclectic collectors of art from around the world. Their home was filled with American pottery, European decorative art, Etruscan gems, Japanese screens, oriental jade, and rare jewelry from France and India. This collection was bequeathed to the Boston Museum of Fine Arts, but nothing in it was on the massive scale of the representation of St. Michael overcoming Satan that Brewer envisioned as a dominating piece of art for his home. He contacted a distinguished sculptor, Scipione Tadolini, in Rome and asked him to convert his vision into stone. Tadolini obtained a single block of the finest Carrara marble and, with his assistants, spent nearly four years completing the statue and its pedestal. Mr. Brewer became impatient after three years, but the conscientious artist insisted that his love and respect for his work would not allow him to settle for anything but perfection.

In February 1869 the group was completed and drew many admiring visitors to Tadolini's studio, including the Holy Father himself, Pope Pius IX. In March the Vatican newspaper *Osservatore Romano* published a lengthy appreciation of the sculptured group. A few excerpts give a professional contemporary reaction to the sculpture:

> The group is elevated upon a marble pedestal embellished with pieces of sculpture and ornamental work, the entire height being eleven feet, three inches. . . . The vanquished Satan lies with his breast on the ground, from which through various crevices fierce flames are issuing. With his horrible left fist closed tightly, he presses the earth with his right hand as if trying to raise himself, disdaining to continue in his humiliating posture and looking at the heavenly warrior with a face distorted by infernal hatred. . . . We think it may be said that *the spirit of the pit* could not be better expressed than in this work of Tadolini.
>
> The Angel standing over Lucifer is refulgent with divine beauty. With uplifted right hand he grasps the avenging sword; in his left hand he holds the thunderbolts of heaven committed to him by the

> Almighty. He does not rest upon his feet, for the fluttering mantle that extends downwards from his left arm to the back of Satan serves him for solid support, the pleasing illusion being thereby produced that he is sustained by his huge wings.

The pedestal contains three bas-reliefs of the Archangel Michael. One, extrapolated from the Old Testament book of Daniel (chapter 10), depicts Michael assuring Daniel on the bank of the Tigris that his prayers have been answered. A second represents Michael driving away the demon who had hidden the body of Moses. This struggle is mentioned in the first chapter of the Epistle of St. Jude. The third bas-relief portrays the body of Moses about to be carried by angels to heaven on the command of Michael. This theme reflects the belief of some Jews as expressed in *The Assumption of Moses,* a Pharisaic apocryphal work of the first century A.D.

In commissioning a sculptured group of Michael conquering Satan, Gardner Brewer was extending a long line of similar representations in art. The Princeton Index of Christian Art has over 900 index cards for artistic representations of the Michael-Lucifer struggle prior to the year 1400, in painting, sculpture, relief, and illuminations.

Tadolini encased his massive work and accompanied it across the Atlantic to Boston, where it was installed in a great hall in Brewer's Beacon Street home. The patron had only five years to enjoy and show his mighty group of statuary: He died in 1874. In 1901 the St. Michael group was purchased by the art dealers Julius and Henry Koopman, whose establishment was across the way at 18 Beacon Street.

As Tadolini's masterpiece stood available for sale on Beacon Hill, in the South End the Jesuits had begun to plan to move Boston College to a new location. By 1907 the Chestnut Hill Campus was purchased. By 1908 the first building, with its great tower and lofty rotunda was planned. By 1909 the building was under construction and a Jesuit who had often stopped at Koopman's gallery to admire the St. Michael statue asked Father Gasson if he could raise money to purchase the statue for the rotunda. Permission was granted and the class of 1910 voted to raise the necessary funds. However, an anonymous donor purchased the statue for the College in the name of Father Charles

Lane, a faculty member. St. Michael and Lucifer had to wait four years before finding their present home in the rotunda of Gasson Hall in 1913.

It may be noted that Ashton Rollins Willard's *History of Modern Italian Art,* published in London in 1898, mentioned the statue. In one chapter, "Recent Sculptors," he had a footnote on "the present group of Roman sculptors." After mentioning the father of the sculptor, Adamo Tadolini, he adds: "One of the principal works of his son Scipione—a marble group representing St. Michael triumphing over Satan—is now in the Gardner Brewer house at Boston."

The journey from Beacon Hill to Chestnut Hill proved more hazardous for Tadolini's work than that from Rome to Boston. The wings of Michael were broken, as well as his sword and the thunderbolts held in the left hand. Plaster wings and thunderbolts were substituted. Not until 1925 were marble wings restored to the statue, and the other defects were remedied later.

Surrounding the massive Tadolini sculpture are four smaller marble statues representing four Jesuit saints: Ignatius of Loyola, founder of the Society of Jesus, and three saints who died in or barely beyond their teens, namely, Stanislaus Kostka, John Berchmans, and Aloysius Gonzaga. In the 19th century Aloysius was named the patron saint of youth. All three young Jesuits were about the age of American college students when they attained a high degree of sanctity. It was no doubt for these reasons that the College proposed them as religious models for the students.

The statue of Ignatius, at the west end of the rotunda outside the assembly hall, represents him in cassock, his left hand clasping a crucifix to his breast, a scroll in his right hand, with the rosary of Mary suspended from his cincture. Apart from his thousands of letters, Ignatius' principal written works were his *Spiritual Exercises,* a handbook for guiding souls from indifference or tepidity toward God to a commitment to seek to know God's will and fulfill it perfectly, and the Constitutions he composed for the government of the Society of Jesus. Both documents have worldwide influence even in our day. The scroll probably represents the *Spiritual Exercises,* since they are directed to people in every state of life, not just to Jesuits.

St. Ignatius needs little introduction to Boston College readers.

St. Ignatius of Loyola.

Born in the Basque section of what is today northeast Spain, he came from a family of some means and standing and spent his youthful years as a courtier and soldier. At age 30 he underwent a dramatic conversion, almost as dramatic as Paul's on the road to Damascus. After a prolonged period of solitary prayer and asceticism, during which he outlined his *Spiritual Exercises,* he was told that if he intended to urge others to reformation of life, he needed theological training. This meant he had to learn Latin, the language of theological discourse. So at age 33 he took his place with beginners learning Latin declensions and conjugations at several Spanish universities—Barcelona, Alcalá, Salamanca. But it was at the queen of European academic centers, the University of Paris, where he was awarded the M.A. degree in 1535, that Ignatius' life took its final direction and the Society of Jesus was, in a way, incubated. Ignatius drew to himself a group of younger men who came to share his own commitment to God and who in 1540 became the first members, with Ignatius, of the Company of Jesus, approved as a religious body by Pope Paul III.

In 1540 St. Ignatius had only 16 years of life remaining. In those few years his young religious order grew from 10 to 1000 members. Before his death he had established 33 schools across Europe. His followers had already carried the Gospel message to Africa, Latin America, and the Far East. Ignatius was beatified in 1609 and canonized in 1622 along with his fellow student at Paris, Francis Xavier, the missionary to India and other Far Eastern countries.

The statue of St. Aloysius, at the east end of the rotunda outside the assembly hall, represents the young Jesuit in cassock and surplice, a vestment worn by assistants at liturgical functions. Rosary beads are wound around his left hand, while both hands clasp a book which could be a missal (Mass book) or bible. His face is slender, somewhat frail, reflecting his noble lineage.

Aloysius Gonzaga (1568–1591) was born in the castle of Castiglione. In his teens his father brought him to Spain, where he became a page to the son of Philip II and later attended the University of Alcalá. Aloysius entered the Society of Jesus in Rome in 1585. He had completed his noviceship and was well advanced in theological studies when in 1591 a pestilence broke out. Attending the sick in hospital, he contracted the disease and died at age 23. Young Gonzaga had the good fortune to be associated with two men who were also declared saints: He received his first Communion in Brescia from St. Charles Borromeo and his Jesuit confessor in Rome was St. Robert Bellarmine. Aloysius was raised to the ranks of the blessed in 1621, only 30 years after his death. A little more than a century later he was declared a saint, in 1726.

St. Aloysius Gonzaga.

The statue outside the Honors Program room at the east end of the rotunda represents St. John Berchmans in his Jesuit cassock covered by a cloak, his hands entwining rosary beads and holding St. Ignatius' rules for the Society of Jesus.

John Berchmans (1599–1631) lived an unspectacular life. Born in the Netherlands, he attended the Jesuit College at Mecklin.

St. John Berchmans.

After completing the course in rhetoric (which would be the equivalent of sophomore year in college today,) he entered the Society of Jesus and was pursuing philosophical studies at the Roman College where he died at age 22. John's holiness in his too brief sojourn in the Society of Jesus consisted in his unforced and unpretentious conformity to every rule. He slept with the rule book under his pillow as other youths might sleep with a likeness of their loved ones nearby. It is of note, in the context of our rotunda statues, that on his deathbed Berchmans had read to him the life of the then Blessed Aloysius Gonzaga, who had died 40 years earlier. John Berchmans was declared blessed in 1865 and was canonized 23 years later.

The statue to the right of the entrance to the Honors Program room represents St. Stanislaus Kostka, dressed in cassock and surplice, holding the Infant Jesus. Born in Poland in 1550 (be it noted: six years before the death of St. Ignatius), Stanislaus Kostka was sent as a teenager by his parents to Vienna, where the Jesuits had established one of their classical schools. After a few years with the Jesuits, Stanislaus asked to become one of them, but the Austrian provincial refused him, fearing family opposition. Thereupon young Kostka decided to take his case to the superior general of the Jesuits in Rome, traveling the many hundreds of miles in the old fashioned way—on foot. The general at the time, St. Francis Borgia, accepted Stanislaus as a Jesuit novice. His life in the Society of Jesus was brief—ten months—for he died in 1568.

Stanislaus had extraordinary devotion to the Blessed Mother, and it is said that to reward him she placed the Infant Jesus in his arms. This is represented in our statue. Stanislaus Kostka was beatified in 1605 and canonized in 1726. He is the patron saint of novices seeking membership in religious orders.

Over the four arched exits from the rotunda—those leading to the east and west corridors of the building and those giving access to the assembly hall and the Honors Program room—are Latin phrases. Each phrase is related to one of the statues.

Over the doorway to the assembly hall are the words *Quis ut Deus?* The expression has meaning in itself immediately on reading it: "Who is like unto (or compares to) God?" But, in fact, the archangel Michael's name in Hebrew means just that. In art St. Michael, as a warrior, is sometimes depicted carrying a shield, and often the shield is emblazoned with the words *Quis ut Deus?*, the Latin translation of his name in Hebrew.

Over the rotunda exit heading toward College Road are the words *Ad Majorem Dei Gloriam,* which, of course, is the motto St. Ignatius gave to the Society of Jesus. The Ignatian motto looks down upon its author's statue beside that exit.

St. Stanislaus Kostka.

Over the doorway to the Honors Program room are the words *Mater Dei Est Mater Mea.* These words, "The Mother of God is My Mother," expressed the ardent devotion of St. Stanislaus Kostka for the Blessed Virgin Mary, and they stand just above his statue, at the right of the Honors Program room entrance.

In the archway over the rotunda exit toward O'Neill Library is the inscription *Quid Hoc ad Aeternitatem?* This phrase has for centuries been a familiar challenge of Jesuit spiritual direction. In some contexts it is a challenge of perspective: How can this limited human event, act, crisis, failure, success compare with eternity? But, more often, it is a challenge to weigh the bearing of a given human decision or act or situation upon eternal consequences. How does this promote or impede progress toward eternal union with God? The question is associated with St. Aloysius, whose statue is below it, at the right of the entrance to the assembly hall. A prayer book used by most American Jesuits earlier in this century states, in a meditation on Gonzaga: "God was ever uppermost in his thoughts; *quid hoc ad aeternitatem* was his one standard of action."

James E. Tobin of the class of 1925 wrote a series of articles for *The Heights* that were later printed in a 31-page pamphlet titled, "Art in Boston College."[2] In Tobin's time there were three buildings to describe: the present Gasson, Devlin, and St. Mary's halls. His major emphasis was on Gasson and, as he conducted his readers from the assembly hall into the rotunda to view what he called "the rotundic panorama," he pointed to the four paintings high above the statues of the Jesuit saints and remarked: "Above each of the marble creations is a wonderful example of the work of Brother Francis Schroen, S.J., placed in a commanding position in the clerestory. Each of the four paintings, beneath the ceiling of metallic blue, has a binding thread and shows the work of the Jesuits in different fields under the inspiration of the Trinity."

Before we describe the Schroen paintings, it is appropriate to devote a few paragraphs to the life of this talented Jesuit brother whose art work is such a significant feature of Gasson Hall. Francis Schroen was born in Bavaria in 1857. In his infancy his family moved to the United States and settled in Baltimore. He had a leaning toward art from childhood, and when he left school he was employed as a decorator and painter of mansions and public buildings. Schroen's obituary, published in the *Woodstock Letters,*[3] has some details of his personal life that are given here because of their relation to his work in Gasson rotunda.

Coming from a family of strong Catholic faith, Schroen attended parochial school. But some time after his marriage at age 21, influenced by the reading of infidel (the obituarist's word) writers,

Inscriptions over the exits from the rotunda.

he ceased the practice of his religion. His wife died when he was 35 and things went worse for him. He became obsessed with spiritism and the Ouija board, and he had ever deeper contact with the spirits beyond until the messages he received became so obscene and blasphemous that Schroen demanded in God's name to know the identity of the being moving his hand. With violent trembling his hand wrote the word *B-e-e-l-z-e-b-u-b.*

There is no evidence that Schroen had contact with evil spirits or was possessed by the devil. But he believed he was, and he went to a priest and asked to be exorcised. The priest told him to return in a day or two, but Schroen was convinced that he was cured through Our Lady's intercession and did not return to the priest. Whether Schroen's experiences with spirits were real or imagined, it is clear that they were exceedingly real for him. He held to his story to his death, as is clear from his obituary. Therefore one can imagine the feelings of awe and self-involvement Brother Schroen must have felt in 1913 as he was creating his great paintings on the upper walls of the rotunda and looked down from his scaffolding to see the statue of St. Michael crushing Lucifer. For Schroen the vanquished was Beelzebub, and the massive statuary must have represented the outcome of a battle that had taken place in his own life.

Schroen entered the Society of Jesus in 1898 at age 41. Schroen's paintings and decorative art are found in several Jesuit churches and colleges—Georgetown, Fordham, St. Joseph's (in Philadelphia), the Gesu church (also in Philadelphia), the cathedral of Kingston, Jamaica, and the church of the Holy Name in New Orleans. At Boston College, in addition to the four paintings in the rotunda, Brother Schroen painted the mural over the stage in the assembly room, "The Church, the Educator of Mankind," and he did all the decorations of the Fulton Debating room on the third floor of Gasson Hall, including representations of the six authors whose words are inscribed on the sloped walls and the likeness of Father Robert Fulton, founder of debating at Boston College.

In the rotunda, the painting over the statue of St. Ignatius represents Ignatius during his early student days, with book in hand, reciting his Latin lesson. The students watching him appear in the painting somewhat older than the schoolboys who were

The "Rotundic Panorama."

St. Ignatius among schoolboys.

Loyola's classmates. The Lord is pictured above the class, looking approvingly at the saint. In the space over the painting is the word *EDUCATIO,* and below it are represented the lamp of education and the book of learning, on either side of the phrase, "St. Ignatius puerorum aemulus litteris operam navat," which may be rendered,

"Competing with schoolboys, St. Ignatius diligently pursues classical studies."

The painting over the statue of St. Aloysius, on the assembly hall side of the rotunda, represents Father Pierre Biard offering the first Mass to be said in New England. The priest elevates the sacred host before a large wooden cross. Around him kneel a few colonists, their implements of civilization, plough and anvil, close by. In the background Indian villagers look on with wonder at a rite they had never seen before. The year was 1613; the place was Mount Desert Island, Maine.

Pierre Biard (1567–1622) was born in Grenoble, France. He entered the Society of Jesus and was serving as professor of theology and Hebrew at Lyons when he was put in charge of a Jesuit mission to Acadia. The historian Francis Parkman called Biard's ship, the *Jonas,* "the *Mayflower* of the Jesuits." Biard's colony in Maine was short-lived; it was attacked and destroyed by an English ship from Virginia. Biard was taken prisoner for nine months and, through the maritime misadventures of his captors, was set ashore in Wales. British authorities returned him to France.[4]

Above this painting is the word *RELIGIO,* and below it is the inscription, "Divina litant hostia in his longinquis oris Christifideles" (Christians offer Mass on these far-off shores.) On one side of the inscription are chalice and host, and on the other a stole and cruet.

Across the rotunda, on the wall to the left of the entrance to the Honors Program room, the painting represents Father Jacques Marquette as the first European to set eyes on the upper Mississippi River. Marquette stands in the prow of a canoe paddled by native Americans. Joliet, with European companions, is in the second canoe. Over the painting is the word *Fides,* which means faith. Whatever the motives of Joliet and the French government may have been, the priest's aim in his perilous journey was the spread of the Christian faith. Below the painting are emblems of the missionary and explorer, a world surmounted by a cross and a boat with crossed oars. Between the two is the Latin expression, "Marquette recludit ignotos fluminis Mississippi fontes" (Marquette reveals the unknown waters of the Mississippi River).

Jacques Marquette (1636–1675) was born in Laon, France. He

The first Mass offered in New England.

entered the Society of Jesus and at age 30 was sent as a missionary to the Indians of Canada. He mastered the Huron language and was fluent in six Indian dialects. He was accepted in many native settlements and worked his way west to the southern part of Lake Superior. There Illinois Indians spoke of a great river. Marquette determined to see it. He had special devotion to Our Lady's

Immaculate Conception and promised that if he reached the great river he would name it Conception. Authorities in Quebec sent Joliet to join the expedition. They crossed Wisconsin by river and portage, and the Wisconsin River brought them to the Mississippi. They continued down the Mississippi as far as the mouth of the Arkansas River, only a few hundred miles from the present city of New Orleans. Because the city was then controlled by Spain, the expedition turned back. The diary that Marquette kept during this momentous and daring journey is a treasure for historians of the exploration and opening of the American continent. Marquette's name for the great river was not adopted, but, writing two centuries later, Francis Parkman remarked that Marquette would have rejoiced when in 1854 the doctrine of the Immaculate Conception of Mary was declared a dogma of the church.[5]

The fourth painting, over the statue of St. Stanislaus, represents one of the leading scientists in Jesuit history, Athanasius Kircher (1601–1680). Under the word *SCIENTIA,* God the Father extends a guiding hand toward Kircher, who is surrounded by scientific instruments and two piles of books. These no doubt represent the 44 folio volumes on scientific subjects he wrote during his long scholarly career. The inscription beneath the painting is, "Kircher arcana naturae pandit" (Kircher discloses nature's secrets).

Athanasius Kircher was born near Fulda, in Germany. He attended the Jesuit school in Fulda, at the same time taking lessons in Hebrew from a local rabbi. He entered the Society of Jesus in 1618. Fascinated by the relations between languages, he mastered many of them, including Chaldean, Syrian, Egyptian, Coptic, Armenian, and Arabic. His scientific interests were truly manifold. Some of them are the study of earthquakes and volcanoes, magnetism, hieroglyphics, medicine, music, astronomy, archaeology, and comparative religion. He invented the magic lantern and tried to develop a universal language. He founded a research museum in Rome that contained a large number of astronomical instruments, hydraulic organs, obelisk models, preserved animals, and ancient coins, as well as ethnographic materials collected by Jesuit missionaries in the New World and China. A scholar at Colgate University calls Father Kircher the last of the polymaths.[6] It should be noted that Burns Library has 13 of Kircher's books, all printed in the seventeenth century.

Marquette entering the Mississippi River.

One can speculate on the reasons Father Gasson or his advisors had in choosing the themes for the four paintings. Two seem obvious: St. Ignatius and Father Kircher. Although Ignatius is represented in the statuary, Ignatius as a delayed vocation student is a natural inspiration for college-age youth. As for Kircher, not only is he perhaps the most prominent scientist in Jesuit history,

Athanasius Kircher, S.J., scientist.

but Father Gasson may have been making a statement by featuring science. In 1907, shortly after he was named president, Father Gasson addressed the alumni and told them he needed a large amount of money to establish a new campus for the College which would have improved science facilities. So science was a priority with Father Gasson.

Surely Fathers Marquette and Biard had dramatic roles in Jesuit history, but there are so many more directly academic models who could have been chosen—for example, St. Edmund Campion, Oxford man, or St. Robert Southwell, poet, both martyrs under Elizabeth I of England; and St. Robert Bellarmine or St. Peter Canisius, both learned theologians and doctors of the church. The reason for the choice of Marquette and Biard seems, in a sense, to have been patriotism. Both had significant roles in the development of America. Boston school children have always been steeped in the story of the Mayflower and the Pilgrims. It is not insignificant that Parkman called Father Biard's ship "the Jesuits' *Mayflower.*" Schroen's painting depicts a scene of Jesuits in Maine seven years before the Protestant English were at Plymouth Rock.

The heroic movement of Americans westward to Colorado, California, and Oregon was antedated and to some extent promoted by Marquette's discovery and exploration of the Mississippi: So two of the rotunda's paintings show Jesuits and the Catholic church as pioneers in the development of America.

Gasson's rotunda is, indeed, a gallery of art, history, and religion. All by itself it proclaims what some people take to be the message of the words that were added to the Boston College seal after Father Gasson's day: *Religio et Bonis Artibus*.

ENDNOTES

1. In the 1950s the author posted a newsclipping on the bulletin board of St. Mary's Hall. It quoted a journalist in Minneapolis whose hobby was visiting college campuses around the country. He declared the most beautiful campus in the United States to be that of the University of Washington on Puget Sound. He awarded second place to Boston College.
2. Tobin's excellent articles appeared in ten issues of *The Heights,* from January to March, 1924. Another well-researched article by a student, to which this chapter is indebted, is "A Great Art Gift to Boston College" by Joseph E. Kelly of the class of 1911. It appeared in *The Stylus* in April 1909.
3. *Woodstock Letters,* 54 (1924), 81.
4. Lyon Gardiner Tyler, ed., *Narratives of Early Virginia, 1606–1625* (Charles Scribners, 1909), contains a 1614 letter from Father Biard to Father General Claude Aquaviva describing the British attack on the Mount Desert settlement, his capture, and eventual release after perils at sea.

5. Francis Parkman, *LaSalle and the Discovery of the Grest West* (Boston: Little, Brown, 1897), I, p. 59.
6. Joscelyn Godwin, *Athanasius Kircher: A Renaissance Man and the Quest for Lost Knowledge* (London: Thames and Hudson, 1979), p. 5.

10

Boston College's Streets

THE STRETCH OF THOROUGHFARE from Lake Street up the hill past Voute Hall, St. Mary's Hall, and Bapst Library did not carry the name Commonwealth Avenue until 1894. Before that it had been known both as Ward Street[1] and South Street.[2] College Road, so dubbed in 1918 for obvious reasons, was formerly called South Street, though at different times in the nineteenth century it was also known as Brighton Road[3] and Ward Street.[4]

Such changes in street names should not surprise anyone familiar with local tradition. Indeed, early Boston had four different names for different pieces of the present Washington Street, running from Dock Square to the South End: Cornhill, Marlborough, Newbury, and Orange Streets. In honoring the republic's first president, the town fathers shifted three of the original street names to new locations.

Until the last decade of the nineteenth century, the principal access to Newton from the east, north of Beacon Street, was Ward Street. An 1830 street map in the Newton Historical Society's Jackson Homestead shows Ward Street running from its present westerly terminus at Center Street to Brighton line, right past the future site of Boston College. An 1874 map shows South Street originating at the juncture of Beacon and Hammond Streets, meeting Ward Street at the northwest corner of Amos Lawrence's farm, where Bapst now stands, then turning east and sweeping down the hill to Brighton. South Street did not stop at the Brighton line but continued past the Evergreen cemetery, known earlier as the Congregational cemetery. The present South Street, between Commonwealth and Chestnut Hill Avenues, is undoubtedly the last remnant of the route that once brought traffic south from Brighton to Brookline via South and Hammond Streets.

Downtown Commonwealth Avenue emerged as one of the topographical triumphs of the filling of the Back Bay, starting in the 1860s. By the 1880s, with enlightened help from the landscape architect Frederick Law Olmsted, the impressive boulevard had pushed as far west as the juncture of Beacon Street, the Brighton Road, and Punch Bowl Road, the original name of Brookline Avenue (so called because it led to the Punch Bowl Tavern in Brookline Village).[5] The juncture of these thoroughfares is now Kenmore Square.

In 1887 the name Commonwealth Avenue was given to the section of Brighton Road[6] from Kenmore Square to Malvern Street, where Brighton Avenue now starts, and to the road left from Malvern onto Chestnut Hill Avenue[7], which at that time was called Massachusetts Avenue.[8] In 1895 Commonwealth Avenue was extended from Chestnut Hill Avenue (formerly Rockland Street) through property taken from the Chestnut Hill Reservoir and over the former South Street to the Newton line.

Boston's pushing of Commonwealth Avenue to the Newton line helped Newton planners to settle on the location of an east-west boulevard they felt was needed by the 1890s. A boulevard commission was established and several alternate routes were proposed. The project was seen by some citizens as a business venture of large landowners, and doubt about the quality of connections for the proposed boulevard at the Boston end was cited as an argument against construction. Once Boston had brought a similar boulevard to Newton's doorstep, however, objections ceased, and by 1896 Commonwealth Avenue reached the Weston line. The historian of Newton's tercentenary, Henry K. Rowe, described the boulevard commission's ideas for the new thoroughfare:[9]

Amos Lawrence's Chestnut Hill estate, eyed by developers in 1907 but purchased that same year by Father Gasson for Boston College.

> The plan was to make a road one hundred and twenty feet wide where it was feasible, with two macadamized roadways each twenty-four feet wide. Between them a thirty-foot space should be set aside for a double streetcar track in the middle laid on a grassy surface. The enthusiasm over the possibilities of the electric car was being felt, and it seemed certain that a street railway over the new boulevard would become popular and profitable.

Fortunately the commission's plans were carried out in all details. We can thank the advent of the electric streetcar for the lovely ribbon of grass from Lake Street to Route 128, happy haunt of joggers and dog-walkers. At the western end of Commonwealth Avenue on the site now occupied by the Marriott Hotel, the Norumbega Park recreation center was opened in 1897, and a trolley line was run along the Avenue to Lake Street. Boston College alumni of the twenties and thirties remember the open air trolleys that served the line in warm months. In those days the Lake Street terminal was considerably larger and, of course, busier than at present. Because of the crowds drawn to Norumbega, the terminal had something of a holiday atmosphere.

The completion of Commonwealth Avenue in Newton and the introduction of the streetcar line led to the development of property in the area. An 1895 map shows all the land on both sides of Commonwealth Avenue from Hammond Street to Grant Avenue divided into lots, with the words "Newton Boulevard Syndicate" printed across the property.[10] The map shows no development plans for the land bounded by South Street (College Road), Commonwealth Avenue, and Hammond Street; only five existing houses are shown on all of that property.

Not the name but the location of Beacon Street near Boston College has been changed. When Amos Lawrence bought the Chestnut Hill property that is now Boston College's middle and lower campus in 1862, his farm fronted to the south on Beacon Street. Just at the east end of his land, where Chestnut Hill Drive is now, Beacon Street veered left on a direct line to Cleveland Circle over land now covered by the reservoir. To make a reservoir of sufficient capacity, land on both sides of Beacon Street's original location was taken in 1868, and Beacon Street from the Lawrence property to Cleveland Circle became an elaborate curve.

One more example of street-name indefiniteness: Lake Street was given its name in 1860 by the town of Brighton, yet an 1886 city document speaks of it as "Lake Street or Foster Street."[11]

But perhaps the most important street names for Boston College are Howland, Fessenden, Southgate, and Hill Streets, and their importance is that they were not built! A 1907 map shows a developer's plans for dividing about 60 percent of the former Lawrence farm into 45 house lots, embracing our present middle campus from Commonwealth Avenue south to about Cushing and Fulton Halls.[12] The lots were arranged on four streets with the names listed above. Howland and Fessenden eventually became street names elsewhere in Newton. Hill is apparently a topographical reference and Southgate, heading south toward Beacon Street, probably refers to a gate house that appears on mid-nineteenth-century maps.

So in 1907, planners were dividing up the heart of the present campus and running residential streets through it. This year was a fateful one for Boston College. In January Father Thomas I. Gasson became the thirteenth president of the College, and in December of the same year Gasson purchased the Chestnut Hill property and buried Howland, Fessenden, Southgate, and Hill Streets. A man of less vision and courage might have waited a year or two into his presidency to undertake the relocation of the College from South End to Chestnut Hill. It seems likely that a

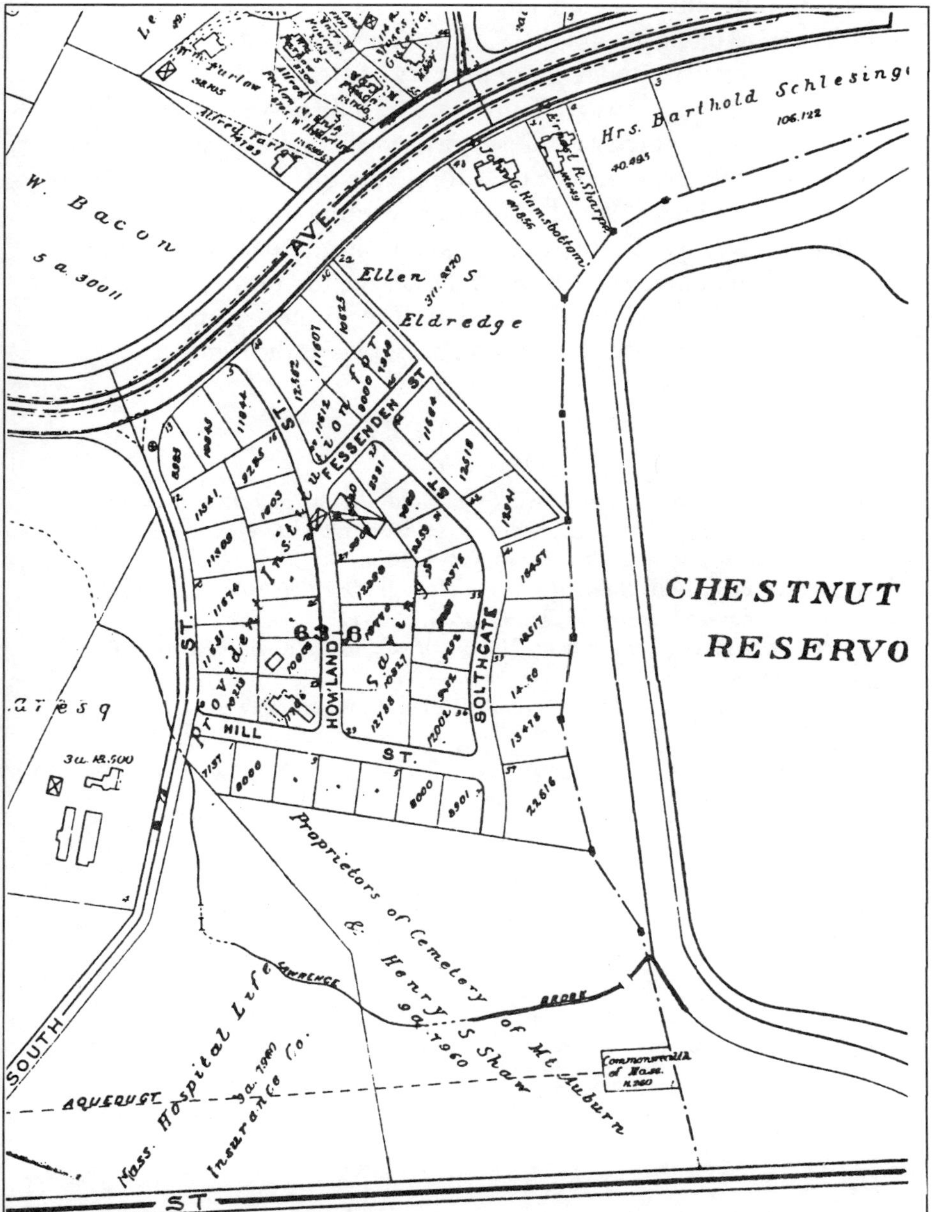

W. Bacon
5 a. 30011
Mrs. Barthold Schlesing
106.122
40.893
Ellen S Eldredge
AVE
FESSENDEN ST
HOWLAND
SOLTHCATE
ST
HILL
ST.
Proprietors of Cemetery of Mt Auburn & Henry S Shaw
9 a. 7960
CHESTNUT
RESERVO
SOUTH
ST
AQUEDUCT
Mass. Hospital Life Insurance Co.
LAWRENCE
BROOK
Commonwealth of Mass.

year or two later the present location would not have been available. Boston College is, indeed, grateful that Thomas I. Gasson, not the "Newton Boulevard Syndicate," became the developer of Chestnut Hill's choicest site.

The map on page 135, showing what is now most of the middle campus, is taken from *Atlas of the City of Newton,* G.W. Bromley Co., Philadelphia, 1907. The owners of four parcels of land that Father Gasson purchased are named on the map: Massachusetts Hospital Life Insurance Co., proprietors of Cemetery of Mt. Auburn and Henry Shaw, Provident Institution for Savings, and Ellen S. Eldredge. South Street is now College Road, so named in 1918. Commonwealth Avenue shows at the top of the map, while Beacon Street shows at the bottom. The former small Chestnut Hill reservoir, now the lower campus, shows at the right.

ENDNOTES

1. Information concerning Ward Street and the streets cited in notes 2 through 4 and 6 through 8, and note 11, is from the street card files in the Engineering Department, Newton City Hall.
5. Walter Muir Whitehill, *Boston: A Topographical History* (Cambridge, Mass.: Harvard University Press, 1963), p. 181.
9. Henry K. Rowe, *Tercentenary History of Newton* (City of Newton, 1930), pp. 277–8.
10. *Atlas of the City of Newton* (Philadelphia: G.W. Bromley and Co., 1895), in Newton Free Library.
12. *Atlas of Newton.*

PART THREE

Vignettes of College Life

11

Alumni Recollections of the 1890s

IN THE ACADEMIC YEAR 1950–51 the author involved a Graduate School class in a project on Boston College history. Class members were to contact and interview Boston College alumni who had graduated in the decade from 1891 to 1900 to garner from them recollections and impressions of their college years.

In the nineteenth century, graduating classes were small. In the century's last decade the total number of alumni was only 217. In the fall of 1950, 40 of these graduates—all of them Golden Eagles in their seventies or perhaps eighties—were identified as living. All but one were in the Greater Boston area.

The class members developed a one-page list of 36 topics on many aspects of college life, which was sent to the alumni with a description of the research project and a request for an interview. The list of topics was intended both to stimulate the graduates' recollections and, hopefully, to give a roughly similar shape to the interviews.

Nineteen of the alumni were able to cooperate in the project. Sixteen were interviewed, while three chose to write letters. As will be seen, two of those letters were the richest product of the class project. But the professor of that 1950–51 class set aside the reminiscences of those gentlemen of the 1890s because in 1951 he was told to start a School of Education. The project was forgotten until the summer of 1990, when it surfaced in the author's quarters in St. Mary's Hall. So these alumni recollections, unanalyzed and unreported in 1951, take on added significance 40 years later, now 90 to 100 years after the events remembered.

The prize response was a 14-page letter from a venerable priest, Monsignor Michael Splaine, pastor of St. Mary's parish in Brookline. Michael Splaine graduated in 1897. His name is on the wall of the Fulton room in Gasson Hall as winner of the Fulton prize debate in 1896. Upon graduation from Boston College, young Splaine entered the North American College in Rome to study for the priesthood. There his rector was also a Boston College alumnus, William H. O'Connell ('81), later archbishop and cardinal. After ordination in 1901, Father Splaine served as chancellor of the archdiocese and rector of the cathedral, and in 1928 he moved to his pastorate in Brookline. A priest of the archdiocese, Father John Saunders, B.C. '34, reports that when he was a seminarian and young priest, Monsignor Splaine was revered as one of the giants of the archdiocese.

Monsignor Splaine's letter is printed below in its entirety. A copy of the handwritten first page is reproduced on the opposite page, showing his large bold script. There is no formal letterhead; he wrote on plain paper. But he made his own pious letterhead—a cross above St. Ignatius's motto AMDG (*ad majorem Dei gloriam,* for the greater glory of God)—to which is added per M (*per Mariam,* through Mary), a piety that was not uncommon in Monsignor Splaine's day.

> I was a student at Boston College at the old headquarters in the South End of Boston from Sept. 1894 until graduation in June 1897. The Boston College High School was conducted under the same roof as the college. I remember that some of the College students resented being housed with the High School, but, as far as I was concerned, it did not matter, because we were all students, some young, some older, but all intent on getting an education. This attitude stood me well in life, because I have never been a snob or resented younger students associated with me, as we both struggled for an education. We were all, for the most part, boys from poor homes, & I could never understand the snobbery of some who thought they were entitled to special privileges because

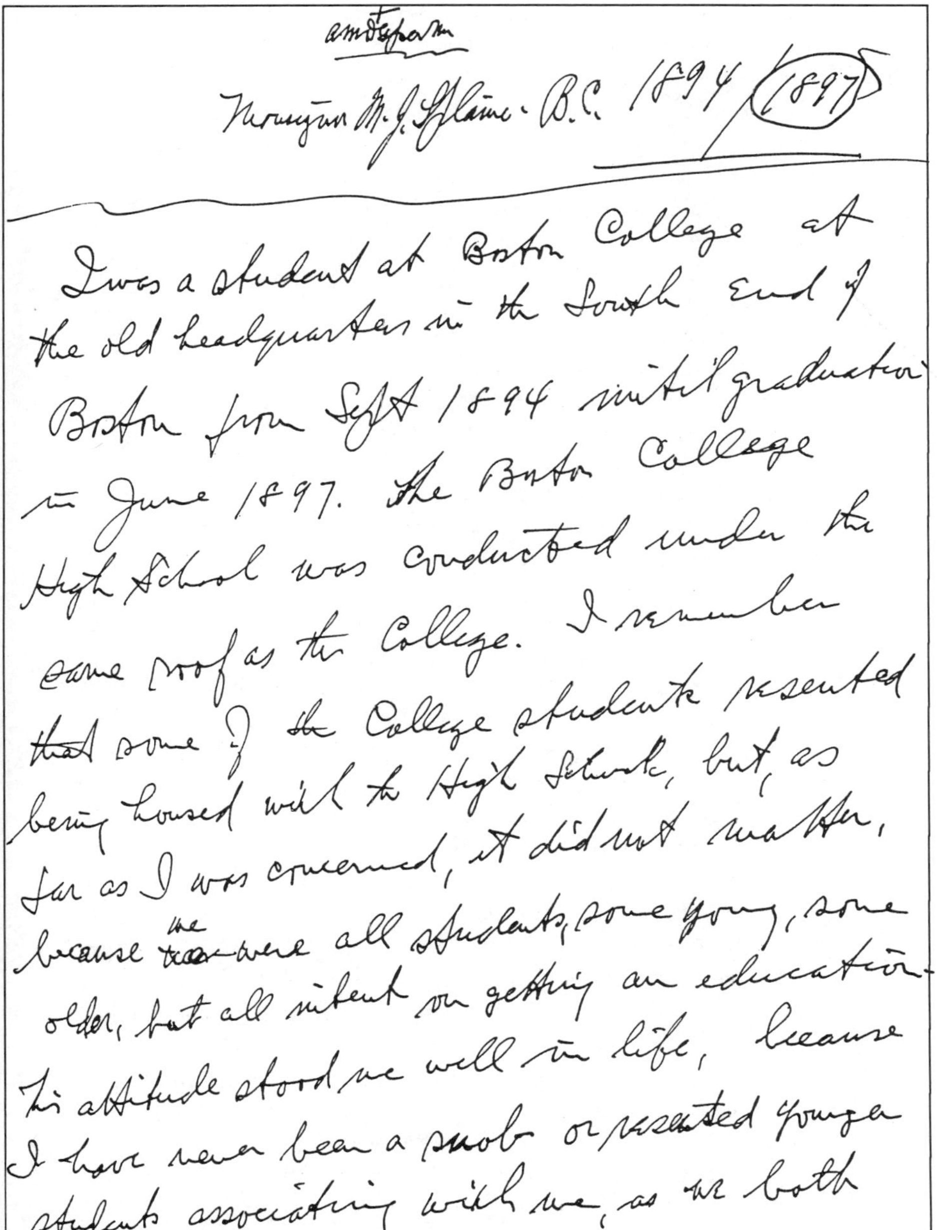

[illegible]

Monsignor M. J. Splaine · B.C. 1894 / (1897)

I was a student at Boston College at
the old headquarters in the South End of
Boston from Sept 1894 until graduation
in June 1897. The Boston College
High School was conducted under the
same roof as the College. I remember
that some of the College students resented
being housed with the High School, but, as
far as I was concerned, it did not matter,
because we were all students, some young, some
older, but all intent on getting an education.
This attitude stood me well in life, because
I have never been a snob or resented younger
students associating with me, as we both

Letter from Monsignor Michael Splaine in 1951.

their parents had a little more money. I am happy to say that that spirit was pretty well broken in my time, because decency & good sense finally prevailed. It taught me a lesson which I have used to good advantage all my life. I thank God that I have always been a Commoner.

We were all together in both College & High School about 450 in number when I entered Boston College. I remember well the day when we reached the extraordinary number of 500. We were granted a holiday by good dear old Father Tim Brosnahan, Rector, but he never knew that it was by drafting a likely young fellow from the Ash Cart that circulated around the College we were able to reach the 500 mark. Father Tim Brosnahan was the Rector magnificus all through the 3 years I spent in Boston College. To say that he was a most impressive and dynamic Rector would be putting it mildly. He was a most extraordinary scholar and possessed of an administrative ability that made him one of the outstanding College Presidents of his Day.

It was during his tenure of office that President Eliot of Harvard made an attack on the *Ratio Studiorum* of the Jesuit Order. Eliot advocated the Elective system which was quite in opposition to the *Ratio Studiorum*. Father Tim Brosnahan made reply in the Stylus, the official student publication of Boston College. The debate continued for some months & was duly published in the Stylus.

The replies of Father Brosnahan caused a great stir in the Educational Circles of that day. It was the general consensus of the intelligentsia of that period that Father Brosnahan had won a decisive victory. Alas, I have lived to see the day when Boston College has more or less abandoned the *Ratio Studiorum* of St. Ignatius & gone over to the rival system. "O tempora, O mores." This change of attitude brought forth severe criticism from President Hutchins of the University of Chicago who castigated the Jesuits for abandoning their safe & sure mooring & endeavoring to imitate the example of the Elective system, which he defined as purely experimental. "You have a fixed & stable system. Stick to it," said Hutchins.

The faculty of my day consisted of learned & devoted professors. For absolute dedication to his task, I give priority to the Rev. Thomas Gasson, S.J. He was an English Convert from Kent in England, close by Canterbury, where he imbibed the Spirit of St. Thomas, the martyred archbishop of that celebrated Minster. He studied in Innsbruck & entered Boston College as a Professor on the same day that I entered as a Student. He was my home room professor all through my course. He spoke German fluently & was still under the spell of that language when he came fresh from his studies to Boston College. I was the first student to be examined by him for admission in 1894. It so happened, that, at my High School in Watertown, I had for 4 years a German professor, by the name of Zuligg. He was a Gymnasium graduate from Germany & he insisted upon giving us a conversational course as well as a reading course in German. Nothing but German was spoken in his classes. He used to take us on long hikes every day &, again, nothing but German was spoken. Naturally I became very fluent in German & when Father Gasson inadvertently addressed me a question in German I replied with the finest of high German pronunciation. A link of friendship was immediately formed which lasted, through the years of my student-hood, out into the years when he was President of Boston College, the founder of Boston College at Chestnut Hill, yes out into the day when he lay dying & sent to me to come & give him a final Blessing. God rest the soul of one of my dearest friends, Father Gasson.

Two of the most brilliant professors under whom I have ever studied were the Reverend Father Fargis in Physics & Chemistry and Father William Duane in Philosophy & Ethics. They were natural imparters of learning & culture. I owe a tremendous debt of gratitude to these two gentlemen which I can only repay by praying for the eternal rest of their dear good souls. They were not only learned & cultured gentlemen themselves but they possessed the knack of being able easily to impart it to others.

A course of immense value to us in connection with our researches in Philosophy was the Physiological course given us by a most eminent Physician of Cambridge, Dr. Francis Barnes. It opened up a vast vista of scientific knowledge. I am happy to pay this tribute to a devoted Boston College man, not only because of his merit & devotion to Boston College, but also, because he was for many years previous to my Boston College Days, my Sunday School Teacher in the old Parish of St. Patrick's in Watertown. He was very strict as a Sunday School Teacher & also as a College Professor, but we all realized it was for our own good, and, by respectful obedience & cooperation, we all profited immensely from his instructions. He died a most respected & honored Catholic Citizen of Cambridge. May God reward & rest his Apostolic Soul.

I must make proper & well deserved reference to Mr. Joseph Willis our dramatics Instructor. He was indefatigable in his efforts to improve our pronunciation & enunciation of our native tongue.

He produced a Shakespearean Comedy every year during the Easter Season and a Shakespearean Tragedy during the Christmas Holidays. In appearance he resembled Edwin Booth, the celebrated Actor. He was always earnest & sincere & the students profited immeasurely from his painstaking coaching. I owe him an immense debt of gratitude, because he selected me many times for the leading role & thus, I came under his special & personal direction. I feel that it has helped me to an extraordinary degree in the public appearances which I have been obliged to make over a long period of years. May God rest his dear good self-sacrificing soul.

Another outstanding professor of those early years was the Rev. Daniel Quinn, S.J. professor of Mathematics. He was also the Moderator of our Fulton Debating Society, named after the famed President of Boston College of an earlier day, the Rev. Robert Fulton, S.J., a truly remarkable gentleman.

I joined the Fulton during my first year at College, & was chosen by Father Quinn to be one of the 3 debaters to meet 3 opponents from Georgetown University. It was the first interscholastic Debate held. I regret to say that our side lost, due I am sure to my weakness. The next year I was chosen to be a participant in the fourth Annual Debate of the Fulton, and, and thanks to the charity of the Judges, of whom President Walker of the Massachusetts Institute of Technology was Chairman, I was awarded the medal, which reposes today among my souvenirs.

My companions & fellow students at Boston College in those days were an exceptional group of earnest young men anxious to better their station in life. We were just one generation away from our hard toiling fathers & were the first generation of what was then called the collar and cuff generation. Many of them rose to high positions, in Church, State, Medical & legal professions. In the halls of legislation, state & Federal, they have all given a good account of themselves. As I review the years I note with anguish that most of them have passed to the great beyond. Of my own class only 3 remain.

I look upon Boston College today, with its wonderful equipment, its large enrollment of students, its outstanding faculty, as a fulfillment of the great hopes entertained by its founders & friends over the many years. "Esto perpetua." May Boston College long endure to bring luster to the Church & honor to our Country.

At the beginning of his truly noble letter, Monsignor Splaine acknowledged that some of his fellow collegians resented the presence of high school boys on the premises of the College. Splaine, the "commoner," did not share this resentment. But the Jesuit administration at Boston College, like those at other Jesuit colleges in the decade of the 1890s, was beginning to doubt the wisdom of operating a college and a high school in the same building. In 1898 separate entrances to the single academic building were provided for the high school and college divisions. In 1899, for the first time, the annual Boston College catalogue listed only collegiate courses and only the names of college students. In 1900 the College engaged the services of the real estate firm of Meredith and Grew to locate a site for a new campus for the College, but, while the present Chestnut Hill location was one of the sites recommended, no action was taken on the recommendation until Father Thomas Gasson's accession to the presidency in 1907.

Monsignor Splaine wrote that a holiday was granted when the combined enrollment of college and high school reached 500 (Monsignor Frederick Allchin, Class of 1900, also remembered a holiday when the enrollment reached 500, while John Johnston, '94, recalled a holiday when 300 was reached.) During the three years Splaine was at Boston College, the college catalogue gave as the total enrollment: 1894–95, 404; 1895–96, 419; 1896–97, 443. If a holiday was given for the enrollment meeting a magic number, it undoubtedly was 400, reached in Splaine's first year. But his whimsical story about the "ash can" boy shanghaied to reach the "holiday" number is obviously one of the collegiate myths alumni cherish. Since there were 404 students that year, it would not have been necessary to press anyone into student-for-a-day service. It is also amusing to think that "dear old Father Brosnahan" would be taken in by such a ruse. Incidentally, in 1894 dear Old Father Brosnahan was 38 years old. Undoubtedly to a lad of 20 that might seem old, but it shows the grip of youthful memory when a man of 76 still remembered his youthful rector as old.

It is not surprising that after a lapse of more than 50 years the alumni would err regarding the size of enrollment in the 1890s. But when three or four remember a holiday being given because the College achieved a certain enrollment, the fact of the holiday may be accepted. Similarly several of the graduates in addition to

Rev. Timothy Brosnahan, S.J., president of Boston College, 1894–1898. He was remembered by some 1890s alumni as an outstanding teacher and as the defender of Jesuit education against President Eliot of Harvard.

Monsignor Splaine refer to a Harvard-Boston College tension because of a published debate between President Eliot of Harvard and Father Timothy Brosnahan, president of Boston College. They are correct in reporting a tension and ill feeling involving these gentlemen, but they, along with many later Boston College alumni, have the facts of the matter somewhat muddled. Monsignor Splaine refers to President Eliot's attack on Jesuit education and Father Brosnahan's response as occurring during Brosnahan's presidency—a time reference often repeated in Boston College circles. The fact is that Father Brosnahan's presidency ended in June 1898 and he became a professor of philosophy at Woodstock College, the Jesuit seminary in Maryland. Eliot's broadside against Jesuit colleges appeared in the October 1899 issue of *The Atlantic Monthly*. President Eliot, of course, had introduced a free elective system into Harvard College, with no prescribed courses. For several decades he had come under blistering attack from his peers in the Ivy League and elsewhere for advocating chaos in college education. So when, in his *Atlantic* article, he proposed the elective system for high schools, he was probably addressing his peer critics as well as the general public when he asserted that only revelation from on high could validate a uniform curriculum for all—and he then gave the Jesuit system of education and Moslem education following the Koran as examples of such religiously inspired rigid education.

Naturally Jesuit educators throughout the country were stunned by this unexpected and unprovoked attack by a man of such stature in a prestigious journal. Whether Father Brosnahan was asked to answer Eliot is not known, but there is no question that during his presidency at Boston College he established for himself a national leadership role among Jesuits by reason of a thoughtful essay on the Jesuit system of education which he introduced into the College catalogue in 1894. The statement found its way, either *in toto* or through adaptation, in the catalogs of at least 14 other Jesuit colleges for a quarter of a century after its appearance in the Boston College catalogue, where it was reproduced annually for 57 years. So it was undoubtedly because of his influence *when* he was president of Boston College that he became the person to respond to Eliot two years after he left Boston College.

Unhappily, there were, indeed, tensions between Boston College and Harvard in the 1890s. Harvard historian Samuel Eliot Morison reports that in 1893 (the year before Father Brosnahan's presidency began) "The Law Faculty took the bold step of excluding from the School anyone not a college graduate."[1] The Law School published a list of 40 colleges whose graduates would be admitted without an examination, not including any Catholic college. Father J. Havens Richards, president of Georgetown, sent President Eliot the Georgetown catalogue along with samples of printed examination questions used at the college. In reply, Eliot, though making some disparaging comments about colleges taught and administered by priests, agreed to place Georgetown on the approved list. Thereupon Boston College and Holy Cross authorities pointed out that their curricula and standards were the same as Georgetown's, and the two New England Jesuit colleges were added to Harvard's approved list. But when Fordham made the same representation, not only did Fordham not make the list but Boston College and Holy Cross were dropped from it. The Boston College president who succeeded Brosnahan, Father W. G. Read Mullan, had some testy correspondence with Eliot. Nothing immediately was gained by this, but by 1905 the privileged list was omitted from the Law School catalogue.

Only Father Thomas Garrahan, '98, connected the hard feeling between Boston College and Harvard to Eliot's position on admission to Harvard's Law School. Judge Timothy Ahearn, '98, said that Boston College Students resented Harvard because of its superior attitude to the "poor Irish" college.

Parenthetically (to put Boston College–Harvard relations in better perspective) it might be noted here that 37 Boston College men had received the M.D. degree from Harvard by 1900. Since the first Boston College class graduated in 1877, that means those 37 M.D. degrees were conferred in 23 years. And when the report was made in the 1899–1900 catalogue, there were also four Boston College graduates attending Harvard Medical School. In contrast, by 1900 Harvard Law School had conferred the LL.B. upon eight Boston College men, although six graduates were attending Harvard Law when the report was made. In those days, more law degrees were earned by Boston College graduates at Boston University.

To get back to Monsignor Splaine's letter, he was correct in saying that there was general agreement that Father Brosnahan's reply to Eliot's *Atlantic Monthly* article was a masterpiece of urbane argumentation. Indeed, as recently as the 1970s Brosnahan's reply was being used as a model in a writing course at Harvard. Father Brosnahan was unsuccessful in having *The Atlantic Monthly* publish his reply to Eliot. It appeared in *The Sacred Heart Review,* and in pamphlet form the reply was distributed widely to educators throughout the country. While *The Stylus* had an article on the controversy, it did not print Father Brosnahan's reply as Monsignor Splaine remembered things.

Monsignor Splaine's letter moved from the masterful writing of his former president to a lament that his alma mater had abandoned the Jesuit *Ratio Studiorum.* He wrote in 1951. True, the College had dropped the requirement of Greek for the A.B. in

1935, but Latin was still a requirement for the A.B. until 1957. In 1951 students earned 28 credits in philosophy, considerably more than in Monsignor Splaine's day. In 1951 there were 29 Jesuit moderators of student activities. There were few on-campus resident students in 1951, but as residences were built in the 1950s, 24 Jesuits were serving as dormitory prefects in addition to their academic responsibilities. In 1951 Boston College was closer to the College of 1900 than to the College of 1991. So one fears that if Monsignor Splaine had lived another decade or two, his response to the Boston College query might have been less benign than it was.

The good monsignor gave a lively picture of Father Gasson, fresh from his theological studies in Innsbruck, Austria, meeting the young Watertown high graduate just entering Boston College and a bond forming between them based on their German language facility. Were it not for this letter, we would not know that the bond between the two clerics was so strong that on his deathbed Gasson asked for and received the Monsignor's blessing.

Among teachers singled out for praise by Monsignor Splaine was Dr. Francis Barnes of the class of 1884, a graduate of Harvard Medical School. One of the progressive academic actions Father Brosnahan took when president was to introduce a course in physiological psychology for all seniors, taught by Dr. Barnes. Several of the alumni interviewed noted that the course was invaluable for students planning to enter medical school, but clearly Father Brosnahan was interested in having all seniors become acquainted with a scientific approach to human life, supplementing the approach of philosophical psychology. Obviously in Splaine's eyes, the Boston College president had done him a favor in introducing the course with Dr. Barnes as teacher.

Mr. Joseph Willis of the class of 1890 was a respected and admired member of the faculty. Besides teaching the classics, he was coach of dramatics, and it was this role that the alumni mentioned with feeling. A contemporary, Daniel Gallagher, '92, later Massachusetts attorney general, remembered him as an excellent student and a superb actor. Monsignor Allchin, 1900, called Willis "a regular Mr. Chips." That Joseph Willis had a dramatic flare even when not close to a stage is affirmed by the late Father Francis McManus of the St. Mary's community, who as a boy was a next-door neighbor to Joe Willis and remembers Willis leaving his home in Roxbury for his daily trip to the College decked out in cutaway coat and formal gray striped pants. Monsignor Splaine correctly remembered the Shakespearean tragedy at Christmas time and the comedy at Easter. The College catalogues in the 1890s stated that two plays of Shakespeare were to be read each year by all the students of the College and the Preparatory School—for example, *Julius Caesar* and *Midsummer Night's Dream,* the tragedy to be presented by collegians after Christmas and the comedy by the preparatory students at Easter. So drama involved the entire student body, and several of the alumni mentioned the seasonal plays as highlights of the year, always playing to a full house.

Monsignor Splaine was grateful for his experience as a Fulton debater, as he was for his experience in drama under Mr. Willis' able direction. His letter ends with a benediction on his alma mater—"May she prosper forever." This remarkable letter from a saintly man was probably his last communication to Boston College. He died in October 1951.

A few topics were mentioned by most of the alumni. One of these was the fact that each day started with Mass at 8:30, and students were expected to be there. Daniel Gallagher, '92, who had a lively memory, reported that one South Boston lad who occasionally was late for Mass gave as his excuse that the Ferry St. bridge was open—an excuse that worked until the prefect learned there was no such bridge. This story anticipated a later one, after the College had moved to the Heights, according to which a student using public transportation from Salem was upbraided for being late while a chap who gave his home as Faneuil was excused because the dean of discipline was unaware that Faneuil was a neighborhood at the foot of Lake Street in Brighton.

On the academic side, the feature most often mentioned was the daily themes, said by one alumnus to alternate between Latin and Greek during the week, with a major English theme on the weekend. No one complained about the themes. With the traditional Jesuit emphasis on philosophy, it is surprising that not one graduate commented on the philosophy course except to say that it was conducted in Latin—and that may have had something to do with the lack of enthusiasm for it. Also the gentlemen attending the College in the 1890s had philosophy only in the senior year. As the century ended, philosophy became the major subject in both junior and senior years.

These Boston College graduates had three collegiate years of Latin and Greek, and many seem to have become passingly competent in speaking Latin. Michael White of the class of '94 remembered that on the streetcar the B.C. boys would talk Latin within earshot of young ladies, to impress and "bother" them. White graduated from Harvard Medical School and interned at Carney hospital. During his internship he was asked to accompany a mentally disordered priest to Mt. Hope hospital in Baltimore. During the trip Dr. White was able to maintain rapport with the priest by conversing with him in Latin, but the young doctor was stunned when the priest cursed him (he didn't mention in what language) when they arrived at the hospital. Dr. White was one of several alumni who were emphatically convinced that having senior philosophy in Latin was beneficial. Daniel Gallagher, '92, agreed and noted that some of the professors of subjects other than philosophy occasionally "lapsed" into Latin. Monsignor Allchin, class of 1900, recalled the final 15-minute oral examination in philosophy, with seven Jesuits (including the president) asking the questions and the entire proceeding conducted in Latin. Only Judge Timothy Ahearn, '98, declared that having philosophy classes in Latin was a mistake. Incidentally the senior courses in philosophy continued to be taught in Latin until 1917.

A course that drew uniformly warm praise was the Friday afternoon elocution class taught by Samuel Kelley. The entire student body, averaging about 125 in the 1890s, met in the College hall for the class. Kelley must have been an outstanding teacher to have his course commented on favorably by so many alumni. The subject, the setting (a large auditorium, with a mixed class makeup including everyone from freshmen to seniors), and the time (late Friday afternoon) seem to have had the potential for disaster under unskilled tutelage. But this experience was clearly stimulating and memorable for Kelley's students. Several of the alumni mentioned that Kelley was a Protestant. They may have done so because he was undoubtedly the only non-Catholic professor they had during their college years. Or they may have thought it unusual, if not unthinkable, that a person named Kelley was not Catholic. In any case, their awareness of the teacher's religion in no way influenced their reaction to him as students or their admiration for him as alumni.

There was remarkable consistency among the graduates as to the best-remembered teachers. Easily the most frequently mentioned and most warmly praised was Charles Macksey, S.J., who taught as a scholastic in 1890–91 (when his students were high school lads taking classics, mathematics, and French with him), and as a priest from 1896 to 1898 (when he taught collegians rhetoric, classics, and calculus). So although he was at Boston College only three years, he made a lasting impression. And he was remembered for incidents outside the classroom. Besides Monsignor Splaine's touching letter, the other sterling written response came from Joseph Loughry of the class of 1899. He wrote:

> In my book Father Macksey was outstanding. He taught Junior class and math. He understood boys. One day after class some boys had been engaged in boxing lessons in the gym. As they left they met Father Macksey. He spotted the gloves, said he hadn't had on a pair in years, and asked for a little sparring, just tapping, etc. The best boxer in the group put on the gloves. They were quite fancy with each other but Father Macksey was landing all the jabs, fast as a dancing master on his feet. Finally our boxer, nettled a bit, let go a right swing with plenty of pep. Father Macksey stepped inside and snapped a stinging jab. Then, pretending to be winded, he said "That's all boys. Thanks," and off he went.

The Boston College students correctly spotted a star in Father Macksey, who went on to teach philosophy and theology at the Jesuit seminary in Woodstock, Maryland, served briefly as dean at Georgetown, and then was sent to the Gregorian University in Rome to teach philosophy.

Another teacher mentioned by many of the graduates was Father Patrick Cormican. Joseph Powers, '99, later a headmaster at Boston Latin School, remembered Father Cormican as both strict and humorous, a teacher who found it difficult to stand in front of the class and so conducted class while walking up and down at the back of the room, a peculiarity mentioned by others. He was praised as a poet and literary critic. Powers said that if a student faltered or was unprepared, Father Cormican's standard response, delivered with a deep Irish brogue was, "Sell your books. You're wasting your time."

One thing that emerges from the names of faculty mentioned by the alumni is that the Jesuit Provincial was sending highly talented men to serve Boston College in the 1890s. The Society of Jesus regularly selects men of outstanding leadership and intelligence to be teachers of Jesuits in training for the priesthood, and this is especially true of men assigned to philosophical and theological faculties. We have already noted that Father Macksey taught at Woodstock College and the Gregorian University after his service at Boston College. Other Jesuits mentioned by the alumni of the 1890 to 1900 period who later taught at Woodstock were Father Henry Casten, Father A. J. Elder Mullan, Father William Duane, and Father Timothy Brosnahan. Father Mullan was dean at Woodstock. He also spent a five-year term as part of Father General's secretariat in Rome. Other Jesuit teachers of that decade who held important positions were Father John Quirk, later dean at Fordham and president of Loyola College, Maryland; Father Augustus Duarte, later dean at Gonzaga College in Washington; and Father Francis J. Donnelly, later prolific writer on Jesuit humanistic education and dean of the Province's liberal arts college for its seminarians at St. Andrew's-on-Hudson. When one considers that at this time the sprawling Maryland–New York Province was supplying Jesuits to 10 other colleges, the presence at Boston College of men such as those just listed and others of equal stature not named by any of the alumni is proof that Boston College was receiving very favorable treatment in the assignment of Jesuit talent.

Some interesting points were made by only a single alumnus, but even such isolated declarations are enlightening. For example, Joseph Powers, '99, mentioned that each class day began with the recitation of the Our Father either in Latin or Greek. Since he later was headmaster of Boston Latin School, it is likely that his memory on this point was correct. Monsignor Michael Scanlon, '95, recalled that at his graduation the 17 seniors did not wear caps and gowns because the president, Father Brosnahan, said that would be an imitation of Harvard, which seems to indicate that Brosnahan did not feel kindly toward Harvard even before Eliot's 1899

The cap of the Boston College cadet uniform bore the initials "B.C."

attack on Jesuit education. In place of caps and gowns the seniors wore Prince Albert suits and stovepipe hats, the rental fee for the suits being $2.50. Those who could afford to do so hired hacks and took their parents out to dinner after graduation.

Daniel Gallagher, '92, who gave a long and rich interview, recalled that some Protestants called Boston College the Irish High School, a derisive interpretation of the letters IHS which had been the monogram on the caps of the Boston College cadets of earlier days. His recollection of the derisive comment is undoubtedly correct, but his explanation doesn't stand up, because photographs of the cadet uniforms show the letters B.C. on the cap. However, until 1913 the Boston College seal prominently featured the letters IHS surmounted by a plain cross. It is quite possible that the cadets carried a banner with the College seal on it. (See photographs.)

Dr. Michael Burke, '92, told his interviewer that he enjoyed telling the younger generations of the hardships men of his time underwent to get a college education. Each morning he walked two miles to Wellesley to catch the train to Back Bay, and from there walked to Harrison Avenue. He figured he walked ten miles a day for eight years. Dr. Burke captained the baseball team and, when asked where the team practiced, he replied, "We practiced when we played someone."

Few of the students in the 1890s worked during the school year. Several mentioned that jobs were scarce. Daniel Gallagher said that home chores such as chopping wood and milking cows kept boys from the more rural areas busy.

Monsignor Michael Scanlon, '95, lived in East Boston. His father was a freight shipper, and it was Michael's job to get up at six each morning and see that the men fed the horses. He took the East Boston ferry and walked to the South End from the Boston landing in good weather. He sold hats in a downtown store during vacation time for $2.50 a day and allowed himself a 25-cent supper every day, adding that he was just feeding himself, not the rest of the world. The most common employment during the school year, mentioned by only a few, was ushering in theaters nights and weekends.

The chattiest, most anecdotal response came from Joseph L. Loughry, '99. The College catalogue of 1907 gave the names and occupations of all alumni, listing Loughry as "in business." But by the time of the 1951 survey he was retired, living in Manomet. The class member who contacted him was Sister Mary Michaeline. He wrote her two letters—one of three pages, the second of two pages, single spaced—with afterthoughts typed on the back of the last page of each letter. While he was self-deprecating regarding his college career, his letters show that those many themes written for the Jesuits gave him a style that would have made him a successful journalist or author. Here is the opening of the first letter:

> Your letter of the 9th inst. with enclosed quiz program [list of suggested topics] quickly unveiled the rearview mirror of my mind, or what passes for it. How long indeed the road behind, how short the road ahead! Why are there so many blank spots? Why did the etching needle plunge deeper into the cranial convolution in various instances? And for other periods of time apparently glide along without the faintest scratch?
>
> I fear I never took college seriously. Lessons were so easily learned and alas! so quickly forgotten. I might sum up eight years at B.C., four prep., four collegiate, as a journey during which I travelled by train, trolleycar and on foot a distance of about twenty-five thousand miles to acquire knowledge, and missed the boat.

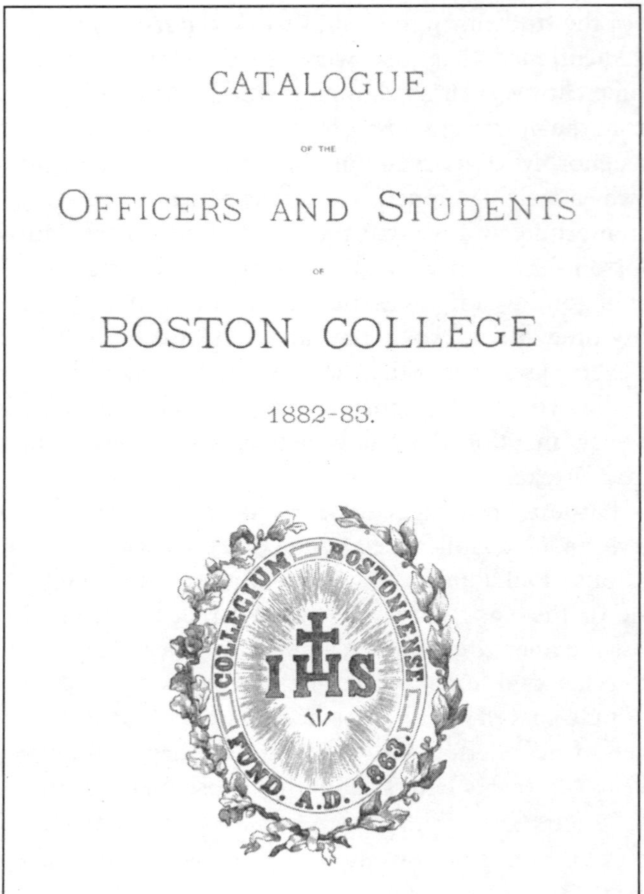

CATALOGUE

OF THE

OFFICERS AND STUDENTS

OF

BOSTON COLLEGE

1882-83.

Cashman, Keating & Co., Printers, Fayette Court, Boston.

The Boston College seal that appeared in annual catalogues from 1882 to 1913 featured the letters IHS.

Loughry went on to name the academic stars and prize winners of his class, and it is good to see that among them he named two men who later taught for many years at their alma mater, one as a layman, the other as a Jesuit. Father Jones I. Corrigan was a truly distinguished and respected professor of ethics from 1917 until his death in 1937. Eugene Feeley was a stalwart in the Classics

Department from 1917 to 1949. Comparing himself with such luminaries, Loughry wrote, no doubt tongue-in-cheek: "My only appearance in that line of endeavor was capturing the prize, *Life of Christ* printed in Greek, for reciting from memory the rules of prosody in record time which still stands, I believe, 3 minutes and 32 seconds." It was also refreshing to read Loughry's encomium on another important person in this survey, Daniel Gallagher, later attorney general and U.S. attorney. Gallagher graduated in 1892, so Loughry would have known him as a student only during Loughry's first two high school years. He wrote: "Of course one amazing fellow was Daniel J. Gallagher, '92, who graduated when 18 and won the Fulton Medal by tearing up (figuratively) his prepared paper and tearing contemptuously into his opponent ex tempore."

Several of the alumni expressed the opinion that the Jesuits were not particularly in favor of athletics, although countering this view is the statement of one graduate that a Jesuit scholastic had visited his home outside of Boston to persuade his parents to let their son play baseball. Here is Loughry's view.

> Athletics! In the eyes of the faculty an athlete was a pariah. The College had a baseball team that played two or three games a year, with Campello Athletic Club of Brockton, Holy Cross, and beginning in 1896 with Bates, Colby and the University of Maine. The Class of '99 had its own ball team in '95 and '96. In the latter year M.I.T. asked us to play a practice game with them in Franklin Field. We were short a couple of players. I brought in from Waltham a wonderful player. He was prematurely bald. He could throw and bat right and left-handed with equal skill. He played second base for us though his pet position was catcher. We were leading M.I.T. along about the seventh inning when they got a couple of men on base. A grounder went down between first and second. Sully (Jack Sullivan) saw he could not make a regulation play. He took off his fielding glove as he tore after the ball, made a left-handed throw to first and then doubled the runner trying for second. While scooting after the ball he lost his cap. The M.I.T. captain called time, quizzed us about Sullivan, and then they called off the game. I later played on the college team, also on the hockey team. But athletics were frowned upon by the faculty.

Boston College men of the 1890s, particularly those not aspiring to priesthood, were interested in the young ladies who lived in the New England Conservatory of Music just across from the College on James Street. Two priests and two laymen commented on the presence of the conservatory girls. Father Thomas Garrahan, '98, chaplain at Marycliff Academy in Winchester, recalled that in his days at the College "the only distracting influence" was the Conservatory of Music nearby. Father James Kilroy, S.J., '96, who had served as rector of the Jesuit seminary and provincial of New England Jesuits, was quoted by his interviewer:

> The New England Conservatory of Music (for girls only then) was located directly across the street and you can well imagine how difficult it was to keep a school full of boys completely aloof from a school full of girls—and vice versa. The sound of girls practicing vocal lessons was a great temptation to the boys.

The laymen had more favorable recollections. One was the former attorney general, Daniel Gallagher, '92, who was described by his interviewer as a white-haired and sage-looking patriarch who made the student feel Gallagher was "The living embodiment of that spirit of mental refinement and excellence that is the goal of the *Ratio Studiorum*." At the end of a long report on the interview—eight and a half single-spaced pages—the conservatory issue came up and is quoted here exactly as the student wrote it:

> The New England Conservatory of Music was then located where the Franklin Square House now stands on James St. and the overwhelming majority of its enrollment was young and female. A "stage" policeman employed by the Conservatory patrolled James St. to assure the young ladies of the proper seclusion. However the Conservatory girls and the B.C. boys used to communicate by flashing a signal code with mirrors and it was not uncommon to see a "lover's light" prancing on the blackboard. Mr. D. J. Gallagher steadfastly denies that he ever practiced this system of communication, used the code, or was aware of the intricacies of its meaning—THE OLD RASCAL!

As the reader by now must expect, the other layman was the lively letter writer, Joseph Loughry. He had two anecdotes, one in each of his two letters of reminiscence:

> There never was any trouble with local families, not even with the girls in the New England Conservatory. An organ grinder was wont to come through James Street about when we had recess for lunch. One day Dixie (Thomas J.) Vahey borrowed the organ and the monkey and serenaded the girls in the conservatory. That was the best collection the organ grinder ever had, but the Faculty clamped down on any repetition.

Loughry's second reflection on the subject came in a postscript to his second letter.

> Memory just whispered, Don't forget Dan Doherty. Rev. Daniel Doherty, S.J., was with us a short while in 1892 as Prefect of Discipline. One day in the Spring after baseball practice five of us snuck up to the attick to play penny ante poker. One boy suddenly said, "Look, fellers, look." We looked. A girl in the conservatory across James Street was in her room dolling up, perhaps for the evening. No more poker. A few minutes later came a rasping voice: "Get out of here and quick." It was Father Doherty. Abashed, we made our exit, that is, all of us except Jack Harte, who was catcher on the ball team. As he sidled by Father Doherty he asked: "How long have you been watching Father?" and successfully dodged a swing aimed at his ear.

One subject on which there was a variety of recollections—not necessarily conflicting—was the accommodations for lunch. Daniel Gallagher, '92, recalled that a Mary Kane ran the lunch concession in the basement. An ample lunch could be purchased for 15 or 20 cents. Milk was 3 cents and a well-filled meat sandwich 5 cents. Thomas Greene ('98) said lunch could be purchased at a counter in the gymnasium, but he said he never ate there. A group of students used to meet at a hotel on Washington Street. Father Henry Brock, S.J., '97, remembered a small cafeteria across the street run by two venerable spinsters where they used to get coffee and doughnuts. A more colorful report came from Monsignor Frederic Allchin, 1900, who said a good woman in the neighborhood operated a boarding house and offered Boston College students a good, warm dinner for 25 cents. When word spread around the College about this wonderful generosity, the boys swarmed to her boarding house, until one day the woman's

The names of two prominent subjects of this chapter, Daniel Gallagher and Michael Splaine, are inscribed on the wall of the Fulton room in Gasson Hall as winners of the prize debate.

daughter told them this magnificent treat would have to stop as there were too many patrons and far too much food consumed.

At this point in the narrative there will be a slight digression to demonstrate the testamentary value of the reminiscences of the gentlemen of the 1890s, but, as will be seen, the digression has to do with lunch, so there is that connection. In November 1989 Father Monan received an inquiry from a group in Canada that was planning an international symposium on athletics. The organizers had a document showing that Pierre de Coubertin, the Frenchman famed for reinstituting international Olympics in 1896, had in 1890 visited Boston College as part of a survey of athletic programs in American universities. In a book, *Universites Transatlantiques,* de Coubertin had this interesting paragraph on Boston College:[2]

> This morning I paid a visit to Boston College, which is run by the Jesuits. 300 students, all externs; building is taking place which allows the number to rise to 500; old classical education and use of the Latin tongue to ask permission to leave class. Outside of that everything is rather modern. The Fathers do not encourage sports, but they do not belittle them in any way; there is a tennis court and a gymnasium for the brief moments of recreation. On the ground floor I spotted a saleslady behind her counter. She sells the students, at strictly controlled prices, bread, meat, beer and chocolate for their lunch.

That was de Coubertin's summary of his Boston College visit. Unfortunately nothing in any Boston College record noted the fact of his visit. So we were not able to satisfy our Canadian correspondents, but thanked them profusely for de Coubertin's delightful little vignette. During Father Robert Fulton's second term as president, from 1888 to 1891, he extended the college building at both ends by 100 feet on James Street. So the French visitor was correct about the expansion and the increased capacity of the building.

The assertion by de Coubertin that students had to ask in Latin to be excused from the classroom could be neither affirmed or denied by any written evidence or collective memory, until Dr. Michael White, '94, said to his interviewer in 1951 that "even if necessary to be relieved one had to ask permission in Latin." That corroborates de Coubertin's observation.

The tepid or ambivalent attitude of Jesuits towards sports that came out of the interviews is also confirmed by our French visitor. And since he was keen on sports, his mild interpretation of the faculty attitude means he saw no overt hostility.

The most intriguing sentence in de Coubertin's brief sketch is the one about beer available at lunch. The visitor's observations during his short stay were so sharp and accurate, that we began to think that maybe serving beer to young men was so common at that time that its being served at lunch never deserved mention in College records. So we were in a state of doubt on the subject until the sophisticated Joseph Loughry of Manomet wrote two simple sentences: "Lunch could be bought daily in the recreation hall in the basement of the college. Most students brought lunch from home and bought only coffee or milk." Had beer been available, would Joseph Loughry have missed it? Hardly. So where did de Coubertin get the idea about beer and chocolate? From the saleslady, whose English he could not understand? But though de Coubertin was an honorable and respected world figure, when it comes to the credibility of his report on liquid refreshment on the basis of a one-day visit compared with Loughry's eight-year experience, we must go with Loughry. Our 1951 class exercise, examined in the summer of 1990, helped solve historical questions of 1890.

There is another example. The college catalogue of 1893–94 was the first to list each student's home town or neighborhood. Some of the cities and towns named were Holyoke, North Brookfield, Fall River, Lowell, Lawrence, and Worcester. Each year during the 1890s the first information the catalogue gave under the rubric "Admission" was this: "Boston College is for day-scholars only. No student will be admitted who does not reside with his parents or immediate relatives, or, if this is impossible, with persons duly approved by the President of the College." The question for the historian is, were students in the 1890s able to commute from distant localities because of the excellent train service that developed at that time or were some given permission to live near the College? University records are silent on the subject. Dr. Michael White, '94, supplied the answer: There were no boarders in his time; out-of-towners rented rooms near B.C. White himself lived in Plymouth and, because he worked nights at the railroad crossing in Plymouth, he had a pass on the train for Boston, and he added that the service was good. It was sad to read in the report of the interview with Dr. White's classmate, John Johnston, that the good doctor died in January 1951 very shortly after his helpful cooperation with a graduate student.

The students enjoyed the historical project as much as did the men of the 1890s. One student concluded his report of his interview with Thomas Greene, '98, with these words: "With this his wife Anne came in and she began giving him a hard time about B.C.'s 1950 football fortunes [the team went 0–9–1 that year!] and before civil war broke out I thanked them and safely made my exit with joy and happiness for the opportunity to have visited such a fine intellectual and spiritual man, a true B.C. man."

The noble gentlemen of the 1890s, as well as the class members who interviewed them in 1951, deserve a salute from all concerned about the history of Boston College. Let Monsignor Splaine have the last word, with his benediction: "*Esto perpetua.* May Boston College long endure to bring luster to the church and honor to our country."

ENDNOTES

1. Samuel Eliot Morrison, *Three Centuries of Harvard* 1636–1936 (Cambridge, Mass.: Harvard University Press, 1946).
2. Pierre de Coubertin, *Universites Transatlantiques,* Paris, 1890.

12

The Classical Curriculum

FOR NEARLY A CENTURY after its founding, Boston College made Latin and Greek a required and substantial part of the curriculum for the Bachelor of Arts degree. For example, in 1898 freshmen and sophomores had five classes a week in Latin and four in Greek. Juniors had two classes a week in both Latin and Greek. Seniors had two classes a week in Latin and two classes a week in classical literature. Such emphasis on a classical curriculum was the norm rather than the exception in American colleges at the time the Jesuit fathers welcomed the first collegians to James Street. Early nineteenth century catalogues of Harvard and Yale show that Harvard freshmen spent two-thirds of each day, sophomores nearly half of each day, and juniors a quarter of each day in Latin and Greek classes, and that Greek and Latin classes had comparable prominence in the Yale curriculum.[1]

The ancient languages and philosophy were the principal studies for the bachelor's degree in the medieval and Renaissance universities of Europe and England, and that curriculum was brought by graduates of Cambridge University to Cambridge in New England when the Puritan colonists decided they should have a college. The curriculum model of Harvard was followed at the other colleges established in the colonial period and by the burgeoning number of colleges that sprang up in the decades before the Civil War. But in establishing its classical curriculum, Boston College was not imitating the course of studies prevalent in American colleges of the time, nor was it simply copying the plan of studies in vogue in the 11 American Jesuit colleges founded prior to 1863. Rather, Boston College and the other Jesuit colleges were adhering to the prescriptions of the *Ratio Studiorum,* the official guidebook for Jesuit education, the first edition of which appeared not many decades after the death in 1556 of the Jesuits' founder, Saint Ignatius of Loyola. The *Ratio Studiorum* was faithful to the founder's directive that Jesuit institutions be structured *juxta ordinem et modum Parisiensem,* on the model of his alma mater, the University of Paris.[2]

Cambridge University is an academic descendant of Paris through Oxford, so the Jesuit colleges and the American colleges on the Harvard-Cambridge model derived from a common tradition. Thus, the Boston College curriculum, rich in Cicero, Pliny, Plato, and Aeschylus, might seem antiquarian or monastic or "alien" to today's collegian, but in the early decades of the College's history it was, in fact, as "American" as baseball and church on Sunday. In 1870 not just some, but all candidates for the A.B. degree at Princeton or Muhlenberg or Rutgers or Wooster or Hamilton spent a substantial part of their time on the same classical studies as all students at Boston College or Georgetown.

There were some challenges to the dominance of the prescribed classics curriculum. In the early 1820s George Ticknor, the first of the influential German-educated scholars, won a minor victory at Harvard as professor of modern languages. A partial elective system was adopted whereby modern languages could be substituted for some previously prescribed parts of the curriculum.[3] This anticipated President Eliot's sweeping curriculum changes by fifty years, but it was a weak and short-lived assault on the fixed curriculum.

It was at Yale that the most serious re-evaluation of the classical course took place. In 1827 the Connecticut legislature criticized the "unpracticality" of Yale's classical curriculum.[4] The Yale faculty set up a committee to look into the criticism and, after a year of deliberation, issued the famous Yale Report, an uncompromising defense of the traditional classics curriculum. The report became an educational bible for the smaller colleges of the country and established for Yale a conservative role that led to a major Yale-Harvard confrontation later in the century when Eliot introduced electivism at Harvard.

Eliot became president of Harvard in 1869, five years after the opening of Boston College and eight years before the College granted its first Bachelor of Arts degree. Eliot's establishment of the elective system at Harvard set off an academic debate unique in educational history for its intensity and public involvement. As one historian notes, "Every journal opened its pages to the controversy—*Atlantic Monthly, Century, Princeton Review, North Ameican Review, Bibliotheca Sacra.* Special bulletins came from Noah Porter (President of Yale) and Daniel H. Chamberlain (Governor of South Carolina) both in 1884. The same year at a meeting of the National Education Association, John Bascom, then president of the University of Wisconsin, concluded that Greek and Latin were antidotes to the materialism of the Age."[5] Charles Francis Adams came out on Eliot's side, attacking the Greek curriculum in an 1885 Phi Beta Kappa address at Harvard, *A College Fetich* [sic], which earned him a rebuke from Harvard's retired professor of moral philosophy, Andrew Preston Peabody, and a strong dissent from the Phi Beta Kappa chapter at Amherst.[6] Along with Yale's Noah Porter, Princeton's president James McCosh took up the cudgel against Eliot in defense of the classical curriculum. One of the highlights of the controversy, widely reported in the press, was a debate sponsored in 1885 by the Nineteenth Century Club in New York between McCosh and Eliot on the Eliot reforms.[7] In 1887, when Greek was about to be dropped as an entrance requirement at Harvard, the presidents of eight New England colleges begged the Harvard Overseers to overrule Eliot.[8]

It was against this background of curriculum controversy, but also in an academic milieu in which the traditional classics courses remained entrenched, that Boston College spent its early decades. That the Boston College community was aware of the controversy is clear from an article that appeared in the student publication, *The Stylus,* in 1886 entitled, " 'A College Fetich' Vindicated," in which the author praised an address by James Russell Lowell at the commemoration of Harvard's two hundred and fiftieth anniversary which the author interpreted as a reply to Adams' Phi Beta Kappa address three years earlier. As the nineteenth century wound down, the Jesuits at Boston College must have felt the need of an explanation, if not a defense, of the traditional curriculum. For as soon as he became president in July 1894, Father Timothy Brosnahan drew up a statement concerning the nature and method of Jesuit education that appeared in the catalogue for the academic years 1894–95. The statement was expanded for the catalogue of the following year, and in that form it appeared yearly in the catalogue of Boston College until 1952. It was borrowed or adapted by a number of Jesuit colleges from coast to coast, so it had for Jesuit colleges something of the standing of the earlier Yale Report. Brosnahan's four-page statement presents a rationale for the entire curriculum and method of Jesuit education, indicating its derivation from the *Ratio Studiorum.* It contains the following succinct justification of the classical curriculum:

> The acquisition of Language especially calls for delicacy of judgment, and fineness of perception, and for a constant, keen, and quick use of the reasoning powers. A special importance is attached to the classic tongues of Rome and Greece. As they are languages with a structure and idiom remote from the language of the student, the study of them lays bare before him the laws of thought and logic, and requires attention, reflection, and an analysis of the fundamental relations between thought and grammar. In studying them the student is led to the fundamental recesses of language. They exercise him in exactness of conception in grasping the foreign thought, and in delicacy of expression in clothing that thought in the dissimilar garb of the mother tongue. While recognizing, then, in education the necessity and importance of Mathematics and the Natural Sciences, which unfold the interdependence and laws of the world of time and space, the Jesuit system of education has unwaveringly kept Language in a position of honor as an instrument of culture.

Brosnahan stressed the disciplinary value of the ancient languages rather than their cultural content, a line of argument that had been used in the Yale Report and, in Brosnahan's day, particularly by President McCosh of Princeton.

While the classical curriculum remained a *sine qua non* for the

A.B. degree in most nineteenth century colleges, alternate curricula leading to some other degree were introduced by many institutions. Starting in 1851 Brown offered a three-year program in practical subjects, without Latin or Greek, for the completion of which the Bachelor of Philosophy (Ph.B.) degree was awarded.[9] The following year Yale began granting the Ph.B. to students following the non-classical scientific course in Sheffield Scientific School. The Ph.B. became quite common. Harvard chose the B.S. degree in 1851 for graduates of its Lawrence Scientific School.[10] As will be seen, Boston College, at different periods of the present century, employed both the Ph.B. and the B.S. degrees for various non-classical curricula.

The non-classical or English curriculum was often called the commercial or mercantile curriculum because it included bookkeeping. Many of the Jesuit colleges—among them Holy Cross, Fordham, and St. Louis—had such a curriculum dating from the first half of the nineteenth century.[11] It was partly at a high school and partly at a collegiate level, and, if completed, it led to a diploma, not a degree. Particularly in Midwest Jesuit schools, the commercial course was popular. For example, the catalogues of St. Louis, Detroit, and Xavier toward the end of the century show that at times enrollment in the commercial course was larger than the classical collegiate enrollment.

But, particularly in the eastern Jesuit colleges, there was opposition to the inclusion of the commercial course. Ten years before Boston College opened, the Provincial of the eastern Jesuits, Father Charles Stonestreet, wrote Holy Cross College: "I wish you would confine yourself to the classics. . . . The English course, or Commercial, is humbugging. . . ."[12] While Holy Cross and Fordham continued the commercial course for some decades, Father

Facing page: The first book published by a Boston College faculty member was Father Russo's Latin textbook on logic and metaphysics. The "Ed. Kenney" at the top of the page may have owned the book. An Edward Kenney graduated in 1897 and became a priest of the Boston archdiocese. Whoever wrote Bacon's maxim on the page set before himself a lofty goal not unlike the αἰὲν ἀριστεύειν that later became part of the Boston College seal: "Choose the best and practice will make it sweet and easy." Father Russo served for one year as president of the College in the late 1880s upon the sudden death of the sixth president, Rev. Thomas Stack, S.J.

Ed. J. Kenny S.J.

SUMMA PHILOSOPHICA

JUXTA SCHOLASTICORUM PRINCIPIA

"Optimum elige, suave et facile illud faciet consuetudo" Bacon.

COMPLECTENS
LOGICAM ET METAPHYSICAM

AUCTORE P. NICOLAO RUSSO, S.J.
IN BOSTONIENSI COLLEGIO PHILOSOPHIÆ LECTORE

EDITIO ALTERA

Veritas in se manens nec proficit, cum plus a nobis videtur, nec deficit cum minus; sed integra et incorrupta et conversos lætificat lumine, et adversos punit cœcitate. — S. AUG. *de Lib. Arb.* lib. 2 c. xi.

BOSTONIÆ
APUD THOMAM B. NOONAN ET SOCIUM
(17, 19, AND 21 BOYLSTON ST.)
1889

Stonestreet's lofty dismissal of that curriculum may have accounted for no commercial course being offered by Boston College in its early years. But in 1879 the Archbishop of Boston, Most Reverend John Williams, asked the Jesuits to include a nonclassical course. There was a somewhat apologetic tone in the announcement of the new curriculum in the catalogue of 1879–80: "To the original classical course was added, September, 1879, at the special instance of the Most Reverend Archbishop, a department in which the study of the ancient languages is superseded by exclusive application to English, the modern languages and the sciences." That reference to the special instance of the Archbishop was repeated in each subsequent catalogue for the 20 years the so-called English course was offered. To the above announcement of the English curriculum was added the following in the catalogues of 1880 and subsequent years: "This course is intended to offer the advantages of a thorough English and business education to that large class of our youth, who, not intending to follow the professions, stand in no immediate need of classical training; but for whom it is of such vast importance that they be well grounded in their faith, and spend a few years at least under healthy religious influence."

The English curriculum consisted of courses taken by the classical students in English composition and rhetoric, French, German, history, mathematics through calculus, physics and chemistry. It included courses in logic, metaphysics and ethics, but these were taught in English, whereas Latin was the language of the philosophy classes for A.B. candidates, a feature that lasted until 1917. The only "commercial" subject was bookkeeping, to which were added in the 1890s stenography and typewriting.

Enrollment in the English course at Boston College was never large. It reached a high of 36 in 1887 and averaged 24 during the two decades of the program's existence. Not only was the enrollment small, but very few completed the four-year course. The great majority of students in the English course stayed only one or two years, a circumstance possibly related to the fact that the business courses were all in the first two years. The poor response to the College's English curriculum led to a rather plaintive addition to the course description in the catalogue of 1893 and the ensuing three yearly catalogues:

> Although this course has been open for four years, and nothing has been spared that could be availed of to make it successful, comparatively few have patronized it; and, so far, the foundation has not been laid for the regular succession of graded classes, as in the longer, classical course. It is hoped that friends of the College will call the attention of the large number of the community, who have sons intended for business, to the fact that a first-class business, literary, and Christian, Catholic education may be had in the English and Commercial course at Boston College.

In the catalogue for the academic year 1888–89, on the page outlining the curriculum of the "English Department," after the courses of the Fourth Year there appeared the words: "when will be conferred the degree of B.S." The same addition appeared for the next four years. One B.S. was awarded at commencement in June 1889, one in June 1890, and one each in 1892 and 1893.

In 1887 the Jesuit colleges of the Missouri Province reduced their commercial courses to the status of terminal high schools.[13] Since the midwest colleges had been the early exponents of the non-classical curriculum, the elimination of the so-called English program from their colleges must have been unsettling to the Jesuits along the East Coast. In 1895 Boston College took collegiate status away from the commercial program. The catalogue of that year noted: "At present the [English] Course consists of four years, during which the student is engaged in the studies of an English High School. On completion of the Course a diploma of graduation is given, but no degrees are conferred."

The catalogues for 1900–1901 and for the three succeeding years contained this statement: "The College offers at present only one course, that leading to the degree of Bachelor of Arts. The faculty, however, is preparing to establish another course, leading to the degree of Bachelor of Science." There are no documents to throw light on what kind of program, obviously non-classical, the faculty were thinking of. Indeed, since Archbishop Williams, who had inspired the English course, was still active and since the English course was abandoned entirely at this time even at the high school level, perhaps the vague and unproductive promise of an alternative collegiate degree program was intended to assuage the Archbishop. It was not until the 1920s that formal alternatives to the classical A.B. program were introduced.

While liberal arts colleges were tinkering with various non-classical, non-A.B. degree programs, the battle for and against the classics themselves continued. Since Yale was the most vocal exponent of the traditional curriculum, the struggle between conservative and liberal forces at Yale is illuminating. Yale's historian, George Pierson, presents the growing faculty uprising against the domination of the classical curriculum (he refers to it as the Thirty Years War[14]) in epic terms and perhaps rightly, since this was undoubtedly the clearest, best-focused educational debate in American collegiate history.

After recounting the preliminary strategies and skirmishes of the anti-classics faction in the post-Civil War period, Pierson summed up the trend of the battle by the title he gave to Chapter 11 of the history of modern Yale: "Farewell to Greek." He starts the chapter with the following statement of the anti-Greek case:[15]

> Greek was the nub of the problem. With philosophy out of the way, Greek, Latin, and mathematics stood as the last survivors of the ancient disciplines. And of these Greek had been singled out as the crucial, symbolic study—the most irritating, the most vulnerable, the next victim of the elective movement. It was difficult, "useless," and aristocratic. It represented the private schools and the well-to-do classes, the old order of privilege in the professions. To the swelling high school systems Greek was the club held over their head by the exclusive colleges: it prevented new studies and stood for interference in their concerns. To more and more parents, who had made their way in business and who sought for their sons a social rather than an intellectual training, Greek seemed old-fashioned and quite impractical.

The reference to the high schools is significant. The reason the eight New England presidents protested Eliot's proposal to drop

Facing page: The senior year courses in philosophy continued to be taught in Latin until 1918. Father Charles Macksey, who had been a popular professor of philosophy at Boston College in the 1890s, had the distinction of rising to the faculty of the Jesuits' Gregorian University in Rome. The "Tower Ref. Library" stamped on the title page was the first student library at Chestnut Hill. It was located on the first floor of what was then called the Tower Building. The Arts and Sciences Honors Program now occupies the original library. It was not until 1952 that the Tower Building became Gasson Hall.

C. MACKSEY S. I.

DE ETHICA NATURALI

PRAELECTIONES SCHOLASTICAE

ABBREVIATAE

AD USUM PRIVATUM SCHOLARIUM

IN

UNIVERSITATE GREGORIANA

ROMAE

EX UNIVERSITATE GREGORIANA

—

1914

Greek as an entrance requirement was that they felt many high schools would seize Harvard's decision as an excuse to downgrade or drop Greek and thus limit the applicant pool for those colleges still insisting on Greek as an entrance requirement.

Pierson comments:[16]

> Most of the church schools and the smaller denominational colleges were still not prepared to abandon the language of Protestantism and the Renaissance—this study that for three hundred years had been used to turn plowboys and townsmen into a responsible leadership. Yet with the rise of the newer studies and the modern multipurpose universities, the pressure from within as well as from below had become almost intolerable.

Harvard dropped Greek as a required part of its curriculum in 1884, seven years after Boston College issued its first A.B.s; and in 1887 Harvard dropped Greek as an entrance requirement. Yale held on for a while longer, but in 1904 it, too, said "Farewell" to the Greek requirement.

Boston College maintained the Greek requirement just a half century longer than Yale, but in the year of Yale's capitulation on Greek the College had to recognize the fact of applicants for admission without any preparatory studies in Greek—just what the non-Jesuit New England college presidents had predicted. In outlining requirements for admission, the 1904–1905 Boston College catalogue added this important concession as a footnote:

> In the case of students from High Schools, who have had no Greek, but have pursued an equivalent branch, special arrangements may be made by which they may enter the Freshman class, and take Greek in the special Greek class. The quality of the degree which they receive will depend on the amount of Greek in their first three years of college.

The public high schools are singled out here as curricular culprits, since no preparatory school or preparatory division of a Jesuit College would graduate a young man without Greek. But Boston College decided not to cut off graduates of the high schools. Still, even though three years of Greek at the college level were insisted on for all applicants without Greek, the A.B. degree was not guaranteed. The superior standing of the A.B. degree is underscored by the phrase about the "quality" of the degree. In other words, if a student were not to master enough Greek in his three college years, the A.B. would be denied and a degree of lower quality—e.g. Ph.B.—would be awarded. In establishing this discrimination between the A.B. degree and all other degrees, Boston College was following an educational view that the A.B. was sacrosanct and special, a view enshrined in the thought of most college people during the nineteenth and early twentieth centuries.

So Greek remained a required subject for the A.B. degree for both students with a high school Greek background and for students entering without Greek. The first breech in the solid Greek-Latin wall at Boston College came in 1935 when the catalogue announced that, as of June 1937, the Ph.B. degree would be discontinued and that only two degrees would be granted: the A.B. and the B.S. However, there would be several paths to the A.B., the most distinguished being A.B. Honors, the traditional Greek-Latin course with special standards of admission and performance. There would also be the A.B. with Greek but without honors, covering the same curriculum as the honors A.B. but less intensively. Finally, the innovation was to be the A.B. without Greek. Concerning this the catalogue stated:

> Hitherto, following the Classical Tradition in liberal education, and accepting the traditional significance of the Bachelor of Arts degree, the College authorities have considered the study of the Greek language and literature as a necessary subject in the curriculum leading to the degree of Bachelor of Arts. . . . However, following the practice now generally accepted in American colleges, beginning in June 1938, the College will confer the degree of Bachelor of Arts without required Greek as a necessary subject in the curriculum.

The announcement went on to explain that premedical students, who for several decades had been taking a non-classical B.S. degree, might pursue an A.B. curriculum if they wished.

The A.B. Honors program lasted 20 years. In 1954 the "Honors" designation was dropped, and through 1956 there were two A.B.s: Program 1 with Greek and Program 2 without Greek.

Starting in September 1957, there was no program requiring Greek. Boston College had valiantly sought to prolong and preserve the ancient Greek-Latin curriculum. Indeed the battle for Greek was longer and more elaborate than the defense of Latin, as will be seen. But students prepared to follow the intensive Greek program of the A.B. honors course diminished in numbers. In 1940, 50 of the 299 graduates took the A.B. Honors degree, 159 the A.B., and 90 the B.S. Ten years later 29 graduates (or only about 3 percent of the class of 865) were A.B. Honors, and 626 of that class earned the B.S. degree. So in 1957 Boston College bade its "Farewell" to Greek.

Back in 1904 Boston College had mentioned degrees of lesser quality than the A.B. for students unable to meet appropriate standards in the classical curriculum. In 1918 the College announced a B.S. program without classics, for premedical students, but prior to 1923 there was no mention of any Ph.B. program even though 14 graduates had received that degree. The 1923 catalogue stated under the heading, "The Ph.B. Course":

> This course is intended for those who have not studied Latin and Greek in High School, and who are consequently ineligible to pursue the A.B. Course. As alternatives for Latin and Greek in Freshman and Sophomore, they study Modern Language, Analytic Geometry and General Chemistry in Freshman; Modern Language, Analytic Chemistry, College Algebra in Sophomore. The course in Junior and Senior is identical with the A.B. course.

Thus the Ph.B. as an alternative to the A.B. was formalized and lasted for some fourteen years. But it did not become a dominant factor in the College. In the class of 1935, for example, only 29 graduates earned the Ph.B. in contrast to 359 A.B. and 15 B.S. degrees. After 1937, successors to the Ph.B. became various kinds of B.S. degrees (Education, History, Social Studies), for although an A.B. curriculum without Greek began in 1935, Latin was required for the A.B. Suddenly Latin became the bone of contention rather than Greek, and the number of graduates earning B.S. degrees greatly surpassed those earning A.B.s.

In a chapter titled, "The Passing of Latin and the Ph.B.," Pierson writes of Yale:[17]

> In the spring of 1931, after a month or two of quiet debate, the College proceeded to drop both the requirement of Latin for the B.A. and the degree for non-Latinists, the Ph.B. . . . From the pedagogical point of view it seems astonishing that so practiced a schoolmaster, so knowing a pilot to the arts of living should now be dropped overboard—still more astonishing that he could be dropped so quietly, with hardly a cry heard.

Maybe not a cry but at least a whimper. Hearing of Yale's decision on Latin, the *New York Herald Tribune* editorialized under the caption "Et Tu, Eli!": "This ancient university is merely mimicking a general tendency in American education. . . . Henceforth her bachelor of arts need have no taint of classicism to interfere with his salesmanship."[18] But that was outside criticism probably written by a journalist who appreciated the richness of his own classical education twenty or thirty years earlier. Pierson is right that Yale's action in dropping Latin caused no outcry in academe similar to that which greeted Harvard's dropping of Greek almost a half century earlier.

The passing of required Latin at Boston College in 1958 just one year after the demise of required Greek seems more sudden and unexpected than what happened at Yale. But Boston College's action on Latin came after a decade of earnest but quiet discussion and negotiation on the subject involving all of the Jesuit colleges in the country. The Jesuit Education Association was established in 1934. Under its auspices college representatives met annually to discuss mutual interests and problems. In 1948 the representatives of the Jesuit colleges at the annual JEA meeting voted to ask the Board of Governors (the Provincials of the American Jesuit Provinces) to allow each Province to decide independently what to do about requiring Latin for the A.B. degree.[19] The liberal arts deans meeting the following summer discussed the Latin requirement and were evenly split on it pro and con.[20] The Provincials set in motion a factual and theoretical inquiry on the subject that revealed a drastic decline in enrollment in the A.B. (that is, the Latin) curriculum between 1940 and 1948—a drop from 41 to 17 percent.[21] The war and the special arrangements for returned veterans may have had something to do with this decline. The study also showed considerable variation nationally, with the A.B.

enrollment higher in the east than in other parts of the country, as shown by the table[22] below reporting the percentages of seniors in the A.B. program by Province for 1940 and 1948.

	1940	1948
California	22	2
Chicago	18	10
Maryland	54	14
Missouri	30	12
New England	67	33
New Orleans	26	23
New York	37	21
Oregon	8	14

A similar study in 1955 showed only Holy Cross and Boston College with more than 30 percent of their students enrolled in the A.B. program. The national average had slipped to under 11 percent.[23] The deans of Jesuit liberal arts colleges met for a 10-day institute at Santa Clara in August 1955. After prolonged debate on the Latin requirement for the A.B. degree, the deans voted: "Resolved: that the members of the Institute respectfully request the Fathers Provincial of the American Assistancy to seek explicit permission of Very Reverend Father General to change the current regulation which requires Latin for the A.B. throughout the Assistancy, so that the place of Latin in the A.B. program may hereafter be determined on a Province basis as are other major changes in the curriculum."[24]

In the various formal discussions on the topic, principal reasons advanced for keeping the Latin requirement for the A.B. were the following.[25] The classical curriculum is identified with Jesuit education and Jesuit tradition. Latin is a key to Catholic culture as well as the language of the Church and its liturgy. (Of course these arguments were advanced before Vatican II and the vernacular liturgies.) Jesuit colleges, it was pointed out, are the last stronghold of Latin and stand out as unique among American colleges in preserving the Latin requirement. Furthermore, because of the intercommunication among Jesuit colleges, abandonment of the Latin requirement in some regions would make it hard for colleges in other regions to maintain it, since abandonment anywhere would be seen as a sign of Jesuit disbelief in the value of Latin.

Indeed, if Jesuit colleges were to give up the Latin requirement, the Latin curriculum of Jesuit high schools might be put in jeopardy. It was argued that dropping the Latin requirement would be an unpraiseworthy yielding to pressure. Finally, there were those who characterized advocates of abandonment of the Latin requirement as "futurists" and anti-traditionalists.

Those who favored dropping the Latin requirement contended that it seemed odd for Jesuit colleges to grant their most prized degree (A.B.) to so few graduates, while the majority of students were enrolled in programs for which the A.B. degree was given elsewhere. Indeed, the B.S. degree earned by many Jesuit college graduates was deceptive because it represented little science. It was argued that the requirement of Latin for the A.B. kept many students from attending Jesuit colleges because they wanted an A.B. degree. The Jesuits, it was said, could not stand alone against the national understanding of what an A.B. degree is. Besides, few high schools were any longer graduating students with four years of Latin. To the argument that Latin is the language of the Church, the reply was given that Latin is the pagan parent of modern languages, and the study of modern languages can give both language discipline and Christian cultural content. Finally, the Latin requirement was criticized as a fossilized and nonfunctional curriculum.

During these years of discussion of the Latin requirement for the A.B., the A.B. program was in a healthier state at Boston College and Holy Cross than in many of the other Jesuit colleges. But the problem was handled on the national level. After weighing the matter for a decade, the Fathers Provincial petitioned Father General John Janssens in January 1958 that the American Jesuit colleges be allowed to offer the A.B. degree for programs not including Latin.[26] In September of that year Father General granted the permission.[27] The Boston College catalogue for the College of Arts and Sciences for 1958–89 omitted any reference to Latin as a requirement for admission or for graduation.

The following is a summary timetable of the retreat at Boston College from the original full Greek-Latin curriculum:

1905 Greek may be begun at Boston College.

1935 A.B. with Honors started—a degree with Greek and Latin.

An alternate A.B. program without Greek but requiring Latin started.

1954 Latin required for A.B. but may be begun at Boston College.
A.B. Honors dropped, replaced by A.B. Program 1, requiring Latin and Greek, with A.B. Program 2 as an alternate, requiring Latin but not Greek.

1957 Greek required in no A.B. program.

1958 Latin not required for entrance or for A.B.

Harvard's historian, Samuel Eliot Morison, had this to say of the passing of the old curriculum:[28]

> It was due to Eliot's insistent pressure that the Harvard faculty abolished the Greek requirement for entrance in 1887, after dropping required Latin and Greek for freshman year. His and Harvard's reputation, the pressure of teachers trained in the new learning, and of parents wanting "practical" instruction for their sons, soon had the classics on the run, in schools as well as colleges; and no equivalent to the classics, for mental training, cultural background, or solid satisfaction in after life, has yet been discovered. It is a hard saying, but Mr. Eliot, more than any other man, is responsible for the greatest educational crime of the century against American youth—depriving him of his classical heritage.

It was probably inevitable that the required Greek-Latin part of the curriculum would succumb, particularly in the twentieth century, because of a perception of the classical curriculum as elite in an egalitarian society, because of a general antipathy to anything prescribed, because of the inability or unwillingness of preparatory schooling to teach "hard" subjects, because of the knowledge explosion and because of the growing necessity of graduate education and the perceived need to devote more and more undergraduate time to pre-professional studies. But to those who experienced it, the passing of classical education is cause for lament, not just for a particular alma mater, but for western civilization. The old classical course was a great education and instrument of education. It fostered literacy, cultural perspective, and mastery of one's own tongue. Morison's judgment is still valid: no substitute has been found that does for students what the classics did.

ENDNOTES

1. Miguel A. Bernad, S.J., "The Faculty of Arts in the Jesuit Colleges in the Eastern Part of the United States" (unpublished doctoral dissertation, Yale, 1951), pp. 139, 143.
2. Allan P. Farrell, S.J., *The Jesuit Code of Liberal Education* (Milwaukee: Bruce Publishing Co., 1938), pp. 13–17, 359.
3. Charles A. Wagner, *Harvard: Four Centuries and Freedoms* (New York: E.P. Dutton, 1950), p. 103.
4. Frederick Rudolph, *Curriculum: A History of the American Undergraduate Course of Study Since 1636* (San Francisco: Jossey-Bass Publishers, 1977), p. 66.
5. Rudolph, *Curriculum,* p. 184.
6. Rudolph, *Curriculum,* p. 183.
7. Rudolph, *Curriculum,* p. 194.
8. Samuel Eliot Morison, *Three Centuries of Harvard 1636–1936* (Cambridge, Mass.: Harvard University Press, 1946), p. 359.
9. Rudolph, *Curriculum,* p. 109.
10. Walter Crosby Eells, *Academic Degrees* (Washington, D.C.: U.S. Government Printing Office, 1960), p. 24.
11. Bernad, *The Faculty of Arts,* Chapter V.
12. Bernad, *The Faculty of Arts,* p. 259.
13. Bernad, *The Faculty of Arts,* p. 267.
14. George Wilson Pierson, *Yale College: An Educational History, 1871–1921* (New Haven: Yale University Press, 1955), p. 46.
15. Pierson, *Yale College,* p. 186.
16. Pierson, *Yale College,* p. 187.
17. George Wilson Pierson, *Yale: The University College, 1921–1937* (New Haven: Yale University Press, 1955), p. 315.
18. Pierson, *Yale: The University College,* p. 315.
19. *Proceedings of the Institute for Jesuit Deans,* August 3–13, 1948, Denver, Colorado Education Association), p. 165. Boston College Archives.
20. Jesuit Education Association, *Proceedings,* p. 164.
21. Jesuit Education Association, Minutes of the Executive Committee Meeting of April, 1949, p. 6. Boston College Archives.
22. Jesuit Education Association, Executive Committee, p. 7.
23. Jesuit Education Association, Minutes of the Executive Committee Meeting of April 1955, p. 26. Boston College Archives.
24. *Proceedings of the Santa Clara Institute for Jesuit College Deans,* August

3–13, 1955 (printed for private circulation by the Jesuit Education Association), p. 188. Boston College Archives.

25. See principally *Proceedings of Institute for Jesuit Deans,* Denver, 1948, p. 164; also Minutes of JEA Executive Committee Meeting, April 1949, pp. 9–10. Boston College Archives.
26. Report of the President of the Jesuit Education Association to the Board of Governors, April, 1958, p. 18. Boston College Archives.
27. Jesuit Education Association, Report of President, p. 23.
28. Morison, *Harvard,* p. 389.

13

Rules of Gentlemanly Conduct

AT THE TIME Boston College was founded (1863), American colleges were conservative institutions in matters of student discipline. Many of them had codes of conduct that would have done credit to a seminary. There were few colleges with officers whose specific responsibility was student discipline, so the enforcement of rules of conduct fell to the president or, in many colleges, to the entire faculty. Reflecting a still influential Calvinist tradition, faculties often had stern and pessimistic views of their students, as illustrated by the sentiments of a professor at Davidson College in 1855:[1]

> Indulged, petted, and uncontrolled at home, allowed to trample upon all laws, human and divine, at preparatory school . . . [the student] comes to college, but too often with an undisciplined mind, and an uncultivated heart, yet with exalted ideas of personal dignity, and a scowling contempt for lawful authority, and wholesome constraint. How is he to be controlled?

The historian of the University of Georgia blames the influence of Puritan Yale for the "flood of petty restrictions and commands" that bound the Georgia students:[2]

> These rules were the law of the land as far as the University was concerned and just as sacred. The student's passport to classes was a set of laws [incidentally, sixteen pages long] signed by the president; he was given ten days to digest them and thereafter he fell hard under their inexorable pains and penalties. His every action was guided by them. A law got him out of bed and put him back again. He ate by them, he studied by them, he recited by them—they were with him always.

Among the things the laws forbade were profanity, playing billiards or cards, association with vile persons, blasphemy, theft, robbery, and forgery. Perhaps the young Georgians were a fractious group, since they were warned: "If any scholar shall assault, strike or wound the President, a Professor, or a Tutor—or shall designedly break their doors or windows, he shall be expelled." Similarly students were forbidden to keep any gun, pistol, dagger, dirk, sword cane or other offensive weapon in their rooms.[3]

Boston College students seem never to have been so mettlesome, since there was never in their rules any mention of carrying weapons. Indeed, that was an injunction of the *Ratio Studiorum,* the sixteenth century Jesuit code of education, that Boston College never adopted. The *Ratio's* fifth rule for students was Regulation on Side-Arms, which stated: "None of our students should bring into school any side-arms, small-swords, poniards, or other weapons of this type. . . ." Apparently sixteenth century European Jesuit college students had more in common with the collegians of nineteenth century Athens, Georgia, than those of Boston's South End. But students at Indiana Asbury University, now DePauw, received admonitions similar to those of Georgia. Among proscribed activities were profane swearing, drinking intoxicating liquors, gambling or playing at games of chance, wearing firearms or weapons, using obscene language, and disorderly deportment.[4]

Faculty involvement in disciplinary matters was commonplace. At Georgia the faculty met "in secret" every Tuesday night after prayers to consider violations of the student code.[5] Frederick Rudolph says that one year the Dartmouth faculty devoted 68 sessions to student conduct, while at mid-century the University of North Carolina faculty addressed 282 cases of delinquency from a student body of 230.[6]

An alumni committee of Haverford College writing at the end of the nineteenth century reported:[7]

> . . . The minutes of the Faculty during 1870–71 teem with chronicles of disciplinary small-beer, and display a spirit of pettiness and triviality in the conception of college government. Peccadilloes of small moment are recorded with solemn iteration, reported to the Committee on Instruction, considered in both bodies, and decided with infinite splitting of hairs. Every case of discipline is a triangular duel, the poor culprit, however, getting his shots from both the other parties. . . . Cases of disorder were met without any sense of perspective.

In contrast to such records of disciplinary minutiae and adjudication, from the beginning discipline at Boston College received no great emphasis. The first published catalogue, for 1868–69, devoted just three sentences to discipline, and the same sentences, without addition, were repeated in the annual catalogues for the following eight years:

> When religious motives are continually appealed to, less need is experienced of frequent or severe punishments.
>
> Flagrant offenses, such as are detrimental to the reputation of the College, or are obstructive of the good of the pupils, are grounds for expulsion.
>
> For faults of ordinary occurrence—such as tardy arrival, failure in recitations, or minor instances of misconduct,—a task, consisting of lines from some classical author, is committed to memory during the hour after the close of school.

The contrast between the brevity of the Boston College rules and those of colleges cited above can, in part, be accounted for by the fact that Boston College catered to "day-scholars" only, as the catalogue said, while the other institutions were residential colleges responsible for the welfare and conduct of the students 24 hours a day for many months of the year. Even so, the contrast is impressive. The directness and brevity of the Boston College approach to discipline seem to reflect a sensible and self-assured attitude on the part of the administration. The first sentence is a generalization, the statement of a principle, religious motivation, that not only explains the relative infrequency of "punishments" but justifies the absence of a long litany of rules and regulations. The following two sentences treat of flagrant offenses and minor faults. Examples of major offenses are not given; rather, they are defined by their results: damage to the College's reputation or impairment of the students' welfare. For such misconduct, expulsion is a possible penalty. Faults of ordinary occurrence include non-disciplinary matters such as failure in recitations and tardiness. The impression is given that "minor instances of misconduct" are indeed minor, such as noise in a corridor or some instance of mischief in a classroom. The brief and nonthreatening catalogue statement about discipline in the earliest years of the College's operation manifests a confident and mild attitude on the College's part in the matter of student conduct.

After 13 years of experience, it was evidently felt that a few more particular guidelines regarding deportment should be published. In the catalogue for the year 1877–78 and with little change for the rest of the century, the following directives and warnings were placed before the three sentences cited above about religious motivation, flagrant offenses, and faults of ordinary occurrence:

> The candidate for admission should be acquainted with and prepared to observe the following rules:—
>
> On arriving, the students will repair immmediately to the cloak-room, where they will deposit their books, overcoats, etc.; thence directly to the gymnasium, where they will remain till time for Mass.
>
> Those who are exempted from Mass, if they arrive during Mass, will remain in the gymnasium.
>
> No class is to leave the gymnasium for the school-room, unless accompanied by the teacher.
>
> When any one obtains permission to leave the class-room, he is to return without unnecessary delay.
>
> The places for recreation are the gymnasium and the court. All the rest of the premises are "out of bounds"; except when the Prefect gives permission to walk by the Church, or to members of the Debating Society to recreate in their own room.
>
> The use of tobacco is prohibited.
>
> Playing ball, snow-balling, pitching, and all games that endanger the windows are prohibited.

Rev. Edward V. Boursaud, S.J., president from 1884 to 1887.

Whoever damages the College property must make compensation.

No boisterous conduct is allowed in the corridors or class-rooms at any time. Even in the gymnasium and during recreation, the behavior should be decorous.

In fine, any conduct unbecoming the character of a gentleman will be regarded as a violation of the College rules.

We learn from these added rules that attendance at Mass was required each morning. That reflects common practice at denominational colleges, where daily chapel remained a feature of college life well into the twentieth century. It is clear that exemptions from attendance at Mass were possible.

We need to remind ourselves as we read these rules that the majority of the students attending the Jesuit institution in the South End were of high school age, since Boston College in its early decades offered a seven-year curriculum embracing preparatory and collegiate divisions. In the 1880s the collegians were outnumbered four to one, and in the 1890s two to one. Thus the rules may have been aimed mostly at the high-spirited youthful scholars, but by that very fact they could have been all the more restrictive and burdensome for the sophisticated students of the poetry, rhetoric, and philosophy classes.

The ban concerning tobacco, which would be applauded by many today, was repeated in each year's catalogue through 1894–95. No mention was made of tobacco in College regulations through all the succeeded years until the 13-year period from 1934 to 1947, when smoking was forbidden except in designated places—a rule that represents a restriction rather than a total ban on tobacco.

The admonition concerning conduct unbecoming the character of a gentleman emphasizes a worldly-religious ideal of civility and manners that was not infrequently held before college students in the nineteenth century. For example, the 1867 college catalogue at Duke warned: "Every student must observe such propriety of language, form in manners, and gentlemanly deportment, as are proper for cultured, Christian people; any departure therefrom will be cause for reprimand, suspension, or dismission."[8]

A similar tone was set in this excerpt from Notre Dame's 1864–65 catalogue: "Whether in class or in recreation, when permitted to converse at table, or during their walks, students should endeavor to improve the purity of their language and cultivate urbanity of manners. A few years in college would be profitably employed if nothing else were learned but to converse and behave with the dignity and propriety of gentlemen."[9]

The Jesuit college in Detroit translated the gentlemanly ideal into the practice of awarding monthly "elegant cards" for polite conduct. In the catalogue for 1891–92, under the heading "Politeness," the following exhortation appeared:

> The College expects from all its students the manners and deportment of gentlemen. Politeness is deemed a very important element of education. Whatever, therefore, is contrary to good breeding, and would be out of place in respectable society, is generally out of place in the College. Any and every violation of good conduct, especially if it occur on the way to and from the College, is liable to punishment, and, if the violation is gross, to dismissal. On the premises, smoking, tobacco chewing, low or profane language, uncouth games of any sort, are not tolerated. With a view to encourage the practice of politeness and gentlemanly manners,

elegant cards, or testimonials of good conduct, are given to deserving students every month.

Any nineteenth century reader of Newman's *Idea of a University* was familiar with his warning that a gentleman, be he ever so urbane and civil, is not necessarily a Christian. The ideals of politeness and gentlemanliness may in some quarters have been promoted as purely secular goals. But, as in the Duke statement, we may assume that the Jesuit colleges expected that religious motives would underlie and elevate polite conduct. Indeed, in all the years from 1877 through 1908 the Boston College catalogue statement on the character of a gentleman was followed in the very next sentence by the allusion to the religious motives that are habitually appealed to.

The Boston College statement concerning conduct unbecoming the character of a gentleman disappeared after the 1912–13 academic year but was revived in an altered form from 1934 through 1947, when the following paragraph was printed under the heading "Gentlemanly Conduct": "Students are held responsible to the College authorities for the requirements of gentlemanly conduct not only within the precincts of the College but at all times and in all places. Any violation of these requirements within the College precincts is subject to the disciplinary sanction specified below." The disciplinary sanction referred to was a system of demerits that was introduced in the 1930s. Ungentlemanly conduct earned anywhere from one to five demerits, and five demerits entailed probation.

The author recalls being told mildly but firmly by his freshman dean in 1929 (when the "character of a gentleman" paragraph was not in the College catalogue) that certain high jinks in the corridor between classes was conduct not becoming "a Boston College gentleman." So the ideal of gentlemanliness was very much alive as a standard of conduct for generations of Boston College students.

Going back to the expanded disciplinary rules first published in 1877, the restrictions on playing ball and snowballing were necessary because of the extremely limited outdoor property. When planning the College, Father McElroy originally wanted to purchase a larger piece of property on Harrison Avenue, but he ran into public protest, on religious grounds, against what was termed an "audacious attempt on the part of ecclesiastical authorities to acquire undue and colossal power."[10] So McElroy compromised and won the city's approval to purchase only a section of the city block he had hoped to have. On the property bounded by Harrison Avenue, James Street, and Concord and Newton Streets were erected the imposing Church of the Immaculate Conception, a residence for the Jesuits, and the college building, which was expanded in 1889. The buildings pretty well occupied the space, and a very limited "court" was left for student outdoor recreation. In no modern sense could the property be called a campus. Hence the ban on ballplaying, and the gradual conviction on the part of the College authorites by 1900 that a new and larger location for the College was a necessity.

We learn from the restrictive rules about places for recreation that from very early days, students engaged in debate enjoyed special status. The Debating Society was privileged, in tight quarters, to have a room of its own.

There is a certain inertia or stability in the texts of college catalogues. The formal expression of a college's ideals and code of conduct tends not to change from year to year. Thus the above-quoted rules from the 1877 catalogue were modified piecemeal and over a long time. The admonitions about ballplaying and places of recreation were dropped after 1893. The reference to after-hours memorizing of literary lines as a punishment for misbehavior appeared for the last time in 1898 (through the practice of "jug," as this disciplinary expedient was called in many American colleges, continued into the twentieth century). The paragraph on faults of ordinary occurrence disappeared the same year. The reference to an appeal to religious motives was dropped after 1908, not, one can assume, because religious motives were no longer in the picture but because the section on discipline was sharply reduced and entirely omitted from the catalogue between the years 1914 and 1924. Incidentally, it may be of significance that 1914 was the year the College left the high school and opened on its new Chestnut Hill campus.

Added to the catalogue in 1895 was a section on parental cooperation that had more to do with students' academic interests than discipline, but it was printed directly after the paragraph on discipline. This is the section:

> The efforts of teachers and prefects will be much facilitated if the co-operation of parents can be secured.
>
> Parents are, therefore, earnestly requested:
>
> Ist.—To insist upon daily study at home, for two or three hours at least.
>
> 2d.—To notify the Prefect speedily in case of the withdrawal of their sons, or of necessary detention from, or tardy arrival at, school; of failure to receive the monthly report.
>
> 3d.—To attend to notifications, always sent by the Prefect on the second day of an unexplained absence, or for lessons signally bad during a considerable length of time.
>
> 4th.—Not to pass over, without inquiry, averages for lessons falling below seventy-five.

An exhortation on parental cooperation appeared in the catalogue from 1895 through 1899, then, after an omission for 10 years, from 1909 through 1933 and again from 1937 through 1951. By the latter year the statement on parental cooperation had undergone slight modification:

> The efforts of teachers and prefects will be much facilitated if parents or guardians will cooperate with them in maintaining discipline and insisting on obedience to regulations made for the purpose. Parents are therefore asked:
>
> 1. To insist that the required amount of time be devoted to home study.
> 2. To notify the Dean of Men immediately in case of withdrawal of the son or of necessary detention from, or late arrival at, class.
> 3. To give immediate attention to notification always sent by the Dean of Men in case of unexplained absense and also to any complaint registered by the Dean of Studies in regard to any considerable deficiency in class standing.

Both the 1895 and the 1951 versions of the plea for parental cooperation refer to home study. During the 38 years from 1913 to 1951, with the exception of the three years from 1934 to 1936, the catalogue had a paragraph on home study, placed just before the section on parental cooperation. Following is the 1895 version:

> Home Study—All the endeavors of the faculty will fail to insure success for the students unless they apply themselves to their studies with diligence and constancy outside of the class hours. Approximately twenty-five hours a week are spent in class work; and to prepare recitations and exercises for this work, as well as to review the matter previously seen, at least three hours of home study daily are required. Parents and guardians are, therefore, urged to insist on this application.

By 1951 the hours of class had decreased, but in turn the expectation of hours of home study increased. After the same first sentence, the 1951 statement read: "Approximately nineteen hours a week are spent in class work, and approximately two hours a day should be spent in the preparation of each class assignment."

For a brief period, from 1934 to 1939, the catalogue contained a paragraph on "Dishonesty in Examinations":

> Any student acting dishonestly or attempting to act dishonestly in the course of a major examination is subject to suspension, and if readmitted must repeat the semester's work in the course in which he was taking the examination. Any manifestation of dishonesty or any attempt at dishonesty in the conduct of class repetitions, written or oral, is subject to the sanction to be determined upon at the discretion of the Professor of the class and the Dean of Studies.

The year 1934 saw major additions and innovations in the catalogue concerning student conduct. In addition to the new admonition regarding dishonesty in examinations, there appeared for the first time a section about parking on campus and a demerit system for breaches of discipline. The rules on parking, which were headed "Automobiles" and appeared in the catalogue in the years from 1934 to 1947, indicated that student cars, with clearance from the dean of discipline, were restricted to what was called the College parking area. That was the parking lot that used to lie to the east of Gasson Hall before construction began on the new library. It accommodated fewer than 130 automobiles, but that was at a time when the student population was under 1500. Students were forbidden to park anywhere else on campus or on any streets near the College. Parking privileges were liable to forfeiture if the campus speed limit of 12 miles an hour was exceeded.

The system of demerits was announced in the catalogue for 16 years, from 1934 to 1950. This explanation (with minor variations) appeared in the catalogue each of those years:

> Problems of Discipline are regulated by a system of Demerits. All Demerits are imposed by the Dean of Discipline.
>
> Disorder during College exercises: 1 to 5 demerits.
>
> Smoking in forbidden places: 1 for first offense; 3 for each subsequent offense.
>
> Ungentlemanly conduct: 1 to 5 demerits.
>
> Defacement of property: 1 to 3 demerits.
>
> Deliberate violation of rules: 1 to 3 demerits.
>
> Deliberate neglect to attend College exercises: 1 to 3 demerits.
>
> A student who incurs five (5) demerits is put on probation. One who is on probation will be debarred from all participation in extra-curricular activities, and may be obliged to report for special work at 9:30 A.M. on the four Saturdays following the imposition of probation.
>
> A student who incurs ten (10) demerits in any year will be dropped from the College. At the end of the year all demerits will be cancelled except in the case of students who incur probation after May 1st. The probation of these students will be continued during the First Semester of the following year.

The postwar period brought to campus the hordes of mature students who were veterans as well as a new breed of student for whom the exhortation to "home study" was inappropriate, namely, the resident student. More complicated times required more detailed rules covering varied situations and these came to be recorded in documents other than the College catalogue. Early in the 1950s there appeared a small booklet titled, "Boston College Student Hand Book," which gave information about student government, extracurricular activities, annual academic awards, academic regulations, and religious customs, with a final four-page (out of 40 pages) section on discipline. In the one year 1956–57, the College catalogue—as if to explain its own silence on a number of topics of interest to undergraduates—called attention to the existence of the Student Hand Book.

From that time on there were no references in the catalogue specifically under the heading of discipline. But it is interesting

Father Edward J. Hanrahan, dean of students from 1965 to 1986.

that two matters that are deportment-related came to be included under "College Regulations" for the first time. From 1957 through 1965 there was an item on the annual retreat, a practice that had been in effect for over 90 years. The statement was the following: "All Catholic students are required to make a Retreat sometime during the academic year. Failure to comply with this requirement will result in the student's withdrawal from the College." These were late pre-Vatican II days when there was little embarrassment about compulsion in matters religious and less sensitivity to freedom and conscience than became the vogue a decade later. Perhaps there were rumblings of discontent and it was felt that a severe sanction had to be attached to failure to comply with the retreat rule.

The second new item to be introduced under "College Regulations" appeared in the catalogue from 1957 through 1966 under the heading "Dress." It read: "Students will not be admitted to class unless they conform to minimum standards of good taste in the matter of dress. They are expected to wear suit coats and ties, together with other articles of clothing that show respect for themselves and others." By 1967, with the advent of flower people and hippie haberdashery, the College ran down the flag on dress standards, at least in the catalogue.

This chapter has been a brief review of Boston College's public statements, specifically, catalogue statements, about student deportment. It is worth concluding with a comment about the first student handbook in the 1950s which, though its section on discipline was brief (containing the paragraph on gentlemanly conduct that had appeared in the catalogue in the 1940s and the same rules on automobiles as had entered the catalogue in 1934), was preceded by a general statement that may be called a philosophy of collegiate discipline that seems to have undergirded administrative thinking and ruling on students conduct since 1868. The handbook stated:

> The college reserves the right to dismiss at any time a student who fails to give satisfactory evidence of earnestness of purpose and active cooperation in all the requirements of conduct and academic work. In this matter the college believes itself to be the better judge of what affects the best interests of the college and the student body. Once a student registers and attends college, he is held responsible for the regulations and traditions of the college.

The statement reflects the paternalistic and institutionally self-assured approach to matters disciplinary that was common throughout academe until the advent in the 1960s of student activism and litigations, with ensuing "due process" procedures and elaborate judicial boards for disciplinary problems. Besides its statement of a philosophy of disciplinary action, the Student Hand Book contained another feature that reflected the fatherly and simple spirit of an earlier time, namely, a series of moral exhortations or generalizations sprinkled throughout the text of the booklet. At the bottom of every other page or so, printed in bold face type, were maxims or warnings such as these:

> Boston College men are always conscious of the importance of their position, whether at the College or away from it.
>
> The use of slang, even in sports, is not the mark of an educated gentleman.
>
> Boston College students always raise their hats as a mark of respect to their professors, both clerical and lay.

Upper classmen at Boston College take a brotherly interest in the members of the Freshman class.

Jackets, not sweaters, may be worn in the classrooms.

Noise in the college corridors creates a general disorder and confusion. Order is the rule of your College.

Boston College men are always good sports, even when losing.

Does your example inspire others to aspire to the "Heights"?

Such an open approach to the inculcation of order, urbanity, and civility seems closer today to the 1860s than to the last years of the twentieth century, even though the Hand Book was in circulation only a few decades ago. Styles and expressions of moral leadership change with changing times, and colleges are not so direct today in their attention to decorum and order.

For the better part of a century Boston College's only, or principal, expression of rules for student conduct was contained in the annual catalogue. The nature and brevity of the rules suggest an unworried and unpetty administration, and a civilized and unboisterous student body.

ENDNOTES

1. Frederick Rudolph. *The American College and University* (New York: Alfred Knopf, 1968), p. 105.
2. E. Merton Coulter, *College Life in the Old South* (New York: Macmillan, 1928), p. 77.
3. Coulter, *College Life,* pp. 78–79.
4. George B. Manhart, *DePauw Through the Years* (Greencastle, Ind.: DePauw University, 1962), vol. I, p. 145.
5. Coulter, *College Life,* p. 81.
6. Rudolph, *The American College,* p. 106.
7. Committee of the Alumni Association, *A History of Haverford College* (Philadelphia: Porter and Coates, 1892), p. 356.
8. Nora Chaffin, *Trinity College, 1839–1899: The Beginnings of Duke University* (Durham, N.C.: Duke University Press, 1950), p. 281.
9. Arthur Hope, C.S.C., *Notre Dame: One Hundred Years* (Notre Dame, Ind.: University Press, 1943), p. 142.
10. Charles F. Donovan, S.J., David R. Dunigan, S.J., and Paul A. FitzGerald, S.J., *History of Boston College: From the Beginnings to 1990* (Chestnut Hill, Mass.: University Press of Boston College, 1990), p. 15.

14

Debate at Boston College:

People, Places, Traditions

THE YEAR WAS 1868. In September Boston College admitted its fifth class of students, and the total enrollment, including collegians and high school boys, was 117. The dean, Father Robert Fulton, decided that there were enough mature students for the College to establish a debating society.

Eloquentia perfecta or *eloquentia Ciceroniana*—perfect or Ciceronian eloquence—was an ideal embodied in the Jesuit *Ratio Studiorum* and practiced in Jesuit colleges since the sixteenth century, so Father Fulton was not innovating but rather continuing at Boston College a cherished ideal of Jesuit education. The "Minutes of the Debating Society of Boston College" report that on Saturday, November 21, 1868, "At a meeting of the upper classes of Boston College, Rev. Robert Fulton presiding, the constitution of the Debating Society was unanimously adopted."

Father Fulton personally assumed the role of director of the new debating society. However, after two years, he was raised to the presidency of the College. During his long service as president (twice), from 1870 to 1880 and from 1888 to 1891, Father Fulton—clearly by his own choice—continued to serve as dean as well as president. He undoubtedly found that he could not handle an extracurricular activity along with the twin burdens of administration, but the debating society (later named for him in 1890) had a special place in his priorities. He kept a ledger during his early deanship containing the advice he gave to his teachers as well as rules for the conduct of the school and for the movement and behavior of the students. Some of the rules seem paternalistic today, but it must be remembered the dean was legislating for youths of high school as well as college age. Students were told that playing ball, snowballing, pitching, and all games that endangered the windows were prohibited. Further, no boisterous conduct was allowed in the corridors or classrooms. Even in the gymnasium and during recreation, students' behavior was to be decorous. Recreation was to take place in the gymnasium or the court (the small plot of land in front of the College on Harrison Avenue, between the church and the Jesuit residence). All the rest of the premises were out of bounds except when the dean gave permission to walk by the church or, *to members of the Debating Society, to recreate in their own room, where no other students might be admitted.*

The College catalogues in the 1870s and 1880s gave a full page to each of four student activities, listing the moderators, officers, and membership. Always listed first was the Sodality of the Immaculate Conception; second, the St. Cecilia Society (choir); third, the Debating Society; and fourth, the Foster Cadets. There is no mention of a special room for any activity except debating. At a time when there seem to have been more rules than privileges, the College made it clear that debating was uniquely privileged.

The book of minutes shows that the topic of the first debate held by the new organization was: "Is the art of printing productive of more good than evil?" The topic afforded the gentlemen of the negative side an opportunity to present some imaginative and humorous arguments as advocates of a poor cause. Some of the debate topics reveal that the students were quite conscious of their ethnic and political status. For example, in 1868 they debated "Whether the power of Great Britain is or is not likely to decline." In 1870 there was a tendentious topic: "Do the later immigrants contribute more to the welfare of America than the descendants of the early settlers?" One wonders how a team was found willing to defend the Yankee position.

Is there reason to question how committed to or emotionally

involved in the Civil War Boston Irish were when only seven years after the war ended Boston College students debated the proposition "That the South had the right to secede." Later in the century, in 1891, the topic for the prize debate was "That the Emancipation Proclamation was unwise." If the debaters seem to have been faced with defending some socially unthinkable propositions, they were no less daring regarding religion, since in 1898 they argued the pros and cons of the proposition "That the Papacy in the middle ages was a beneficent power in European affairs."

As late as the catalogue for 1889–90, the Debating Society was described as cultivating extemporaneous debate, dramatic reading, and declamation. The minutes show that brief dramatic pieces were sometimes part of the regular meetings. For example, a notation in October 1871 informs us that seven or eight members were given two weeks notice for the presentation of the second act of *Macbeth*. Father Fulton ended his second term as president of the College early in January 1891. He was succeeded by Father Edward Devitt. The catalogue for 1890–91, published at the conclusion of the academic year, for the first time listed the "Fulton Debating Society of Boston College," with no description of its purposes, but with the significant bottom-line information: 75 members. On the next page is announced "Boston College Athenaeum," with the subjoinder: "The object of this society is to promote the study of dramatic art and conduct the College plays." The new organization had 40 members. In a brief history of Boston College that Father Devitt wrote after his presidency ended, he noted that in 1890 a student organization called the Boston College Athenaeum was formed "to take over the Thespian chores until then performed by the debating society."

The year 1894–95 was memorable in the history of debate at Boston College because in that year occurred the College's first intercollegiate debate and the first between two Jesuit colleges—Boston College and Georgetown. It is hard, almost a century later, to understand the excitement and the high level of negotiations involved in arranging the debate. Letters went back and forth for months between the two presidents, both of whom were among the most sophisticated to lead their respective colleges in the nineteenth century: Fathers Timothy Brosnahan of Boston College

On the front wall, above a seal of the Fulton Debating Society, is a good rendition of the standard photograph of Father Fulton, painted by a gifted Jesuit brother, Francis Schroen.

and J. Havens Richards of Georgetown. The presidents discussed details such as the location of the debate and the choice of judges, and decided to seek the approval of the Provincial for the whole project. Father Brosnahan wrote to the Provincial and reported to Father Richards:

> I asked that three boys be allowed to come and promised that they should be given quarters at the College & consequently all

appearance of undue liberty to be taken away. They are to come direct from Georgetown to Boston and to return in the same manner. This is important, because if anything should happen to give grounds for complaint, the scheme would end with its beginning.

There were no accommodations for putting up visiting students overnight at Boston College, so obviously the Georgetown men were welcomed to the Jesuit residence, another measure of how important this visit was.

The much-heralded event took place—after two postponements—on May 1, 1895. Among the distinguished guests in a capacity audience in the Boston College Hall that night were the auxiliary bishop of Boston, John Brady, and the vicar-general, Monsignor William Byrne; Father Edward Devitt, former president of Boston College, who accompanied the Georgetown debaters from Washington; and Georgetown's president, Father Richards, who came from an engagement in Buffalo for the occasion. This first intercollegiate Jesuit debate was considered of such national interest that an account of it was printed in *Woodstock Letters*. The Boston College debaters were recorded as Michael J. Splaine, '97, Michael Scanlan, '95, and John J. Kirby, '95. (Splaine and Kirby were later to win the Fulton medal.) The *Woodstock Letters* account said the Boston debaters brought credit to their alma mater by their able defense of "The Equity of the Income Tax Law as passed by the last Congress," but in a close decision, decided finally by the vote of the chairman, they lost to the young men from the shores of the Potomac. The philosophical Bostonians found consolation in the thought "that victory still remained in the Society [of Jesus]."

The next recorded intercollegiate encounter for the Fulton Debating Society was with the Forum of Harvard University in the College Hall on the evening of March 24, 1898. As was true of the earliest intercollegiate debates, those between Harvard and Yale in 1892, it was a debate without a decision, on the topic "Resolved: That the adoption of an inheritance tax is advisable." *The Stylus* reported that Boston College chose the topic and Harvard chose the affirmative side. Presiding at the event was one of the city's outstanding lawyers, Thomas J. Gargan, whose widow

Seal of the Fulton Debating Society.

many years later funded Gargan Hall in Bapst library in her husband's memory. *The Stylus* admired the printed program for the historic debate, artistically decorated with the college colors of the rival debaters. How we would love to have that program in our archives and how we lament the short-sightedness of those who deprived us of that pleasure. Incidentally, it is worthy of note that Georgetown and Harvard, the first colleges the Fulton Society met in debate, are, nearly a hundred years later, frequent opponents of the Fulton in tournament debates.

In the last decade of the nineteenth century the annual prize debate featured a number of the most distinguished citizens of Greater Boston as judges. In 1890, only a few months before his death, John Boyle O'Reilly, poet and editor of the *Pilot,* Boston's Catholic paper, was a judge. The following year the Hon. Josiah

Quincy, a member of the state legislature and Boston's mayor from 1895 to 1899, together with James Jeffrey Roche, successor of O'Reilly as editor of the *Pilot* and later O'Reilly's biographer, judged the debate. In 1892 Patrick Collins, who had been a member of Congress and became the second Irish Catholic mayor of Boston after the turn of the century, was a judge.

College presidents did honor to the Fulton Society at its prize debate—Francis Walker of Tufts in 1896, Charles W. Eliot of Harvard in 1897, and Elmer Capen of Tufts in 1898. Eliot's gracious participation should be noted by Boston College people who tend to think of him in relation to Boston College only in terms of the Eliot-Brosnahan controversy about the college curriculum.

The fact that the College extended invitations to such eminent gentlemen to participate in the prize debate shows the esteem in which the Jesuits held debating; and the acceptance of the invitations by such men indicates the stature that the young college itself and its debating society had achieved.

In the early part of the twentieth century the big event for Boston College and the Fulton Debating Society was the move to Chestnut Hill, where the college swelled with pride in its magnificent new building and the Fulton men gloried in the special amphitheater built for them. Father Gasson followed the example of Father Fulton in providing the debating society a room of its own—and what a room! The Boston College club of Cambridge made a gift (the amount is unrecorded) specifically for the Fulton room, and all generations of Boston College people are in their debt for their role in creating one of the architectural gems of the campus. The ceiling of the room forms a Gothic arch, reflecting the building's architecture. The sloping ceilings on either side were, fittingly, adorned with six examples of or tributes to oratory: in Greek by Demosthenes, in Latin by Cicero, in Jerome's Latin rendition of St. Paul, in Italian by Paolo Segneri, S.J., in French by Louis Bourdaloue, S.J., and in English by Daniel Webster. Three of the quotations are from secular and three from sacred eloquence. From the vantage of the platform in the Fulton room the quotations from Cicero, Webster, and Demosthenes are on the left wall and those from Segneri, St. Paul, and Bourdaloue on the right wall. The unknown selector of the quotations has provided

The Fulton room.

generations of Fultonians with gems of eloquence and exhortation. They are called, as aspiring orators, to selfless patriotism, to respect for human dignity, to lofty life goals, to sincerity springing from high intellectual and moral force. Truly these are guidelines that challenge the mind and stir the heart.

The selection from the great Greek orator Demosthenes is taken from his speech, "On the Crown." The translation given here is from the Loeb Classical Library. The style is a bit old-fashioned, but that is perhaps appropriate to the time when the Greek was copied on the Fulton wall, with some wrong accents and erroneous letters, by Brother Schroen. Father David Gill, S.J., of the Department of Classical Studies, identified the selections from Demosthenes and Cicero in their respective works.

> But it is not the verbal fluency of the orator, Aeschines, nor the stretch of his voice, that is valuable, but that he should choose the same ends as the bulk of his countrymen, and should hate and love the same persons as his country. For the man who has his soul thus ordered will say everything with loyal intentions; but the man who courts those persons from whom the city anticipates danger to herself, does not ride at the same anchor with the multitude, and consequently has not similar expectations of safety. But, mark you, I have; for I adopted the same interests as my hearers, and have done no isolated or individual act.

Cicero is represented by some lines from his treatise on the orator, *De Oratore,* Book I, viii, 32 and 34. Again the translation is from the *Loeb Classical Library.*

> What function is so kingly, so worthy of the free, so generous, as to bring help to the suppliant, to raise up those that are cast down, to bestow security, to set free from peril, to maintain men in their civil rights? Not to pursue any further instances—wellnigh countless as they are—I will conclude the whole matter in a few words, for my assertion is this: that the wise control of the complete orator is that which chiefly upholds not only his own dignity, but the safety of countless individuals and of the entire state. Go forward therefore, my young friends, in your present course, and bend your energies to that study which engages you, that so it may be in your power to become a glory to yourselves, a source of service to your friends, and profitable members of the republic.

The most interesting of the citations from the point of view of writing this chapter was that from St. Paul, because it took some literary sleuthing to discover that the selection is composed of 13 excerpts from 6 of the Pauline letters. A translation is presented unannotated. The same translation with scriptural references for each separate quotation will be found in the appendix to this chapter.

> Take strength, my son, from the grace which is ours in Christ Jesus. Stand by what you have learned and what has been entrusted to you, remembering from whom you learned it. Run the great race of faith; take hold of eternal life. Test everything; keep hold of what is good. Turn from the wayward passions of youth. Pursue justice, piety, integrity, love, fortitude, and gentleness. In everything set an example of good conduct: in your teaching, your integrity, your seriousness. Have nothing to do with superstitious myths, mere old wives' tales; keep yourself in training for piety. While the training of the body brings limited benefit, the benefits of piety are without limit, since it holds out promise not only for this life but also for the life to come. What you say must be in keeping with sound doctrine. Never be harsh with an older man; appeal to him as if he were your father. Treat younger men as brothers. Do not dispute about mere words; it does no good and only ruins those who listen. Be on the alert; stand firm in the faith; be valiant, take courage. Let us never tire of doing good, for if we slacken not our efforts we shall in due time reap our harvest.

A scripture scholar, Father Joseph Fitzmyer, S.J., Gasson professor at Boston College from 1987 to 1989, says he knows of no precedent for a concatenation of texts such as that from St. Paul in the Fulton room. He concludes, as we must, that some Jesuit on the Boston College faculty culled sentences from various passages of St. Paul, which fit together rather nicely, and described the new text correctly in the line below the inscription, "From the letters of St. Paul."

Paolo Segneri of the Society of Jesus is one of the great pulpit orators in the history of Italy. He flourished in the second half of the seventeenth century. The citation on the wall of the Fulton room is taken from his fourth sermon for the first Sunday in Lent. Thanks are given to Joseph Figurito of the Department of Romance Languages and to Father Patrick Ryan, S.J., of the Department of Theology for the translation from the Italian.

> What food is for the body, the word of God is for the soul. "Cibus mentis est sermo Dei," says a disciple of Ambrose, and the common language of the saints echoes him. Nor is this surprising. The word of God preserves in the soul the spark of life so that it be not extinguished. It nourishes the soul when exhausted, strengthens it when weak, makes it robust when spent. Indeed this food has a

> wonderful advantage over every other kind of food. For every other food, however choice, however healthful, however substantial, can do nothing for our bodies unless they are alive. But the divine word calls back to life souls that are dead. So which of you would be surprised to hear that Christ affirmed that man does not live by bread alone but by every word that comes from the mouth of God? It can be said, not just metaphorically but really, that when the soul, the noblest part of man, is nourished by the word of God, the whole person is nourished by it.

Like Paolo Segneri, Louis Bourdaloue was a seventeenth century Jesuit and a premier pulpit orator. His reputation in France was perhaps even greater than Segneri's in Italy. Whoever chose the selections from these two talented men again chose a lenten sermon. The Bourdaloue excerpt is from a sermon for the Second Sunday in Lent entitled, "On the wisdom and sweetness of God's law." Father Joseph Gauthier, S.J., of the Department of Romance Languages, kindly provided the translation.

> God's law is at once a yoke and a comfort, a burden and a support. Didn't this law of love change shackles into bonds of honor? Witness a Saint Paul. Didn't it make the cross attractive? Witness a Saint Andrew. Didn't it give refreshing coolness in the midst of flames? Witness a Saint Lawrence. Doesn't it continue to perform countless miracles before our very eyes? If the law seems difficult to you, don't put the blame on the law or its burdens but on yourself and your indifference towards God. The law is difficult for those who fear it, for those who would like to change it, for those whom the spirit of God, the spirit of grace, the spirit of love doesn't quicken, doesn't embolden, doesn't touch because they don't want to be touched. But let us take heart and with a holy desire to please God let us enter into the way of His commandments. We will stride, we will run, we will enjoy the blessed eternity to which we are being led.

The quotation from Daniel Webster is from a discourse, "Adams and Jefferson," delivered in Faneuil Hall in Boston on August 2, 1826. The two former presidents and friends died on the same day, the 50th anniversary of the republic, July 4, 1826. In the chosen excerpt Webster was speaking of the quality of John Adams' eloquence. Let Webster's words introduce the passage on the Fulton room wall: "The eloquence of Mr. Adams resembled his general character, and formed indeed a part of it. It was bold, manly, and energetic; and such the crisis required." He then continued:

> When public bodies are to be addressed on momentous occasions, when great interests are at stake, and strong passions excited, nothing is valuable in speech farther than as it is connected with high intellectual and moral endowments. Clearness, force, and earnestness are the qualities which produce conviction. True eloquence, indeed, does not consist in speech. It cannot be brought from afar. Labor and learning may toil for it, but they will toil in vain. Words and phrases may be marshalled in every way, but they cannot compass it. It must exist in the man, in the subject, and in the occasion. Affected passion, intense expression, and pomp of declamation, all may aspire to it; they cannot reach it. It comes, if it comes at all, like the outbreaking of a fountain from the earth, or the bursting forth of volcanic fires, with spontaneous, original, native force.

The representations of the six authors above their quotations on the side walls, as well as all the lettering in the Fulton room, are the work of Brother Francis Schroen. On the front wall the artist, painting in 1913 and with a long view of the Fulton's future, provided a slot for the name of each year's winner of the Fulton prize debate, starting with 1890 and going as far as the year 2104.

The Fulton room seats 104. The size of the room deserves comment. Since the 1960s the Fulton Society has been, as regards debating, an activity of a small number of intercollegiate debaters. From 1868 to the post-World War II era, the Fulton was a club of 40, 50, or 60 upperclassmen—juniors and seniors—participating in weekly debates. From this membership 6 or 8 were chosen for intercollegiate debates. Many Fultonians who never represented the College in intercollegiate debate profited from the give and take of the weekly debates and later starred in professional fields where public speaking was important. If the topic of a weekly debate was especially provocative, many non-Fultonians might attend, hence the need for ample seating.

However, having their spanking new quarters in Gasson Hall did not insure excellence in debating by the Fultonians, because on

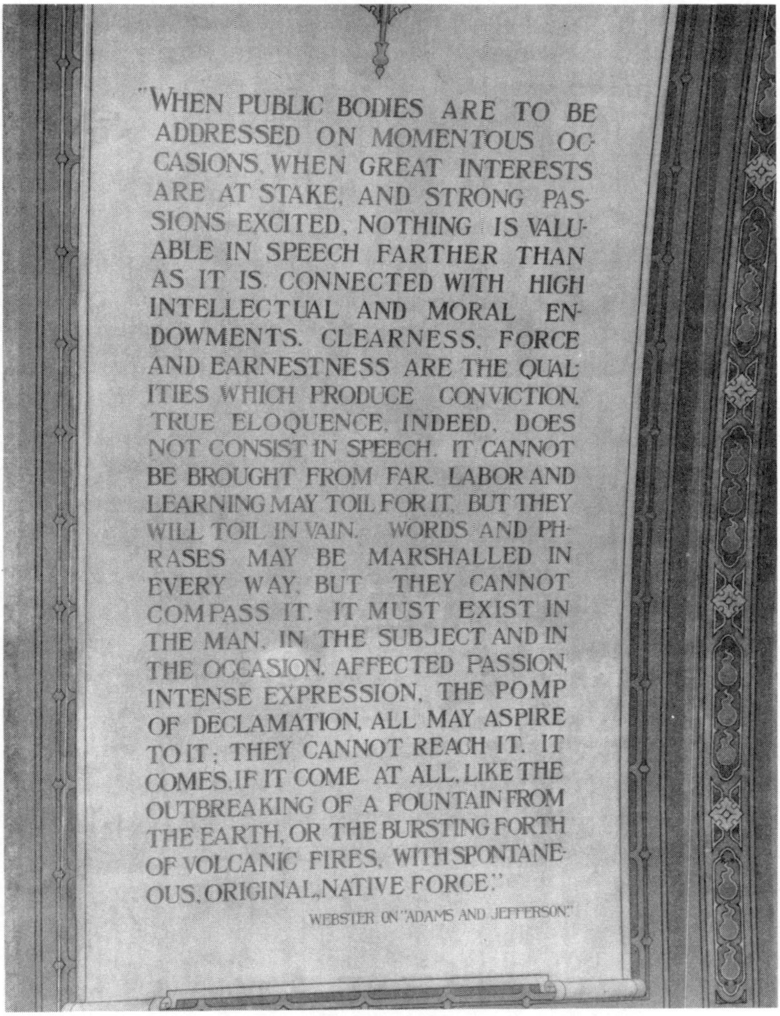

Wall inscription in the Fulton room.

January 14, 1920, the student paper stated, rather pontifically: "*The Heights* would be false to its manifest duty did it fail to direct the attention of the college to the present condition of debating within its walls—did it fail to demand, for the sake of those ancient traditions, of those in whose power it lies, that they spare no effort to bring our leading society, the Fulton, back to the level of its former preeminence."

One cannot measure the influence of *The Heights'* admonition upon the subsequent performance of the Fultonians, but it is surely a fact that the next two decades, from 1920 to World War II, were a golden era for the debating society, and this in part reflected the general strength of college debating at the time. A sort of old world civility and formality was part of the debating scene. For instance it was taken for granted that for major encounters such as Boston College debates with Holy Cross, Harvard, or Oxford and at all prize debates, all parties involved—debaters and judges and masters of ceremonies—would be in formal attire. Intercollegiate debates drew large audiences. A Boston College–Harvard debate in the late 1920s filled Symphony Hall. When Boston College was host team, the Holy Cross debate was held at the old Newton High School, where the auditorium held a thousand.

The prestige of the Fulton Society at this time is attested to in the dean's diary that was kept from 1914 to 1939. For most of that period, from 1920 to 1936, the dean was Father Patrick McHugh, who was warmly regarded by students and alumni. Most of the diary entries recorded routine business such as the appointing of a substitute for an absent professor, the transfer of a Jesuit professor to another assignment, or the hiring of a lay professor. There is no mention of athletic contests and hardly a mention of any other student activity. But year after year, seemingly the entire intercollegiate debate schedule of the Fulton was recorded as the debates occurred. Here are some typical entries:

November 2, 1928—Intercollegiate debate between Fulton and Oxford University at Ford Hall. Won by Fulton.

February 3, 1929—International debate with the University of Australia. Good crowd. Won by Fulton.

March 27, 1929—Intercollegiate debate between Fulton and Harvard at Symphony Hall. 1500 present. Won by Fulton.

October 26, 1932—Debate with Oxford at the Hotel Commander in Cambridge—ballroom overflowing. Splendid debate. Won by Fulton.

March 13, 1933—Fulton vs. Harvard. 600 present. Won by Fulton.

March 16, 1933—Fulton vs. Providence College in Milford. 500 present. Won by Fulton.

Fulton debate winners.

Defeats, of course, were noted. They were few and usually to another Jesuit college, especially Holy Cross and Fordham, which also fielded formidable debating teams in this era.

After World War II intercollegiate debating was transformed radically. In place of debates between teams from two colleges, debate tournaments emerged, bringing together teams from a number of colleges engaged over several days in a round robin of contests. A byproduct of the debate tourney was the establishment each year of a national collegiate debate topic; all debates at a given tourney were on that topic and all tourneys around the country, leading up to the National Debate Tournament in the spring, debated the same national topic.

In the prewar period the Fulton had nine or ten intercollegiate debates a year, usually on seven or eight different topics. The four or five leading debaters, who met the most formidable opponents, may have had as many as four or five different debate topics to research and for which to develop debate strategy. The prewar debaters obviously could not achieve the kind of command of five debate topics that contemporary debaters do for the one annual topic. But there was challenge and diversity in preparing multiple debate topics each year that is absent under the tournament format. There has also been a significant change in debate style. In the earlier period the debater stood on the platform with no podium between him and the audience. There was no podium because debaters made their main presentations without notes, speaking either extemporaneously or from memory. A card or two might be held in the hand during rebuttal. The tournament style is to come to the main podium with an array of documents and notes for main speeches as well as rebuttals, and rebuttal and cross-examination are merged with the main speeches as the debate progresses. The earlier style was platform speaking, where argument blended with oratory. The tournament presentation is more of a courtroom style, stressing argumentation rather than eloquence.

Mention should be made of the faculty direction of the debating society. Father Fulton was the first moderator. In the first half of the twentieth century the moderator usually served a brief term. Between 1910 and 1955 28 Jesuits served as moderator, 16 of them scholastics (that is, unordained Jesuits doing several years of collegiate teaching before entering the theological studies). Among the scholastics were several who became outstanding professors and administrators, such as Ignatius Cox, who was later one of Fordham University's outstanding professors of ethics; William Kenealy, later dean of the Boston College Law School; Leo P. O'Keefe, long a member of the Boston College community, who won the Fulton medal in 1929; and Walter McGuinn, founder of the Graduate School of Social Work.

Professor John L. Mahoney of the English department was the first layman to direct the Fulton Society, from 1955 through 1959.

He led the Fulton during an era of transition. There were still some debates with representatives of one other college—for example, Boston University. But Boston College began to participate in tournament debates involving teams from colleges in the region, including Holy Cross.

The appointment in 1960 of John Henry Lawton, whose doctorate from the University of Iowa was in speech and communication, marked the beginning of an era in which the mentor of the Fulton Society no longer directed debate as an extracurricular activity but as his principal commitment or as a major part of his faculty assignment. The faculty title was changed from moderator of debating to director of forensics. John Lawton began the era of the careerist in charge of debating. He stepped aside in 1968 to pursue other kinds of collegiate public speaking that were then not under the aegis of the Fulton Debating Society. Another professional, Daniel Rohrer, took over the Fulton for 12 years.

Dr. Lawton plunged Fulton debaters into the national tournament circuit. Travel funds for attending tournaments were not liberal in the 1960s, but he managed to have his debaters at many of the most prestigious tourneys. In 1962 he had the first Boston College team to qualify for the Super Bowl of debating, the National Debate Tournament. Between 1962 and 1993 Fulton debaters earned a place in the National Debate Tournament 20 times.

The director from 1985 to 1994 has been Dale Herbeck. He has been entering teams at three levels in debate tourneys—varsity, junior varsity, and novice debaters—and in the 1990s he is fielding as many as nine teams. In addition, since the 1970s the Fulton has also developed contestants for non-debate speaking performance, some of the categories being informative speaking, persuasive speaking, extemporaneous speaking, after-dinner speaking, dramatic interpretation, and rhetorical criticism. Fultonians have been regularly participating in speech tournaments that are independent of debate tourneys. In a sense this diversification of the Fulton's activities goes back to the 1868 to 1890 period, when drama and dramatic readings were part of the debating society's activities. The consistently impressive record of Fulton debaters for the last quarter of a century reached a climax in 1990, when the National Debate Tourney ranked Boston College first among the more than

Dilip B. Paliath, '93, winner of the Fulton Prize Debate in 1993.

100 colleges active in policy debate. The Fultonians were ranked first also in 1992 and 1993.

The list of 96 Fulton Medal Winners on the wall of the Fulton room contains the names of many great and some legendary Boston College graduates. Some standouts are Monsignor Michael J. Splaine, 1896, a revered churchman; Henry Foley, 1921, founder of a distinguished Boston law firm; James M. Curley, Jr., 1928, son of Boston's mayor, whose prospects for a brilliant public career were cut short by an early death; John J. Wright, 1931, later bishop and cardinal, possibly the quickest and wittiest debater in Fulton history; Lawrence J. Riley, 1936, a beloved auxiliary bishop of Boston; John J. Curtin, Jr., 1954, first Boston College alumnus and Law School alumnus to be president of the American Bar Association.

In the tournament debate format, two of the outstanding medalists were contemporaries and teammates, James Unger, 1963, and Joseph T. McLaughlin, 1964 and 1965. Unger, who rivalled John Wright's intimidating intellectual command, has had a distinguished career in the field of intercollegiate forensics. McLaughlin brought his platform skills to the New York bar. The first woman to win the Fulton medal was Jane M. Osborne, 1973, an outstanding accomplishment in the light of the fact that total coeducation had come to Boston College just three years earlier. Osborne took her law degree at Boston College and practices law in California.

The almost frenetic pace of today's Fultonians is seen in a typical 1990s schedule, including as many as 40 tournaments for varsity, junior varsity, and novice debaters as well as for speech. Since each debater may be in five or six debates per tournament, most debaters have as many as 65 debates from September to April. The busiest debaters might have over 80 debates. Tournament locations include the states of Kansas, Illinois, Missouri, Iowa, Kentucky, Georgia, and North Carolina, as well as a number in the Northeast. Not only does the University finance the considerable travel expenses involved in such a schedule, but it supports the young speakers with a staff of seven full-time and part-time professionals: director of forensics, director of debate (John Katsulas, who became director of forensics in the fall of 1994), director of individual events, and four assistant coaches. The ideal of *eloquentia perfecta* that motivated early Jesuit education is being pursued in the late twentieth century. Competitive debating and speaking is sponsored by some of America's finest colleges. Boston College has seen to it that the Fulton Debating Society is one of the highly respected debate and speech organizations in the country.

APPENDIX

The following paragraph gives the scriptural sources of the various sentences that make up the citation from St. Paul's letters:

> Take strength, my son, from the grace which is ours in Christ Jesus. (2 Tim. 2:1) Stand by what you have learned and what has been entrusted to you, remembering from whom you learned it. (2 Tim. 3:14) Run the great race of faith; take hold of eternal life. (1 Tim. 6:12) Test everything; keep hold of what is good. (1 Thess. 5:21) Turn from the wayward passions of youth. (2 Tim. 2:22) Pursue justice, piety, integrity, love, fortitude, and gentleness. (1 Tim. 6:11) In everything set an example of good conduct: in your teaching, your integrity, your seriousness. (Titus 2:6, 7) Have nothing to do

with superstitious myths, mere old wives' tales; keep yourself in training for piety. While the training of the body brings limited benefit, the benefits of piety are without limit, since it holds out promise not only for this life but also for the life to come. (1 Tim. 4:7, 8) What you say must be in keeping with sound doctrine. (Titus 2:1) Never be harsh with an older man; appeal to him as if he were your father. Treat younger men as brothers. (1 Tim. 5:1) Do not dispute about mere words; it does no good and only ruins those who listen. (2 Tim. 2:14) Be on the alert; stand firm in your faith; be valiant, take courage. (1 Cor. 16:13) Let us never tire of doing good, for if we slacken not our efforts we shall in due time reap our harvest. (Gal. 6:9)

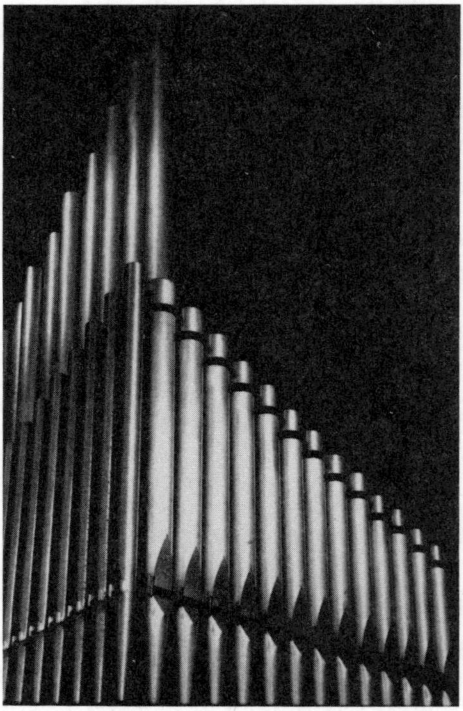

PART FOUR

A Tradition of Service

15

Boston College's Boston Priests

THE FOLLOWING PAGES are about priests of the Boston archdiocese who claimed or claim Boston College as alma mater. It is hoped that focus on this special group of the University's alumni will in no way obscure the happy and productive relations the College has had from the earliest days with Boston priests having no ties to it but those of faith and common goals. The College could not have prospered without the active support of the general body of the clergy, starting with the great shaper of four parishes in Cambridge, Father Manasses Dougherty, who gave both his library and a bequest to the College in its infancy. Many a pastor over the years contributed to the tuition, or even paid the entire tuition, of promising young men. Until the last thirty years, the fund drives of the College were largely parochial, including the $2 million drive of 1921 and the post-World War II drive of 1947. So, although Boston College is justifiably proud of its priest alumni, it acknowledges an incalculable debt to all the priests of the archdiocese and treasures its longtime affiliation with them.

* * *

We turn, in this final chapter, to the priests of the Boston archdiocese who received degrees from Boston College or attended

Boston College and entered the seminary before graduating. Although this noble army of men of God, dating from the 1880s to the present, contains cardinals, archbishops and bishops, distinguished pastors, scholars, and seminary professors, from the Boston College *historian's* perspective the outstanding priest-alumnus was a member of the tiny first graduating class of 1877. He is Rev. Patrick H. Callanan, and he claims pride of place among alma mater's priests because he was Boston College's first historian! Twenty years after graduation, from 1896 to 1899, he published a series of reminiscences—mostly his own, but also some he collected from fellow alumni—concerning the early years of the College, from about 1870 on. These reminiscences were published in 20 articles in the student paper, *The Stylus*. The articles included 268 pages of text and, remarkably, 281 photos and tintypes. Callanan was a modern historian, emphasizing illustration.

Boston College's first historian, who will get more space in this paper than can be given to other priest-alumni, entered the College in October 1870. He was interviewed and assigned to class by Father Robert Fulton, who had become president in August of that year but retained the duties of dean that he had performed since the College had opened in 1864.

During his seven years at Boston College, Callanan achieved academic honors and was a leader of student activities. For three years in a row, he won top honors in classics and French. He received second honors in poetry and the medal in mathematics in his sixth year and second honors in philosophy and the physics medal in his last year. In competitive efforts, he won a $25 prize (tuition was $60 a year) for best English composition, a $25 prize for reading, a $30 prize for the best thesis in Christian doctrine, and the prize for the best centennial ode in 1876, celebrating the nation's first century. Active in debate, Callanan was an officer of the debating society for three years and was prefect of the Sodality of Our Lady twice. One of Father Fulton's pet projects was the Foster Cadets, to which all students had to belong, and Callanan was the dominant figure in the student militia in his day, rising from corporal in his first year to captain and finally to the top rank of major from 1873 to 1876. Father Callanan devoted three of his 20 "Reminiscences" to the Foster Cadets. As military leader, he naturally remembered the cadet experience much more fondly than did many of his contemporaries; the latter chafed at the cost of the uniform, which was almost as much as the tuition.

If the militia loomed large in Callanan's student life, music loomed even larger. Six installments of his reminiscences are devoted to music. But for Callanan's writings, we would have no idea of how prominent music was in the life of the fledgling college. The major musical organization was the St. Cecilia Society, which was given this description in the College catalogue in Callanan's time: "Supplies the music at daily mass, and gives its aid, when needed, at celebrations either of the College or of the Church of the Immaculate Conception." Callanan reproduced the programs of several of the non-liturgical presentations of the St. Cecilia Society that included music of Handel, Von Weber, Mozart, Verdi, Rossini, Gounod, and Schubert. Callanan corresponded with several Boston College students who entered the Society of Jesus before graduating, and the young Jesuits' letters show lively interest in the ongoing musical activity of the College. Were it not for Callanan's reminiscences, we also would not know of a second musical organization, the Glycophonic Glee Club, founded by a Jesuit scholastic, Mr. Jerome Daugherty, in 1871. The name reflected the penchant in American colleges of the nineteenth century for giving student organizations Greek names. In this case, the glee club's Greek-derived name meant "sweet-sounding."

After graduating in 1877, Patrick Callanan entered St. Joseph's Seminary in Troy, New York, where he was ordained in 1880. He noted with pride in his *Stylus* reminiscence that he was the first alumnus to be named a pastor. He was the first pastor of St. John's Church in Wellesley, appointed in 1890.

Boston College honored Father Callanan twice. In 1906 he delivered the baccalaureate address, and in 1927, the year the first graduates reached their golden jubilee, he was most deservedly awarded an honorary doctorate.

Father Callanan proudly documented the number of Boston College graduates entering the priesthood from each succeeding class. Of course, he included those entering religious congregations as well as those becoming diocesan clergy in other parts of the country. For our purposes here, the number becoming priests for the Boston archdiocese and the number of graduates each year are given in the table on page 223.

Reverend Patrick H. Callanan.

The Number of Graduates Becoming Priests for the Boston Archdiocese

YEAR	NUMBER	YEAR	NUMBER	YEAR	NUMBER
1877	7 of 10	1882	8 of 18	1887	9 of 16
1878	5 of 10	1883	6 of 13	1888	4 of 14
1879	9 of 13	1884	6 of 15	1889	13 of 19
1880	12 of 17	1885	13 of 19	1890	7 of 15
1881	9 of 16	1886	1 of 9		

Another dramatic view of the number of Boston College men who went on to serve the Boston archdiocese as priests can be gleaned from the 1907 College catalogue, which listed graduates and their occupations and addresses. By that year, 587 men had graduated, of whom 243 (or 41 percent) were either Boston priests or seminarians preparing for service in the archdiocese.

The third volume of *History of the Archdiocese of Boston*, published in 1945, covers the years 1866 to 1943.[1] That period, starting in the days of Boston College's infancy, was marked by explosive growth of the Catholic population. The church historians fill their pages with accounts of the openings of new parishes and the construction of new churches throughout the archdiocese. Of the priests named as starting new parishes, we identify 42 as sons of Boston College. Among the church builders named, 47 were Boston College men, and their edifices include landmark structures such as the Church of the Sacred Heart in Roslindale, St. Mary's in Charlestown, and Blessed Sacrament in Walpole. Eighteen of the priests just counted both started a parish and built a church, which means that 71 Boston College priests are cited as pioneers in the expanding decades of the Boston archdiocese.

A history of the archdiocesan seminary, St. John's, was published in 1945. In an appendix, it listed all priests who had attended the seminary since its inception in 1884,[2] giving the names of 536 priests. When these names were checked against Boston College student rosters in the annual catalogues through the year 1920, it was found that of the 536 St. John's alumni, 219 (or 41 percent) were also alumni of Boston College. In addition, 102 graduates of St. John's had first studied at Boston College and entered the seminary before earning the bachelor's degree. So 321 (or 60 percent) of the Boston priests listed in the 1945 history of St. John's Seminary had attended or graduated from Boston College.

Actually, the number of Boston College men who became diocesan priests is slightly larger than the above statistics show because some, like William O'Connell and Michael Splaine, did theological studies in Rome, not at St. John's Seminary.

A more recent study by a current professor at St. John's Seminary, Father Robert E. Sullivan, corroborates the above data and carries them beyond 1920. Father Sullivan writes: "Over 70 percent of those ordained between 1900 and 1944 had been students at Boston College."[3]

The dry statistics so far presented demonstrate that Boston College was a training ground for St. John's Seminary, almost as if it had been established as such by negotiations between the archbishops of Boston and the Jesuits—negotiations that actually never took place. With the outbreak of World War I, the relationship became formalized. When the United States entered the war, there was concern that the flow of students to the seminary from Boston College would be cut off by conscription. But when Boston College was declared a Petit Seminary for the diocese, the supply of clergymen was assured.[4].

In *Catholic Boston*, Father Robert Sullivan commented on the Boston College–St. John's Seminary relationship: "Himself an alumnus of Boston College, [Cardinal] O'Connell resourcefully deflected attempts by the Vatican during the early 1930s to disrupt this longstanding symbiotic relationship [with Boston College] by requiring the archdiocese to conform to Latin practice and support a minor seminary that would admit youths immediately after high school. He finally acquiesced in this recommendation [of the Vatican] in the summer of 1939 as Europe was preparing to go to war once again. Should America become involved, the federal government was unlikely to renew the concession it had granted in the spring of 1917 and declare Boston College a minor seminary whose undergraduates were exempt from conscription."[5]

In 1940 St. Clement's Hall was opened on Foster Street, offering a two-year college-level course for high school graduates to prepare them to enter the seminary. This marked the end of the era when a majority of St. John's seminarians had roots in Boston College, but it by no means ended the entrance of Boston College men into service of the Boston archdiocese as priests. There are

Cardinal William H. O'Connell.

currently 304 priests in the Boston archdiocese who attended Boston College. Some of these men were not undergraduates there, but claim the University as alma mater through graduate degrees.

As we move from statistics that can be stated in a few sentences to persons who are numbered in the thousands, space limitations permit the celebration—or even the mention of—only a small number of Boston College's Boston priests. Let us start with our three cardinals, two of whom were archbishops of Boston.

Boston's first cardinal was Right Rev. Dr. William H. O'Connell, rector of the North American College in Rome when, in 1897, Father Patrick Callanan wrote to him for his reminiscences and a photo for his *Stylus* article. Those who know the many volumes the cardinal later published about his life and work may be surprised at Monsignor O'Connell's restrained reply to Callanan:

> You forget, perhaps, that I entered in '79 and left in '81. Not that I have not scores of happy memories of that brief time, among the very happiest days of my whole life. But they are, perhaps, rather more uninteresting from the fact that they are more personal and uneventful. After one has entered Poetry [at that time equivalent to sophomore year], you know one already begins to miss the heyday spirit of the Humanities [equivalent to present junior and senior years of high school and freshman year of college]. I entered Poetry after the middle term examinations, and our class, though not lacking in merriment, had already taken on the serious air of men who have begun to grow mustaches. I do wish, however, that Ed Flynn, who grew up with the class from rudiments [the beginning high school years] and was its leader in many respects, would put a few of his reminiscences in print for the sake of '81.

William O'Connell became bishop of Portland, Maine, in 1901. In 1906, with the venerable Archbishop John Williams of Boston in failing health, Bishop O'Connell was named Williams' coadjutor bishop with right of succession. Archbishop Williams died on August 30, 1907. Archbishop O'Connell's accession to the See of Boston came at a critical moment for Boston College. In January of 1907 Father Gasson had been named president. He had consulted Archbishop Williams and had received his approval for purchasing property and constructing buildings for a new campus for the College. The plan now had to be resubmitted to Archbishop O'Connell. O'Connell gave the project his blessing and enthusiastically endorsed the Chestnut Hill site for the campus.

At some point after the Chestnut Hill property was purchased, the archbishop evidently became alarmed at the style and scope of what Father Gasson was planning. Perhaps the stunning plan submitted by architects Charles Maginnis and Timothy Walsh for nineteen buildings on what is now the central campus seemed too ambitious. The archbishop, however, was concerned not only about cost and grandeur but also about the authority of the archbishop vis à vis a Catholic university. In June 1910, just a few weeks after the first masonry work began on the tower building, the archbishop wrote Father Gasson what this reader deems a very tough letter, devoted mostly to what he considered necessary limits to fund raising (and the prelate had legitimate concerns here), but with a brief but trenchant paragraph on his role as head of a

Catholic university in his archdiocese. He seemed to feel that this role was agreed to by the provincial and Father Gasson—evidently at the 1907 meeting when he approved the acquisition of the Chestnut Hill property. He believed it was agreed "that when the time came for the erection of a Catholic University in these parts, the Archbishop, consulting with Rome, should be the head and director of such University, and that it should not be merely a growth of the present organization of Boston College." The letter demanded a document of agreement signed by Jesuit authorities. The archbishop may have slept on the letter or sought advice, because he added in a postscript: "I wish to add here that I have no intention of infringing upon any particular privileges or the Constitution of your order."

Although the archbishop never received the document he demanded, he seems never to have pressed the notion that he should head the local Catholic university. When by introducing graduate education and the Law School in the 1920s, the college moved toward university status, he made no objection. He was generous in supporting the 1920–1921 public drive for Devlin Hall and, of course, in 1941—the sixtieth anniversary of his graduation from Boston College—he purchased the Liggett Estate (the present upper campus) for his alma mater.

In the 1930s and 1940s Cardinal O'Connell often took an afternoon stroll on Linden Lane, usually accompanied by his secretary, Monsignor Jeremiah Minihan, and sometimes by his standard poodle. Minihan, who had been a football star at Georgetown, would look for a Jesuit scholastic (that is, a Jesuit in training for the priesthood getting his first teaching experience at the College) during the fall walks. If successful in spotting one, he would commandeer the scholastic to walk with the cardinal while he went to the stadium to watch football practice. The patrician Cardinal O'Connell, though amiable and generous to the College in the last three decades of his life, was somewhat remote compared with his successor, Richard Cardinal Cushing.

Richard Cushing had attended Boston College High School and entered Boston College in 1913 with the first class on the Chestnut Hill campus. He completed two years and entered St. John's Seminary in 1915. Cushing became auxiliary bishop of Boston in 1939, and in 1944 he succeeded Cardinal O'Connell as archbishop

Cardinal Richard J. Cushing, with Father Michael P. Walsh, S.J., president, and classics professor Joseph P. Maguire, breaking ground for Carney Hall in 1963.

of Boston. It was not long before Archbishop Cushing had a significant impact on Boston College. He was anxious to establish a collegiate program for Catholic nurses. Advised by professionals in the field that it would be well to locate such an enterprise at a university, he happily approached Boston College about founding the School of Nursing, which opened in 1947. Located off campus in downtown Boston for 12 years, the School of Nursing moved into its current campus building in 1959, funded by a gift of $1 million from Cardinal Cushing. Apart from Gasson Hall, no building on campus wears its name with more pride than Cushing

Hall. But the School of Nursing was not the only school closely associated with Cushing. He was an annual visitor to the School of Education in the 1950s, persuaded by the gracious director of student teaching, Marie Gearan, to give an inspirational talk on the teaching profession each year to the assembled student body. It was a function the archbishop obviously relished. In 1946 the Alumni Association presented the William V. McKenney award to Archbishop Cushing.

A storied fund-raiser, benefactor of Catholic organizations and causes worldwide, promoter of harmony between Christians and Jews, a power in the pulpit, and one hundred percent priest of the people until the day he died, Cardinal Cushing will always be a towering figure in the history of Boston, of the Catholic Church in Boston, and of Boston College.

Boston College's third cardinal to date is John J. Wright, who entered the College from Boston Latin School and graduated in 1931. He excelled in academics, but his special fame was as the outstanding debater in the history of Boston College—a reputation that has not been challenged to the present time, more than 60 years after his graduation. Wright debated in what may be called the golden age of Boston College debating. Among many outstanding Fultonians, Wright was the star, not as orator but as an intimidating logician with quick wit. In his senior year, a Fulton team composed of Wright and two others was scheduled to debate New York University on the affirmative side of the proposition that the 18th amendment should be repealed. Because of inclement weather, the NYU team did not arrive. Rather than disappoint the audience gathered in the assembly room in Gasson Hall, debate officials drafted a senior from the audience to join Wright in taking the NYU "anti-saloon" position against a two-man Fulton team. In a quick-switch tour de force, Wright carried his game partner—and the day. Besides winning the Fulton medal, Wright was valedictorian at his commencement.

After a year at St. John's Seminary, John Wright did his theological studies in Rome, where he was ordained. He earned a doctorate in theology at the Jesuit Gregorian University. He served as secretary to both Cardinal O'Connell and Archbishop Cushing and, at age 37, was named auxiliary bishop of Boston in 1947. Three years later he became the first bishop of the new Worcester diocese.

Bishop John J. Wright, with Boston College librarian Terence L. Connolly, S.J.

In 1959 Wright became bishop of Pittsburgh. Ten years later Pope Paul VI named him a cardinal and placed him at the head of the Vatican Congregation for the Clergy.

Cardinal Wright remained close to Boston College and, like other older alumni, he was concerned about his alma mater's share in the unrest and turbulence that swept American campuses in the 1960s and 1970s. Not long into the presidency of Father Monan, the senior vice president and dean of faculties received a call one afternoon from the switchboard at St. Mary's Hall saying that Cardinal Wright was there and would see Father Monan in the vice president's office. That seemed like a bit of Roman protocol to let the cardinal meet the president on "neutral" ground. The cardinal and the president met in the Hopkins House office, with the vice president waiting in the outer office. During the lengthy meeting, there was some anxiety outside of the office, but apparently none inside. When the office door finally opened, the cardinal emerged, his left arm draped around Father Monan's shoulders. As they left the building, a relieved vice president reflected that with all the examinations Father Monan had faced in his Jesuit course of studies and for his Ph.D. in philosophy at the University of Louvain, he had just passed his toughest ecclesiastical test, as the saying goes, with flying colors!

Boston College is proud that before he was called to Rome as cardinal, Bishop Wright was known as perhaps the leading intellectual in the American church. As such he became episcopal adviser to such groups of Catholic academics and intellectuals as the American Graduate and Professional Commission (Pax Romana); the Albertus Magnus Guild, an organization of scientists; and the Catholic Renaissance Society, a group devoted to letters and the arts. In 1952 Bishop Wright received the Alumni Association's McKenney Award.

Including Cardinals Cushing and Wright, 11 Boston College men have served as auxiliary bishops of Boston. The first was Bishop Joseph Anderson of the class of 1887. He became Archbishop O'Connell's auxiliary in 1909. In the spring of 1913, when the archbishop was in Rome, Bishop Anderson blessed the cornerstone of Gasson Hall on June 15 and three days later presided at the first commencement held on the Chestnut Hill Campus. He was pastor of St. Peter's Parish in Dorchester.

Louis F. Kelleher was valedictorian of the class of 1910. He did his theological studies in Rome and was awarded the degree of Doctor of Divinity. For 17 years he taught dogmatic theology at St. John's Seminary. He was consecrated auxiliary to Archbishop Cushing in 1945 and died a year and a half later at age 57. In his latter years he was pastor of St. Catherine's Parish in Somerville.

Bishop Eric MacKenzie graduated from Boston College in 1914. He was a senior and Richard Cushing, the future cardinal, a freshman in Boston College's first year on the Chestnut Hill campus. After ordination, MacKenzie did graduate study at Catholic University in canon law and dogma. For nearly a quarter of a century he taught moral theology and canon law at St. John's Seminary. He was consecrated Archbishop Cushing's auxiliary in 1950. Bishop MacKenzie served for 25 years as pastor of Sacred Heart Parish in Newton Center.

Bishop Thomas J. Riley of the class of 1922 studied at St. John's Seminary and, after ordination, earned a Ph.D. at the University of Louvain. He taught philosophy and moral theology at St. John's for 11 years, then served as vice rector and rector of the seminary. In 1959 the then Monsignor Riley became auxiliary bishop of Boston. During his years at the seminary and as bishop, he contributed to the diocesan paper, the *Pilot,* a commentary on moral issues and problems under the title, "Theology for Everyman." A dozen other diocesan papers in the United States and Canada carried the column. Bishop Riley was pastor of St. Peter's Parish in Cambridge. Boston College conferred the honorary degree of Doctor of Laws upon Monsignor Riley in 1952.

Another Riley, who left Boston College a decade and a half after the first Bishop Riley, was Lawrence J. Riley. He won the Fulton prize debate and graduated *summa cum laude* in the class of 1936. He studied theology at St. John's and in Rome and, after ordination, earned a doctorate in theology at the Catholic University of America. For 25 years he was associated with St. John's Seminary, 17 years as professor of theology and 8 years as vice rector and rector. For a time he was chaplain of the Harvard University Catholic Club and served as secretary to Archbishop Cushing. He was pastor of the Most Precious Blood Parish in Hyde Park and was consecrated auxiliary bishop of the archdiocese in 1972. Now retired, Bishop Riley remains a faithful and visible son

Auxiliary Bishop Emeritus Lawrence J. Riley.

of alma mater, notably supportive of Boston College families in times of loss and grief. In 1975 Bishop Riley was awarded an honorary LL.D. degree by alma mater, and three years later he received the Alumni Association's McKenney Award.

Continuing its record of producing a man destined to be an auxiliary bishop of Boston each decade, Boston College graduated

Joseph F. Maguire in the class of 1941. While at college, Maguire was a member of the hockey and baseball teams. Monsignor Maguire served as secretary to Archbishop Cushing and was pastor of St. John's Parish in Quincy. He was ordained auxiliary bishop in 1972, in the same ceremony in which his fellow alumnus, Lawrence Riley, was raised to the episcopacy. In 1976 Bishop Maguire was appointed co-adjutor bishop of Springfield, and he was installed as bishop of Springfield in November 1977. Boston College conferred an honorary Doctor of Laws degree on Bishop Maguire and awarded him a Bicentennial Râle Medal in 1976. Bishop Maguire retired in 1991. He has been an active alumnus and a close friend of many Boston College Jesuits.

Thomas V. Daily entered Boston College during World War II, in September 1944, as a member of the Boston College class of 1948. When he had completed his freshman year and the first semester of this sophomore year, he transferred to St. John's Seminary. After serving in St. Ann's Parish in the Wollaston section of Quincy, he became secretary to Archbishop Medeiros and later chancellor of the archdiocese. In 1975 he was ordained auxiliary bishop, and the following year he was named vicar general of the archdiocese. Upon the death of Cardinal Medeiros, he became administrator of the archdiocese and, after the accession of Bernard Law as archbishop of Boston, he was installed as bishop of the new Diocese of Palm Beach in 1984. In 1990 he was named bishop of the Diocese of Brooklyn. His brother, Father Vincent Daily, graduated in 1951.

Bishop Daniel Hart is the only Boston priest to earn an undergraduate degree at Boston College after his ordination. Ordained in 1953, he attended the then College of Business Administration, earning the B.S. in Business Administration in 1956. He became vice chancellor of the archdiocese in 1964 and was consecrated auxiliary bishop to Cardinal Medeiros in 1976. Bishop Hart received the Almuni Association's Award of Excellence in Religion in 1979.

Bishop John Boles takes care of the decade of the sixties for Boston College priest alumni becoming auxiliary bishops. In 1965 he earned the D.Ed. degree. Father Boles' priestly career has been close to education. Shortly after ordination in 1955 he joined the faculty of St. Sebastian's Country Day School. While there he earned an M.Ed. degree at Boston College in 1959. He became headmaster of St. Sebastian's and later was named vicar of education for the archdiocese by Cardinal Medeiros. In 1976 Boston College awarded him a Bicentennial Râle Medal. As pastor of St. Paul's Parish in Cambridge for 18 years, Father Boles supported, and eventually provided, new quarters for the Harvard-Radcliffe Catholic Center and the Archdiocesan Choir School. Consecrated bishop by Cardinal Law in 1992, Bishop Boles has responsibility for the central region of the archdiocese.

Several Boston College men became bishops elsewhere without first being auxiliary bishops of Boston. In terms of his Boston College connection, the first was Bishop James Anthony Walsh, M.M., who attended the College from 1882 to 1885. He entered St. John's Seminary and was ordained for the Archdiocese of Boston in 1892. While associated with the Society for the Propagation of the Faith, he became deeply committed to foreign missions, and in 1911 he co-founded the Catholic Foreign Missionary Society of America, (better known as the Maryknoll Fathers). He was consecrated a bishop in Rome in 1933. Bishop Walsh has another intimate connection with Boston College. His brother Timothy was a partner in the architectural firm of Maginnis and Walsh, the team that designed Boston College's early Chestnut Hill buildings. Indeed, in 1911, when Father James Walsh was laying the foundations of a uniquely American religious congregation, his brother Timothy was anxiously supervising the construction of the magnificent first building of the new campus.

A man who attended Boston College during the same decade as Bishop Walsh, John B. Delaney of the class of 1887 became bishop of Manchester, New Hampshire, in 1904. Also going north of Boston was Edward F. Ryan of the class of 1901. Father Ryan served in the Boston archdiocese for four decades, completing the great Holy Name Church in West Roxbury. In 1945 he was consecrated bishop of Burlington, Vermont.

In 1946 Father Paul F. Anderson, who attended Boston College from 1937 to 1939, was one of five Boston priests "loaned" by Archbishop Cushing to the diocese of Sioux Falls, South Dakota. In Father Anderson's case, the loan became a permanent assignment. After serving as pastor in the Sioux Falls diocese for 22

Monsignor Charles A. Finn.

years, he was consecrated co-adjutor bishop of Duluth, Minnesota, in 1968, and he became bishop of the diocese in 1969.

It has been noted that four of Boston's auxiliary bishops—Louis Kelleher, Thomas Riley, Eric MacKenzie, and Lawrence Riley—were members of the faculty of St. John's Seminary, as indeed was Cardinal Wright for five years. The two Bishops Riley also served as rectors at the seminary. So many Boston College men shared the honor and responsibility of being seminary professors that, for this one category of priestly service, an attempt has been made to give a complete list, from the first in 1897 to current members of the seminary faculty. This academic apostolate of Boston College alumni teaching the future priests of the archdiocese is surely one of the proud boasts of alma mater. Several of this honored group deserve special comment.

Long the best-known priest alumnus of Boston College was Monsignor Charles A. Finn, who lived to the great age of 104. A graduate of the College in 1899, he not only taught at St. John's but served as rector for five years. He had been pastor of Holy

Boston College Men on the Faculty of St. John's Seminary

Name and B.C. Class	Years at Seminary
Joseph V. Tracy, 1882	1898–1903
George V. Leahy, 1889	1897–1927
Charles A. Finn, 1899	1913–1933
Edward F. Crowley, 1900	1907–1918
Patrick J. Waters, '03	1911–1932
Joseph A. Murphy, '06	1913–1928
Louis F. Kelleher, '10	1918–1935
Eric F. MacKenzie, '14	1919–1943
*Charles D. McInnis ('16)	1927–1941
Walter J. Furlong, '21	1928–1946
Thomas J. Riley, '22	1933–1958
Francis A. Barry ('23)	1946–1949
William J. Gorman ('24)	1930–1944
John J. Downey ('25)	1951–1958
Henry J. O'Connell, '26	1941–1952
Matthew P. Stapleton, '26	1934–1965
Arthur J. Riley, '26	1937–1947
J. Joseph Ryan, '27	1940–1978
Francis S. Shea, '28	1934–1950
Timothy P. O'Connell ('29)	1935–1950
John J. Wright, '31	1939–1943
John T. Feeney ('31)	1949–1961
Francis X. Meehan, '31	1941–1964
Daniel T. McColgan, '32	1941–1953
Joseph P. Monahan ('32)	1937–1941
Russell H. Davis ('34)	1946–1965
Lawrence J. Riley, '36	1941–1966
John J. McManmon ('38)	1952–1969
Robert P. Murray ('38)	1957–1969
James F. Redding ('38)	1955–1960
Alfonso G. Palladino ('39), '46 M.A.	1953–1969
William A. Granville ('40)	1945–1947, 1950–1951, 1968–1969
John W. Connor, '41	1956–1971
John A. Broderick ('41)	1947–1971
James A. O'Donohoe ('43)	1954–1979
John J. Connelly, '44	1958–1983
Joseph Smyth, '49	1965–1990
Joseph G. Lind, '50	1969–1989
James J. Haddad, '53	1967–1977
Paul F. Donelin, '53 M.A.	1949–1951, 1968–1972
Francis V. Strahan ('55)	1965–1983
Arthur J. Driscoll, '56 M.S.	1968–1976
Thomas J. Daly, '57 M.A.	1968–1991
Martin Connor, '58	1977–present
Walter Edyvean, '60	1971–1990
John P. Galvin ('63)	1971–1987
Walter J. Woods ('65) '69 M.Ed.	1979–present
John E. Farrell, '66 M.A.	1968–1990
John L. Sullivan, '70	1980–present
George P. Evans, '73	1985–present

*A date in parenthesis after a name means that he attended Boston College, but left before his class graduated in the year given.

Monsignor Matthew P. Stapleton.

Name Parish in West Roxbury for 23 years when he retired at age 80. At that time he had ahead of him 24 years of lively retirement. Since mention will be made later of Boston College priests who were brothers, note is made here of Father Charles Finn's younger brother Aloysius, class of 1911. Monsignor Aloysius Finn, retired pastor of St. John the Evangelist Parish in Winthrop, died a year before Charles at age 94. Boston College conferred an honorary Doctor of Laws degree on Monsignor Charles Finn in 1939.

Few Boston College priests have had a greater identification with St. John's Seminary than Monsignor Matthew Stapleton of the class of 1926. By far the greater part of Monsignor Stapleton's active priestly career, 31 years, was spent at St. John's where, besides being a professor, he served for 14 years as vice rector and seven years as rector. He was an outstanding biblical scholar and teacher and served as president of the Catholic Biblical Association of America. When he left the seminary staff, Monsignor Stapleton served as pastor of St. Columbkille's Parish in Brighton. In his latter years, his cheerful presence at Father Monan's annual lun-

Monsignor J. Joseph Ryan.

cheons for priest alumni was a welcome benediction. Alma mater conferred on him an honorary Doctor of Laws degree in 1960.

Arthur J. Riley was a classmate of Matthew Stapleton at Boston College. After ordination, Father Riley earned a doctorate in history at Catholic University. He published *Catholicism in New England to 1788,* a meticulously researched volume that contained a remarkable list of books, both anti-Catholic and—surprisingly—Catholic, found in libraries of Colonial Protestant leaders. In 1944 he published *Anti-Semitism* and later co-authored *The History of St. John's Seminary.* He taught history for 10 years at the seminary and, as a monsignor, was pastor of Our Lady of Good Counsel Parish in Quincy.

Monsignor J. Joseph Ryan of the class of 1927 was one of the most distinguished scholars and long-serving faculty members of St. John's Seminary, having been a professor of ecclesiastical history for more than 40 years. After theological studies at St. John's and the Gregorian University, Father Ryan attended the Pontifical Institute of Medieval Studies in Toronto. An active writer, he contributed articles to *The Catholic Historical Review, The Irish Monthly, The Encyclopedia Britannica,* and the *Catholic Encyclopedia,* as well as to the *Pilot.* It is estimated that Monsignor Ryan taught over a thousand priests during his career at the seminary, where he served as vice rector for 13 years.

In celebrating its centennial year in 1963, Boston College declared Monsignor Ryan an honorary doctor of humane letters. In 1976, as part of the University's celebration of the country's bicentennial, the History Department conferred the Boston College Râle medal on Monsignor Ryan for his scholarly achievements and his prized courses in the Graduate School.

Daniel T. McColgan graduated *summa cum laude* in the class of 1932. After ordination, Father McColgan earned a Ph.D. at the Catholic University in the fields of sociology and social work. For 12 years he taught at the seminary, and he also taught at Regis College. In 1953 he became head of Nazareth, the former center for children in Jamaica Plain. That year he also became a monsignor. Monsignor McColgan published a two-volume history of the Society of St. Vincent de Paul.

Monsignor John A. Broderick ('41), had a long association with St. John's Seminary, starting as librarian in 1947. He was a professor of moral theology, church history, and homiletics, and served as rector from 1966 to 1971. He supervised the construction of the Creagh Research Library and later the new seminary library. He presided at the merger of Cardinal O'Connell Seminary with St. John's and became the first president of the seminary college. During his administration the college received full accreditation, and the theologate was the first diocesan seminary to be accredited by the American Association of Theological Schools. In 1971 Monsignor Broderick became pastor of Our Lady of the Presentation Parish in Brighton, where he served until his retirement to Regina Cleri in 1993.

Father John J. Connelly of the class of 1944 attended St. John's Seminary and earned a doctorate at the Gregorian University. In 1958 he began a career as seminary professor that spanned three decades and two years, teaching fundamental theology and theological anthropology. He is now pastor of the Sacred Heart Parish in Newton.

Father Thomas J. Daly is an alumnus by virtue of his master's

Monsignor Walter Edyvean.

degree in French literature, earned in 1957 under the tutelage of Father J. D. Gauthier, S.J. He had a distinguished career of 38 years in what may be called the seminary system. He joined the former Cardinal O'Connell Seminary in Jamaica Plain in 1953 and remained there until 1970, when St. John's consolidated its efforts on the Brighton campus. He continued as a member of the seminary faculty until 1991, serving as rector for the last five years. He currently is executive director of the Synod of the Archdiocese of Boston.

Monsignor Walter Edyvean, class of 1960, did theological studies at St. John's and at the Gregorian University. After ordination and a brief stint of parish work, he returned to the Gregorian University and earned the doctorate in theology. He joined the faculty of St. John's Seminary in 1971 and remained there for 19 years, teaching courses in sacramental theology and in the history of medieval theology, as well as the thought of Pope Paul VI. Since 1990 Monsignor Edyvean has been in Rome, serving in the Vatican's Congregation for Catholic Education. In that congregation he is concerned with the universities section, which is responsible for both Catholic universities and for the ecclesiastical universities and faculties that award their degrees in the name of the Holy See.

Father John Farrell, '66 M.A.—beloved by his seminary students—taught at Cardinal O'Connell Seminary and St. John's Seminary for a quarter of a century. He is now pastor of Our Lady of the Assumption in Lynnfield.

Associated not with St. John's Seminary but with the other seminary located in the Boston archdiocese, Pope John XXIII Seminary in Weston, is Father James W. DeAdder of the class of 1951. After a few years of parish service followed by study in Rome, he was assigned in 1964 to Pope John XXIII Seminary, a national seminary for preparing men with "delayed" vocations for the priesthood. He is now in his twenty-ninth year of service there, including a stint as rector.

In the category of seminary professors, note should be made of three other Boston College priests who were professors at the Catholic University. The first was Father Edmund Shannahan of the class of 1889. Having earned the Doctor of Divinity degree, he joined the faculty of the Catholic University when the institution was in its infancy. He was followed by Father John Creagh of the class of 1891. Creagh attended St. John's Seminary and earned a doctorate in canon law in Rome. He also earned the LL.B. degree at the Catholic University. He was professor of canon law there for 16 years, after which he served for 38 years as pastor of St. Aidan's Parish in Brookline. He left a distinguished canon law library to St. John's Seminary. Father Edward Dowd of the class of 1926 earned a Doctor of Divinity degree at Catholic University and taught theology there twice for a total of 18 years. Monsignor Dowd served as pastor of St. Bernard's Parish in Concord. It should also be mentioned that Father John P. Galvin ('63), who was on the St. John's Seminary faculty for 17 years, has been a professor of theology at Catholic University since 1987, teaching Christology as well as history and method in theology. In addition, he chaired the Department of Theology from 1989 to 1992.

When we turn from priests who served as professors and/or rectors of the seminary to the great number of Boston College men who have spent their careers in pastoral service in parishes of the archdiocese, the possibility of doing justice to them in these few pages is zero. The half hundred who can be even briefly named have not been selected as some sort of clerical elite but as representatives of the edifyingly large body of priest alumni. Some, indeed, are given personal notice because of public prominence they achieved, but most are simply typical devoted, hard-working pastors of their flocks.

From one of the early classes, 1881, came Father John A. Daly. Ordained by Archbishop Williams in 1884, his first assignment was to St. Mary's Church in Waltham. After 10 years he was asked to do what was common at the time: start a new parish. The parish was St. Mark's in Dorchester, and Father Daly, as was also common then, remained pastor there for the rest of his long life. He died 39 years later at age 86, 63 years out of Boston College.

The class of 1891 gave the archdiocese another parish founder and builder in Monsignor Joseph P. Coppinger. After ordination, Father Coppinger was assistant at St. Joseph's Church in the West End, and in 1910 he was asked by Archbishop William O'Connell to start a parish, St. Aidan's, in Brookline. Monsignor Coppinger erected a church similar to English Gothic village churches, with low walls and high-pitched roof, the walls being of rustic stone and half-timber. Later Monsignor Coppinger served as pastor of the significant parishes of St. Augustine's in South Boston and St. Catherine of Genoa in Somerville. As part of its seventy-fifth anniversary celebration in 1938, Boston College conferred on Monsignor Coppinger the honorary degree of Doctor of Laws.

Monsignor Hugh F. Blunt attended Boston College for only one year, as a member of the class of 1896, but his exposure to the classical and literary curriculum seems to have been a stimulating experience, for he was perhaps more widely known as an author than as a pastor. After serving as assistant in three parishes, including St. Peter's in Dorchester, Monsignor Blunt was appointed pastor of St. John's in Cambridge, where he presided over a beautiful church whose architects were the designers of Boston College's early buildings (Charles D. Maginnis and Timothy Walsh). Throughout his priestly career, Monsignor Blunt was a prolific writer. In the early years of the century he contributed regularly to two venerable Catholic journals, *Donahue's Magazine* and the *Sacred Heart Review,* serving for a time as editor of the latter. He wrote more than a score of books of verse and prose, all of them on religious subjects for the edification of the Catholic reader. He served ably for 28 years as pastor of St. John's until his death in 1957 at age 80.

A native of South Boston, Father William J. Farrell graduated in the class of 1898. He had served as assistant in several parishes when the United States entered World War I. Father Farrell became a chaplain of the 102d Massachusetts Field Artillery, A.E.F., and he served with heroism. The *History of the Archdiocese of Boston* gives the following account:[6]

> The late Father William J. Farrell, on April 16, 1918, went to the aid of an American battery in which many gunners had been killed; he carried up ammunition and helped to keep the guns going through the night; he was injured, but refused to have his wound attended to next morning until he had carried a wounded comrade, a Connecticut lad of nineteen, to a dugout dressing station. Father Farrell was officially cited for bravery on this occasion.

After the war, Father Farrell assisted in several parishes before becoming pastor of Sacred Heart Church in Groton, the position he held when he died in 1933.

Another World War I chaplain was Monsignor Frederic J. Allchin of the class of 1900. Before and after his war service he was assistant in St. Paul's Parish, Dorchester. For nearly 25 years he was administrator and pastor of the venerable St. Mary's Parish in Charlestown. He served as director of the Archdiocesan Holy Name Society and was a diocesan consultor for 10 years. He died in 1955.

Monsignor Joseph F. McGlinchey of the class of 1902 was ordained in Rome and, after an assignment as assistant priest in St. Paul's Parish in Cambridge, was named director of the Boston office of the Pontifical Society for the Propagation of the Faith. One of his assistants in that office was a youthful priest with strong missionary fervor, a fellow Boston College man: Father Richard J. Cushing, the future archbishop of Boston. Monsignor McGlinchey's younger brother Henry, who left Boston College after junior year, entered the Society of Jesus. Named by his

Monsignor Joseph F. McGlinchey.

provincial as one who would follow a missionary life, he was sent to Bombay, India, prior to his theological studies. After several fruitful years he died of pneumonia—a promising missionary career cut short. His brother Joseph published in *Catholic Missions* (the organ of the Propagation of the Faith) an account of the sociological and religious insights Henry had developed in a brief period concerning the caste system. After directing the office of the Propagation of the Faith for 16 years, Monsignor McGlinchey became pastor of one of the oldest parishes in the archdiocese, St. Mary's in Lynn, where he served for more than 30 years. He enjoyed being a schoolman and acted as principal of both the grammar school and the high school attached to the parish. During the celebration of its seventy-fifth anniversary, Boston College conferred on Monsignor McGlinchey the honorary degree of Doctor of Laws in 1938. The monsignor died in 1959.

Monsignor Bernard S. O'Kane of the class of 1909 was the oldest diocesan priest in Boston at the time of his death in 1986 at age 99. As an undergraduate he captained the baseball and track teams, and he was an early member of the B.C. Hall of Fame. After service in parishes in Chelsea and Brookline, he was pastor successively of St. Bridget's in Abington, St. Pius V in Lynn, and St. Bernard's in West Newton.

Monsignor Francis A. Burke of the class of 1913 did theological studies in Rome, where he was ordained in 1918. Assigned to the chancery office in Boston, he was named chancellor and secretary to Cardinal O'Connell in 1927. From 1933 until his death in 1959, he was pastor of Blessed Sacrament Parish in Jamaica Plain.

Popularly known as Driftwood Casey because of his *Pilot* column by that name, Monsignor George V. Casey ('16) was a familiar figure in many households not only because of the "Driftwood" column (which appeared weekly in the *Pilot* for 30 years) but also because of a column he contributed to the *Boston Herald* for six years. During World War II he served as an army chaplain in the European Theater of Operations. After the war he did graduate study at Harvard under the G.I. Bill. He was pastor of St. Brigid's Parish in Lexington from 1949 until his retirement in 1972. Boston College conferred the honorary degree of Doctor of Letters on Monsignor Casey in 1971. He died in 1983 at age 87.

A classmate of Monsignor Casey, both at Boston College and at ordination, was Monsignor Daniel J. Donovan, who was an outstanding church figure both locally and nationally. As executive secretary for the Boston unit of the Holy Name Society, he vitalized that organization and promoted a giant Holy Name parade in Boston. He was a national officer of the Catholic Church Extension Society and the Catholic Rural Life Conference. While serving at the Presentation Church in Brighton in the 1930s, he established the Presentation 10-mile road race, which for many years was the sole warm-up for the BAA marathon. He was pastor of St. Agatha's Church in Milton at the time of his death in 1955.

Monsignor James H. Doyle of the class of 1921 was an outstanding member of the football team that in his senior year was undefeated and scored on only twice—one of the greatest records in Boston College football history. Early in his priesthood he was chaplain of a New Deal institution, the CCC (Civilian Conservation Corps). He served as director of the Catholic Charitable Bureau and was pastor of St. Patrick's Parish in Roxbury and, later, of St. Peter's in Dorchester. In 1976 the Alumni Association presented him with the Award of Excellence in Religion. Nominated by the Boston College Jesuit Community that same year, he received a Râle medal. He was named to the Boston College Hall of Fame in 1979.

Father Francis P. Moran, class of 1928, is best remembered as editor of the *Pilot,* the venerable archdiocesan weekly. Father Moran studied for the priesthood at St. John's Seminary and the Gregorian University in Rome. In 1941, while serving as assistant priest in St. Cecilia Parish in the Back Bay, he became assistant editor of the *Pilot,* and he was named editor in 1948. He resigned in 1952 because of ill health. He had been in residence at the Cathedral of the Holy Cross since 1959 at the time of his death in 1967.

Father Charles P. Glennon of the class of 1929 was an army chaplain in World War II. He received two Purple Hearts for his service and was a German prisoner of war for 10 months, gaining release when the war ended. Later he was chaplain of a Knights of Columbus Council and district director of the Holy Name Society. He had served for 16 years as pastor of Holy Ghost Parish in Whitman at the time of his death in 1985.

Deserving of special mention are the McGann brothers, not only because three of them became priests of the archdiocese, but because three other brothers graduated from Boston College. Father Gregory McGann attended for two years before entering the seminary in 1928. In 1930 brother Leo McGann left the College after sophomore year for St. John's. The sixth Boston College man in the family, Gerard, entered the seminary after completing his sophomore year in 1943. The three other brothers were Edward, '29, Thomas, '31, and Emmett, '37. Before any of the McGann brothers entered the College, the family had a framed certificate in their home attesting to a $25 donation to a Boston College drive. It was signed by Father William Devlin, president from 1919 to 1925, who in 1920 launched a fund drive for the first science building, Devlin Hall.

Father William J. Donlon, '31, a luminary in a class that contained such stars as John Wright (future cardinal) and Francis

Meehan (future seminary professor), served in parishes in Methuen, Lynn, Cambridge, and Quincy before becoming pastor of Sacred Heart Parish in South Natick, a position he held for 21 years. In vigorous retirement, he is senior priest in residence in the parish of his pastorate. As an undergraduate, Bill Donlon was a star on the track team and eventually was inducted into the Boston College Hall of Fame. He has the honor of being chaplain and recording secretary of the Boston College Varsity Club. Few alumni can match his boundless zeal as a supporter of alma mater.

Father John E. Foley graduated from Boston College in 1933. His priestly assignments took him to, among other parishes, Holy Name in West Roxbury, St. Patrick's in Natick, and Our Lady Help of Christians in Newton, and he was pastor of St. Rita's in Haverhill and St. Cecilia's in Ashland. The University is proud that so many priest alumni have been bookmen whose priestly lives have been supported and enriched by books. But Father Foley went beyond the status of bookman; he became a bibliophile. In 1985 he donated to Boston College from his ample library 20,000 volumes, most in the field of theology and spirituality. More recently he has added more than a thousand books to Burns Library's Liturgy and Life Collection, which documents and reveals Catholic culture in the first half of the twentieth century.

Father John A. Saunders of the class of 1934 served in St. Bernard's Parish, West Newton, and St. Agatha's in Milton before becoming pastor, first, at Saints Peter and Paul in South Boston and, then, at St. Mary's in Waltham. Blessed with a seemingly inexhaustible store of diocesan history, he has edified his many Jesuit friends with stories of local parish life in much of the twentieth century. The author acknowledges Father Saunders' encouragement and help in this discourse on Boston College men who became priests in the Archdiocese of Boston.

Monsignor John Dillon Day ('34) is known to all who enjoy his acquaintance as, first, a dedicated priest and, second, an ardent Boston College alumnus. There is no question about his priorities, but neither is there a question about his commitments. All but four years of his near half century of parochial assignments were spent in two parishes named for Our Lady: 19 years in St. Mary's in Lynn and 26 years in St. Mary of the Hills in Milton. He was an enthusiastic sponsor of youth activities and sports programs in his

Monsignor Francis J. Lally.

parishes, and it is not surprising that all of his athletic teams wore maroon and gold. He is the only alumnus who had not participated in athletics to be elected to membership in the Boston College Hall of Fame. Monsignor Day has been a leading supporter of Father Monan's annual luncheon for alumni priests, and those gatherings have been blessed spiritually and socially with his opening benedictions. In 1982 the Alumni Association presented Monsignor Day its Award of Excellence in Religion.

Monsignor Robert J. Sennott of the class of 1937 spent a few of his early priestly years on the faculty of St. Clement's Hall, the liberal arts division of St. John's Seminary. There followed a lengthy association with the chancery office, during which he rose to the office of vice chancellor and chancellor. In 1964 he began a 25-year pastorate in the beautiful St. Catherine of Siena Church in Norwood. In 1961 Boston College conferred on Monsignor Sennott an honorary Doctor of Laws degree.

Monsignor Francis J. Lally, '40, was one of the most public of the Boston College priest alumni. He attended St. John's Seminary and earned a Licentiate in Social Sciences at Laval University after ordination. In 1948 he was named associate editor of the *Pilot,* while fellow alumnus Father Francis Moran, '28, was editor. In 1952 he succeeded Father Moran as editor, and for 20 years he gave the archdiocesan paper a quality and reputation that resembled the glory days when poet John Boyle O'Reilly headed it in the late nineteenth century. During those years, Lally assumed the considerable civic responsibility of heading the Boston Redevelopment Authority in its formative period. In 1962 Little, Brown published Msgr. Lally's book, *The Catholic Church in a Changing America.* After five years as pastor of Sacred Heart Parish, Roslindale, Monsignor Lally was called to national church service in Washington as secretary of the United States Catholic Conference's Department of Social Development and World Peace. In 1984 Boston's new archbishop, Bernard Law, asked Monsignor Lally to return to Boston as rector of Holy Cross Cathedral, the position he held when he died in 1987. In 1962 Boston College conferred to Monsignor Lally the honorary degree of Doctor of Letters. In 1953 the Alumni Association presented him with the William V. McKenney award, and in 1976 the University conferred on him the Bicentennial Râle medal.

After a distinguished career as professor of classics and rector of Cardinal O'Connell Seminary for 19 years, Monsignor William A. Granville ('40) served as pastor of Sacred Heart Parish in Newton Centre and was the first president of the Priests' Senate. He is now senior priest in residence at St. Thomas Aquinas Parish in Bridgewater. Nominated by the College of Arts and Sciences, Monsignor Granville was awarded a Bicentennial Râle medal in 1976 and the Alumni Award of Excellence in Religion in 1994.

Monsignor George V. Kerr of the class of 1941 was an academic star and an All-American member of the football team. He graduated as one of only 39 members of the honors course and took his degree *cum laude*. Salutatorian of his class at commencement, he selected the topic, "Jesuit Missionaries," in honor of the fourth centenary of the founding of the Society of Jesus. He was a member of the famed Sugar Bowl team. Coach Frank Leahy said of him years later that he was the greatest scholar-athlete he ever coached. As a priest, Monsignor Kerr was a very public figure because of his 25 years of service as chaplain of the Massachusetts

House of Representatives. Whether it was because of the importance of his House chaplaincy or his clean-jawed, strapping presence, Monsignor Kerr's photo was frequently in local papers. Indeed, for a quarter of a century he was probably second only to Cardinal Cushing as the favorite of news photographers. Among his non-parish assignments were assistant director of the Catholic Charitable Bureau, director of the Nocturnal Adoration Society, and chaplain at the children's home, Nazareth, in Jamaica Plain. He served as administrator and pastor of St. Francis de Sales Parish in Roxbury and was pastor of St. Francis Xavier Parish in Weymouth at the time of his death in 1983.

Father James A. O'Donohoe ('43) did doctoral studies at Catholic University and at Louvain in preparation for a 25-year career as professor at St. John's Seminary, which concluded in 1979. Fortunately for Boston College, he then began a second academic career in the Theology Department, where he has been a distinguished teacher and lecturer in the field of theological ethics.

Father Francis Gallagher ('44) served in parishes in Marlboro, Newton, and Revere before becoming pastor of St. James Parish in Medford. Father Gallagher's family has kept him closer to Boston College than most alumni. His sister Helen was Father Monan's executive secretary before marrying John Smith, the financial vice president who helped Father Monan turn the University's financial status from minus to plus, plus.

Monsignor Stanislaus Sypek holds two degrees from Boston College: a Master of Arts in Sociology, awarded in 1946, and the M.S.W. degree from the Graduate School of Social Work two years later. Throughout his career he has been active among Polish Catholics, most recently as pastor of St. Adalbert's in Hyde Park. For 22 years Monsignor Sypek was a devoted teacher of sociology in the University's Evening College of Arts and Sciences.

Father William Burckhart, '49, assisted at St. John the Evangelist Parish in Winthrop and St. Catherine's in Norwood before becoming the first director of the Permanent Diaconate Program, a position he held for seven years. During that time he became administrator of the ancient German parish, Holy Trinity, in the South End. Since then he has been pastor of two parishes named for St. Joseph, in Medway and in Belmont.

Father Joseph Lind of the class of 1950, after 20 years of service as business manager and assistant to the rector of St. John's Seminary, is pastor of St. Paul Parish in Wellesley. The parochial vicar of the parish is another Boston College graduate, Father David Mullen ('77), who is a leader of the pro-life movement in the archdiocese.

Father Francis V. Strahan ('55) is known far and wide as the voice of the archdiocese—the *singing* voice, that is. For close to 20 years he was professor of music at St. John's Seminary, and an inspiring but daunting model for his students. He also directed the archdiocesan papal choir. In related service he chaired the Archdiocesan Liturgical Commission. He is currently pastor of St. Bridget's Parish in Framingham.

Father James Power, '56, holds three degrees from Boston College: A.B., M.Ed., and Ph.D. Besides parochial service in Revere, Plymouth, and Marblehead, he was chaplain in residence at Xaverian Brothers High School and campus minister at Salem State College. Since 1987 he has been pastor of St. Francis Parish in Dracut.

Father John E. McLaughlin, '57, '68 M.A., served in rural parishes in Holbrook, Concord, Hanson, Abington, and Sherborn and as chaplain of Cardinal Spellman High School in Brockton before his current assignment as pastor of St. Benedict Parish in Somerville. Father McLaughlin is director of the archdiocesan Holy Name Society. He is one of the few priests in the Greater Boston area with a command of the Irish language. His brother, Francis M. McLaughlin, '54, has long been a distinguished member of the Economics Department at Boston College.

Father Carney Gavin, '59, had a spectacular academic record at Boston College and has carried that early promise into his priestly and academic career. He earned the A.B. degree in three years, was a member of the first group in the Arts and Sciences honors program, and was one of the two first Scholars of the College. He studied Greek philosophy and Roman archaeology at Oxford and completed theological studies at Innsbruck and in Germany. Ordained in 1965, he earned a Ph.D. in Near Eastern languages and civilizations at Harvard in 1973. Long associated with the Harvard Semitic Museum, he now is its executive director. A master of many languages, he delights the parishioners of St. Columbkille's Church in Brighton (where he is in residence) with

Reverend Carney Gavin, with Reverend J. Donald Monan, S.J., president, and Richard T. Horan, alumni president, at Alumni Awards of Excellence in 1987.

his discourses in English. Father Gavin was recipient of the Alumni Award of Excellence in Religion in 1987.

Father Richard Harrington, '61, C.A.E.S. '76, has served in parishes in Needham and West Medford and has been assistant director of the Office of Religious Education and archdiocesan director of Youth Ministry. He is currently pastor of St. Mary's Parish in Randolph.

Father Robert Kennedy ('60) has been active in ministry to the poor in Boston. He has served in St. Catherine's in Charlestown and is currently pastor of St. Mary Star of the Sea Parish in East Boston.

Father William Mullin ('61) has the distinction of long service in inner-city parishes: St. Ambrose's in Dorchester, St. Philip's in Roxbury, and St. Mary's in Roxbury. He is currently associate pastor in St. John the Evangelist Parish in North Beverly.

Father Frederick J. Murphy, '62 M.A., taught at the Cardinal O'Connell Seminary from 1960 to 1970. While there, he earned a master's degree in classics at Boston College. For the next 21 years he was a faculty member of St. John's Seminary. In 1991 he became rector of the Cathedral of the Holy Cross.

Father Arthur A. Brown earned an M.A. in philosophy in 1965. In 1976 he received a Ph.d. in higher education. While located at St. Cecilia's Parish, he served as chaplain for college students in the Back Bay area, then as chaplain and professor of philosophy at Bentley College before becoming administrator of the venerable St. James the Greater Parish in Chinatown. He is currently pastor of the St. Catherine of Siena Parish in Norwood.

As an undergraduate, Father Robert J. Sullivan, '66, played Thomas More in *A Man for all Seasons*—a role that may have led him to the seminary, but not directly, because first he earned a Ph.D. in history at Harvard. Ordained in 1978, Father Sullivan's first assignment was at St. Catherine of Siena in Norwood. After later assignments in Malden and Belmont, he is back in the Norwood parish as parochial vicar.

Father James J. Ronan earned a M.Ed. in 1971 and a Ph.D. in higher education in 1972. He became dean of students at Bentley College and was involved in the move of the college from Boston to Waltham. He was vice president for student affairs when he entered St. John's Seminary. After ordination he served for six years in the Immaculate Conception Parish in Malden. Since 1988, as a member of the Society of St. James, he has been pastor of Parroquia de Santa Marianita in Guayaquil, Ecuador.

Father Thomas Maguire, '71, served as associate pastor in Sacred Heart Parish in Quincy, St. Mary's in Dedham, and St. Patrick's in Watertown before his present assignment as associate pastor in St. John the Evangelist in Canton. He is an uninhibited B.C. rooter. His friends predict that, in time, he will match the reasoned fanaticism for Boston College of such stalwarts as Fathers Bill Donlon and John Dillon Day.

Father William Schmidt ('72), an expert in youth ministry, served as associate pastor in the Immaculate Conception Parish in Everett and St. John the Evangelist in Swampscott before becoming secretary for pastoral services in the archdiocesan administrative cabinet.

Father Peter Uglietto, '73, served for 10 years as associate pastor in St. Francis Xavier in South Weymouth and St. Gregory and St. Margaret in Dorchester. From 1990 to 1993 he was an adjunct

Reverend Mark O'Connell.

faculty member teaching moral theology at Pope John XXIII Seminary and chaplain at Regis College. In 1990 he was awarded the S.T.L. degree in the first class graduating from the Pope John Paul II Institute in Washington, D.C., and he began doctoral studies there in September 1993.

Father Brendan Sullivan, '73, served as associate pastor of Our Lady Star of the Sea in Marblehead and St. John the Evangelist in North Chelmsford. He is currently at the Camaldolese monastery in Big Sur, California.

Father Richard M. O'Brien earned an M.A. at Boston College in 1981 when he was a Xaverian Brother. Later he entered Pope John XXIII Seminary, and was ordained in 1992. He serves as parochial vicar for St. Michael's Parish in Hudson.

Father Paul McManus, '82, was ordained in 1987. His first assignment was to St. Robert Bellarmine Parish in Andover. He currently serves with the archdiocesan missionary Society of St. James.

Father Mark O'Connell, '86, was ordained in 1990. His first assignment is as parochial vicar at St. Barbara's in Woburn. Father O'Connell will grace the annals of Boston College and of the archdiocese in his own right, but his B.C. lineage must be mentioned. He is the son of Thomas F. O'Connell, class of 1950, the distinguished university librarian who brought Boston College into the twenty-first century with the planning, construction, equipping, and staffing of the Thomas P. O'Neill, Jr. Library. Proud father of a Boston College Boston priest, the elder O'Connell gave the author the nudge—deeply appreciated—that led to this account.

Father Louis R. Palmieri, '87, is the most recent Boston College alumnus to join the noble ranks of the priests of the Boston archdiocese. Father Palmieri, a native of East Boston, was ordained May 22, 1993, and has been assigned to St. Ann's Parish in Peabody.

Four Boston College priests have been associated with the Catholic Youth Organization since its founding in 1938 by Monsignor George M. Dowd, '24. Monsignor Dowd was succeeded as director of the CYO in 1950 by Monsignor John P. Carroll, '27, who also served as national chaplain of the Boy Scouts of America. In 1968 Monsignor Carroll received the McKenney Award. In the same year he was succeeded as CYO director by Monsignor Robert W. McNeil, '43, who served until 1985. At that time, the Youth Ministry office that included the CYO was established. Father Richard L. Harrington, '61, CAES '76, was director from 1985 to 1992.

Mention should be made of two special subgroups among Boston College priests in the Boston archdiocese: outstanding college athletes and brothers who became local priests. (Some have already been mentioned in the text.) First, on page 257, is a list of Boston College athletes who later served the archdiocese as priests. Two of this group became bishops: Joseph Maguire and Thomas Daily. Then follows a list of priests identified as having brothers who also became priests of the archdiocese.

The most recent members of the honor roll, the Crowley brothers, are all pastors: Daniel, of Star of the Sea Parish in Squantum; John, of St. Mary of the Annunciation in Cambridge; and Richard, of St. Francis of Assisi in Braintree.

In concluding this all-too-brief account of Boston College men who have served or are serving as priests in the Boston archdiocese, an apology is repeated for the small number of priests we have

Boston College Athletes Who Became Priests in the Boston Archdiocese

1896	Henry Lyons (track)
1909	Bernard O'Kane (captain, baseball and track; B.C. Hall of Fame)
1921	James Doyle (football; B.C. Hall of Fame)
1928	Michael Durant (football)
1929	Francis Harkins (track)
1929	James McManus (football manager)
1931	William Donlon (track; B.C. Hall of Fame)
1931	Francis Meehan (baseball)
(1937)	Daniel Hannigan (hockey and golf)
1940	Charles McCarthy (football)
1941	George Kerr (football All-American; B.C. Hall of Fame)
1941	Edward Cowhig (football)
1941	Joseph Maguire (hockey and baseball; B.C. Hall of Fame)
1943	William Commane (football and baseball; B.C. Hall of Fame)
(1948)	Thomas Daily (football)
1949	Charles J. McCoy (football)
(1952)	John McElroy (basketball and baseball)

Brothers Who Attended Boston College and Became Boston Priests

Patrick J. Supple, 1885
David G. Supple, 1898
James A. Supple, 1900

Daniel W. Cronin, 1890
Francis T. Cronin, 1896

Henry M. Lyons, 1896
William F. Lyons, 1897

Charles A. Finn, 1899
Aloysius R. Finn, 1911

Patrick J. Waters, '03
David B. Waters, '11

Neil A. Cronin, '06
James V. Cronin, '10
(Daniel Cronin, S.J.)

John J. Phelan, '12
Francis L. Phelan, '13
(Timothy Phelan, S.J.)

Eric F. MacKenzie, '14
Howard C. MacKenzie ('17)

Patrick J. Flaherty, '14
Francis N. Flaherty, '19

Michael J. Norton, '15
Arthur J. Norton, '31

William B. Foley ('20)
Thomas M. Foley ('23)
Charles J. Foley, '24

George P. McColgan ('21)
Daniel T. McColgan, '32

Michael J. Desmond ('21)
Edward W. Desmond ('25)

Anthony J. Flaherty, '24
Edward B. Flaherty, '31
Walter L. Flaherty, '34

(continued on next page)

Nunzio A. Carrozza ('29) George T. Carrozza ('33)	John M. Donelin, '33 Paul F. Donelin, '53 M.A.
James J. McManus, '29 Paul J. McManus, '37	Thomas F. Sennott ('33) Robert J. Sennott, '37
Bernard T. Rattigan ('29) Paul V. Rattigan, '32	Robert F. Murray, '38 Thomas F. Murray, '52
Gregory M. McGann ('30) Leo M. McGann ('32) Gerard J. McGann ('45)	Thomas V. Daily ('48) Vincent E. Daily, '51, '54 M.A.
John P. Redding ('31) James F. Redding ('38)	Daniel J. Crowley, '58 John D. Crowley, '58 Richard P. Crowley, '59

NOTE: A date in parenthesis means that he attended Boston College, but left before his class graduated in the year given.

been able to identify personally because of space limitations. A list of all Boston College priests in the archdiocese as of May 1994 is given at the end of the chapter.

The University is, of course, proud of all priest graduates—priests who have served in other dioceses and priests of various religious congregations—but the story of the throng of Boston College men who have given priestly service to the parishes and the Catholic people of Greater Boston deserves to stand alone as one of the treasures and boasts of Boston College.

ENDNOTES

1. The authors of *History of the Archdiocese of Boston* were Fathers Robert H. Lord, John E. Sexton, and Edward T. Harrington. None of these priests had a Boston College connection.
2. *History of St. John's Seminary* by Fathers John E. Sexton and Arthur J. Riley. Father Riley was a Boston College alumnus, class of 1926.
3. *Catholic Boston: Studies in Religion and Community, 1870–1970,* Rev. Robert E. Sullivan and James M. O'Toole, editors. Published by the archdiocese in 1985. Father Sullivan's statement is on page 210.
4. *Ibid.*
5. *Ibid.*
6. *History of the Archdiocese of Boston,* page 603.

Current Priests of the Archdiocese of Boston Who Hold Degrees from or Attended Boston College May 1994

BERNARD CARDINAL LAW, '84 HON. S.T.D.
ARCHBISHOP OF BOSTON

LAWRENCE J. RILEY, '36
AUXILIARY BISHOP EMERITUS OF BOSTON

JOSEPH F. MAGUIRE, '41
BISHOP EMERITUS OF SPRINGFIELD

THOMAS V. DAILY ('48)
BISHOP OF BROOKLYN

DANIEL A. HART, '56
AUXILIARY BISHOP OF BOSTON

JOHN P. BOLES, '65 D.ED.
AUXILIARY BISHOP OF BOSTON

Abracinskas, Albert C.	'33
Abucewicz, John A.	('41)
Alves, Eugene L.	'54 M.A.
Alves, Joseph T.	'44, '48 M.S.W.
Anadore, Charles E.	'34
Bailey, David P.	'59
Bailey, Paul F.	'62 M.S.W.
Barrett, Daniel J.	'42, '52 M.A.
Barry, Garrett J.	('59)
Barry, Gerard D.	('46)
Barry, Henry F.	('37)
Beksha, Francis W.	'42
Benoit, Raymond P.	'83
Bernatonis, John F.	('41)
Berube, John J.	('45)
Blackwood, Wallace E.	'62, '73 M.S.W.

NOTE: A date in parenthesis after a name means that he attended Boston College, but left before his class graduated in the year given.

Blute, Robert H.	('51)
Bonfiglio, David G.	('47)
Bourque, Charles J.	'68 M.A.
Bowers, Robert J.	'82
Boyle, J. Leo	('51)
Boyle, Robert J.	('47) '72 M.Ed.
Brady, Richard J.	('53)
Brennan, Gerard M.	('47)
Broderick, James M.	'51
Broderick, John A.	('41)
Brown, Arthur A.	'65 M.A., '76 Ph.D.
Bryson, Robert C.	('43)
Bucke, Gerald L.	('39), '68 M.A.
Buckley, Frederick J.	'50 M.S.W.
Buckley, John E.	('54)
Bullock, Robert W.	'51
Burckhart, William C.	'49
Burke, David M.	'37
Burke, John T.	'75 M.S.W.
Burke, Leonard J.	'37
Butler, James P.	'75 M.A.
Butler, Robert J.	'71, M.S.W.
Carr, Mark V.	'47
Carrigg, George A.	'61 M.S.W.
Carrigg, William J.	'51, '56 M.Ed.
Carroll, John P.	'36
Casey, Walter E.	('45)
Cedrone, Laurence C.	('43)
Clifford, Donald G.	'39
Cloherty, Francis J.	('58)
Clougherty, Paul L.	('55)
Collins, Russell J.	('34)
Commane, William J.	'43
Connelly, John J.	'44
Connolly, James H.	('45)
Connor, John E.	'27
Connor, Martin P.	'58, '72 M.Ed.
Connors, Francis P.	('40)
Conroy, Francis M.	('59)
Contons, Albert	'53 M.A.
Conway, Richard C.	('59)

Conway, Thomas D.	('56)
Corcoran, John W.	'59 M.Ed.
Costello, Robert B.	'48
Cowhig, Edward D.	'41
Craig, Richard J.	'69 M.S.W.
Crispo, John R.	('46)
Crowley, Daniel J.	'58
Crowley, Francis J.	'63 M.Ed.
Crowley, John D.	'58
Crowley, Richard P.	'59
Curran, Richard G.	'73 M.A., '77 M.Ed.
Curran, Thomas M.	'84 D.Ed.
Daily, Vincent E.	'51, '54 M.A.
Daley, Joseph D.	'31
Daly, Thomas J.	'57 M.A.
Daniele, Anthony J.	'51, '63 M.A.
Davis, Russell H.	('34)
Day, John D.	('34)
DeAdder, James W.	'51
Desmond, Hubert E.	('54)
Dewey, Charles F.	('34)
DiFruscio, John A.	'64
Doherty, Henry F.	'51
Donahue, Richard T.	('63)
Donelin, John M.	'33
Donlon, William J.	'31
Donovan, Joseph F.	'67 M.Ed.
Doocey, Michael F.	'69 M.Ed.
Dorgan, Gerard L.	'66 M.A.
Downey, Joseph J.	('42)
Doyle, Lawrence J.	'40
Doyle, Michael J.	'81
Drennan, Lawrence J.	'53
Driscoll, Arthur J.	'56 M.A.
Driscoll, Richard A.	('51)
Edwards, John G.	'46
Edyvean, Walter J.	'60
Evans, George P.	'73
Farrell, John E.	'66 M.A.
Feeney, John T.	('31)
Ferraro, Michael M.	'63

Finnegan, Thomas J., Jr.	'41
Flaherty, Edward B.	'31
Fleming, Thomas J.	'53
Flynn, Arthur C.	'73 M.Ed., '76 C.A.E.S.
Flynn, James B.	'73 M.Ed., '80 Ph.D.
Flynn, John H.	'48
Flynn, Joseph D.	'57
Flynn, Robert G.	('47)
Flynn, William C.	('42)
Foley, John E.	'33
Foley, John J.	('45)
Foley, William B.	('20)
Gallagher, Francis L.	('44)
Gallivan, A. Paul	'39
Galvin, John P.	('63)
Garrity, Paul V.	'74 M.A.
Gaudette, Edward J.	('45)
Gavin, Carney E.	'59
Geary, Edward P.	'59
Geegan, John J.	('36)
Gibbons, James M.	('45), '55 M.Ed.
Gilmartin, Daniel J.	'56 M.Ed.
Glynn, William F.	('44)
Gough, Joseph F.	'30
Graham, Daniel M.	'75 M.Ed.
Granville, William A.	('40)
Guarcello, Russell V.	'39
Guerrette, William J.	'70 M.Ed.
Haddad, James J.	'53
Hannon, John Mark	('56)
Hardiman, Francis J.	('45)
Harrington, James J.	'49, '67 M.Ed.
Harrington, Richard L.	'61, '76 C.A.E.S.
Hart, James P.	'35
Hart, Peter F.	'31
Hehir, J. Bryan	'85 Hon. LL.D.
Hennessey, Joseph M.	('79)
Hever, John J.	'72 M.Ed.
Hobbs, Frederick J.	'29
Hogan, Cornelius J.	'32
Horrigan, Kevin P.	'62

Hyland, Charles H.	'24
Irwin, Francis X.	'70 M.S.W.
Jennings, Henry J.	'52
Jennings, John J.	('45)
Joyce, William F.	'53
Keane, John F.	('59)
Kearney, Philip J.	'50 M.A.
Keating, James J.	'36
Keilty, John P.	'37
Kelleher, Timothy J.	'71 M.Ed.
Kelley, Edward T.	'63
Kelly, John P.	('42)
Kelly, Patrick J.	('45)
Kenneally, William F.	('45)
Kennedy, Robert R.	('60)
Keohan, Edward M.	'54
Keohane, John J.	('41)
Keohane, Mark H.	'24
Kerivan, William C.	('45)
Kirchmeyer, Robert W.	'50 M.A.
Koen, Stephen A.	('54), '60 M.Ed.
LaRaia, Joseph P.	'75 Ph.D.
Larner, James M.	'52
Laurano, Anthony J.	('45)
Lawler, John F.	('42)
Lawler, John T.	'39
LeBlanc, Francis R.	'88 M.A.
Lennon, Richard G.	('69)
Leonard, Francis B.	('46)
Lind, Joseph G.	'50
Linehan, William J.	'31
Logue, Charles D.	('45)
Lombard, Samuel J.	'42
Loscocco, Angelo P.	'48
Lucey, William F.	'70 M.A.
Lucid, Vincent F.	('39)
Lukas, Joseph S.	('43)
Lyons, John P.	'50
MacDonald, Paul V.	'54
Maguire, John J.	'36

Maguire, Thomas H.	'71, '72 M.Ed.
Mahoney, James F.	('42)
Mahoney, John P.	('45), '56 M.Ed.
Martocchio, Peter T.	'52
Mawn, Francis X.	'76 M.S.W.
McAndrews, Walter J.	'39
McAuliffe, Robert J.	'52
McCarthy, Charles W.	'40
McConville, Philip G.	'39, '47 M.A.
McCormack, John B.	'69 M.S.W.
McCormick, John J.	('52)
McCoy, Charles J.	'49
McCue, Richard T.	'50
McGann, Gerard J.	('45)
McGowan, Frederick R.	('45)
McGowan, James J.	('57)
McLaughlin, John A.	'38, '41 M.A.
McLaughlin, John E.	'57, '68 M.A.
McMahon, Edward M.	'57
McManus, Paul G.	'82
McNamara, Eugene P.	'65 M.S.W.
McNeill, Robert W.	'43
McNulty, Joseph P.	'39
McPartland, Paul G.	('53)
McQuade, Richard E.	('53)
Meehan, Francis X.	'31
Minigan, Frederick J.	'32
Mooney, Thomas J.	('44)
Moran, Daniel F.	'43
Morgan, Thomas B.	('51) '90 M.A.
Moriarty, Thomas W.	'37
Motherway, Thomas F.	'64
Moynihan, Paul V.	'47, '59 M.A.
Mulkern, John F.	'40
Mullen, David J.	'77
Mullin, William H.	('61)
Murphy, David C.	'70 M.A.
Murphy, Frederick J.	'62 M.A.
Murphy, Kenneth B.	('42)
Murphy, Timothy J.	('59)
Murray, Frederick J.	('49)
Murray, Thomas F.	'52

Naughton, Thomas J.	('56)
Navien, Thomas A.	'36
Noonan, William J.	('34)
O'Brien, Richard M.	'81 M.A.
O'Connell, Edward T.	'31
O'Connell, Mark	'86
O'Donohoe, James A.	('43)
O'Grady, Robert M.	'81 M.Ed.
O'Hara, Peter J.	'67 M.S.W.
O'Leary, Arthur P.	'56 M.Ed.
O'Neill, Christopher C.	'28
O'Regan, Hugh H.	('52)
O'Sullivan, Francis G.	'64 M.S.W.
Palladino, Alphonso G.	'39 M.A.
Palmieri, John A.	('37)
Pearsall, Ernest P.	'31
Philbin, John J.	'40
Phinn, Gilbert S.	('50)
Pitaro, Mimie B.	('38)
Power, James F.	'56, '70 M.Ed., '83 Ph.D.
Powers, Thomas F.	('62)
Publicover, James L.	('52)
Ready, Francis P.	'42
Regan, John J.	'35
Regan, Michael J.	'71 M.Ed.
Riley, James H.	'53
Roche, Allan E.	'40
Roche, William H.	'44
Rogers, James M.	'41
Ronan, James J.	'71 M.Ed., '72 Ph.D.
Rowan, John M.	'71, '73 M.Ed., '77 C.A.E.S.
Ryan, Paul T.	'53
Rynne, Paul P.	('52)
Saja, Thaddeus A.	('43)
Santerre, Richard R.	'66, '68 M.A., '72 Ph.D.
Saulenas, Simeon W.	('41)
Saunders, John A.	'34
Schmidt, William T.	('72)
Scorzello, Joseph F., Jr.	'78 M.A.
Sennott, Robert J.	'37, '61 Hon. LL.D.

Sexton, Francis J.	'38
Sheehan, John J.	('34)
Sheehy, Charles I.	'40
Smyth, Joseph P.	'49
Stankard, Albert H.	('55)
Stanton, Thomas J.	'84
Stocklosa, J. Walter	'44 M.A.
Strahan, Francis V.	('55)
Sullivan, Brendan J.	'73
Sullivan, Eugene P.	'57, '81 D.Ed.
Sullivan, Gary S.	'84 M.S.W.
Sullivan, John L.	'70
Sullivan, Michael D.	'38
Sullivan, Robert J.	'66
Sullivan, Timothy E.	'31
Sullivan, William P.	'34
Surette, C. Melvin	'73 M.A.
Svirskas, Joseph J.	('47)
Sypek, Stanislaus	'46 M.A., '48 M.S.W.
Taglino, John L.	'35
Thomas, John E.	('45)
Tolland, Cyril E.	('41)
Turke, Francis X.	('45)
Uglietto, Peter J.	'73
Vasaturo, Anthony J.	('51)
Veneto, Joseph P.	'42
Waldron, Robert J.	'53
Walsh, John F.	'76 M.A.T.
Ward, Robert A., Jr.	'68
Wasnewski, Richard P.	'49
Weber, Charles P.	'71 M.A.
Whelan, Thomas J.	'76, '81 M.A.
White, A. Paul	'54
Williams, George J.	('34)
Wilson, Joseph C.	'52
Wolkovich, William L.	'80 M.A.
Woods, Walter J.	('65) '69 M.Ed.
Zuromskis, John D.	'36

Index